William Spottswood White, H. M. White

Reverend William S. White and his Times

William Spottswood White, H. M. White
Reverend William S. White and his Times
ISBN/EAN: 9783337340445
Printed in Europe, USA, Canada, Australia, Japan
Cover: Foto ©Lupo / pixelio.de

More available books at **www.hansebooks.com**

REV. WILLIAM S. WHITE, D. D.,

AND HIS TIMES.

[1800—1873.]

An Autobiography.

EDITED BY HIS SON,

REV. H. M. WHITE, D. D.,

PASTOR OF THE LOUDOUN-STREET PRESBYTERIAN CHURCH, WINCHESTER, VIRGINIA.

RICHMOND, VA.:
PRESBYTERIAN COMMITTEE OF PUBLICATION.
1891.

PREFACE.

OUR father wrote a memoir of his son Hugh, who fell in battle, August 30, 1862; and we undertake to prepare one of him. These are two proverbially difficult tasks. The one is liable to error through excessive complacency, and the other through excessive reverence.

His was the more difficult task, because of the time and circumstances. His eyes were yet wet with tears; the grass had not grown on his son's grave; the war, in which his young life had been quenched, was still raging. Yet *he* succeeded. The love of the father does not color the thoughts of the biographer. Therefore we are encouraged to undertake our task, yet not without misgiving.

We do it from a sense of duty. During his last days, after he had been laid aside from regular work, he wrote out some "Notes" on his life. His reason for so doing is thus given by his own hands: "It occurs to me that a portion of the leisure I now enjoy may be wisely spent in recording, for the good of my children, and especially for my sons who are ministers of the gospel, a few of the incidents of my earlier ministerial life. It may throw some little light upon their paths, and, if not their's, upon those of my grandsons, many of whom, I trust, are to be heralds of the cross."

The fruit of such a labor of love cannot be allowed to moulder in the grave. Our hearts would never bear it.

Moreover, we believe our father did a great work for God; that he was a man for his time, and therefore a man for all times; and that the study of the life of such a man will do good, not only to his children, but to all others.

His personal acquaintance with many of the most distinguished men of his time, both in church and state; his active participation in some of the most stirring events of the church; and his peculiarly close relations to the most prominent institutions of learning, secular and religious, in our commonwealth, give to his memoir a historical significance of singular interest and importance.

He was partly induced to write by the urgent entreaty of one of his sons, whose chief object was to get his mind employed upon daily work, and thus retard that decay of mental faculties which comes on so rapidly when an energetic life is suddenly exchanged for one of inactivity. The work grew on his hands until it became a book, which filial honesty must put in print.

These "Notes," together with other papers, were placed in the hands of a friend and ministerial brother, who had known him long and intimately, and who expressed a warm desire to write his memoir; but this friend was prevented by insuperable difficulties from executing his cherished purpose. After twelve years the papers have been returned to our hands, and at this late day we undertake the work, under many disadvantages.

In a little volume, entitled *The Old Bachelor*, by Mr. William Wirt, a picture is strikingly described. Writing of the influence mothers may exert over their children he says: "I cannot better explain myself than by describing a picture which I saw some years ago, in the parlor of a gentleman with whom I was invited to dine. It was a plate—a colored engraving, executed in the highest style of that art—which represents a mother as reciting to her son the martial exploits of his ancestors. The mother herself had not lost the beauty of youth, and was an elegant and noble figure. She was sitting in a large arm-chair, her face and her arm extended aloft, and her countenance exalted and impassioned with her subject. Her little boy, a fine-looking fellow, apparently about fourteen years of age, was kneeling before her, his hands clasped in her lap, and stooping towards her. His bright eyes were fixed upon her, and swimming with tears of admiration and rapture. Such, said I to myself, is the impulse which a mother can give to the opening character of her child; and such is the way in which a hero may be formed."[1]

If we can set before the descendants of our honored father a delineation of his character and life true to nature, though without any of "the finish" of this prize picture of Alfred the Great, it will be such as we desire and all that we can attain unto.

Believing as we do, that when the materials at hand are sufficient, every biography should be an autobio-

---

[1] This picture now hangs in the parlor of a Virginia gentleman— Frederick Johnston, Esq., of Roanoke County.

graphy, our part in this work has been mainly to reproduce his own work in such an order as will give to it unity. A man's writings delineate himself more accurately than he can be delineated by another. This self-revelation, unconsciously made in correspondence, diaries, anecdotes and narrations, is the true, the express and only reliable portrayal of personal mind and soul that can be made. Through it we can see the heart beating, the blood flowing, and the wonder-working mind performing its subtlest and most vital functions.

No likeness was ever taken of our father that caught the true expression of his countenance. When at rest, a look of sternness always settled upon it, that melted away as soon as he began to speak in public or converse in private, or even when reading. Then his large brown eyes would glow with a strong light, and his warm feelings spread themselves in a smile of animated joy over his large and strongly marked face. This drew to him strangers wherever he went, and made him friends as long as he lived. The likeness prefixed to this Memoir, with this exception, is very good.

CONTENTS.

CHAPTER I.
1800.
PLACE OF BIRTH AND ANCESTRY.

Hanover County, Famous in the Annals of Church and State.—Patrick Henry.—Henry Clay.—Samuel Davies.—First Formal Movement for Religious Liberty.—Drs. B. M. Smith, Theodorick Pryor, and W. S. Plumer, on Dr. White's Life and Work.—The Residence of the White Family.—His Ancestry, 13

CHAPTER II.
1800–1822.

Paternal Grandmother.—Learning the Alphabet.—Washington-Henry Academy.—"Parson Hughs."—A Leader among Boys.—His Father.—His Mother.—Various Schoolmasters.—First Attempt at Teaching.—Enters Hampden-Sidney College.—Room-mates.—How Awakened.—Wrestling in Prayer in the Woods.—(Rev.) Daniel A. Penick.—Students' Prayer Meeting.—Received into the College Church 22

CHAPTER III.
1820–1824.

Teaching in his Father's Family.—A Profitable Prayer Meeting.—Gilbert Tennent Snowden.—Death of his Father.—Seeing his Way into the Ministry.—Dr. John H. Rice.—Mrs. John H. Rice.—Their Home.—Anecdotes about Dr. Rice.—Dr. Rice's Death.—Re-enters College.—How he Gets through College .. 32

CHAPTER IV.
1822–1827.

Graduates.—Teaches School in Farmville.—Taken under Care of Presbytery.—Opening of Union Theological Seminary.—Studies there while Teaching in Farmville.—Anecdote of Dr. B. H. Rice.—Licensed, April 30, 1827.—Anecdote of Dr. Rice; or, How to Treat Other Denominations.—Goes as Home Missionary to Nottoway.—Letter of Encouragement from Dr. B. H. Rice.—Sketches and Anecdotes of the Two Rices, and of Dr. William S. Reid... 43

CHAPTER V.
1827-1832.

Shiloh Church Built.—Fruits of Five Years' Work in Nottoway, Lunenburg, Amelia and Dinwiddie.—Jeter's Race-track.—Dr. Rice's Wise Counsel to him in Despondency.—Baptists and Methodists.—Marriage.—Generosity of Dr. James Jones.—Uncle Jack, "The African Preacher."—Anecdotes of him.—The Dying Infidel.—Encomium by Dr. Pryor 54

CHAPTER VI.
PASTORAL SKETCHES.

Infidelity in Prospect of Death.—"Caught with Guile."—Interested Hearers.—Anti-Presbyterianism Cured.—"The Devil Threw him Down and Tore him."—Early Conversion: E. F. P.; E. W. W.; A. R.; A. H.; E. S.; A. A. B. 69

CHAPTER VII.
1832-1836.

Leaves Nottoway for Scottsville, Va.—Mr. (afterwards Rev. Dr.) Peyton Harrison Builds a Parsonage for him at his own Charges.—Revival.—Rev. Daniel Baker.—Accepts Agency for American Tract Society.—Observations on his Agency and Similar Enterprises Auxiliary to the Church.................. 90

CHAPTER VIII.
1836-1838.

His Field in and about Charlottesville.—Abandons South Plains and Bethel.—Rev. Joseph F. Baxter Called to them.—Confines his Work to Charlottesville.—Opens a School for Young Ladies.—The School a Nursery to the Church.—Declines Entertaining a Call to a Valley Church 97

CHAPTER IX.
1836-1848.

University of Virginia.—Mr. Jefferson Sees his Mistake.—Popular Demand for Religious Instruction.—Denominational Rotation in the Chaplaincy.—Himself Chaplain in 1840.—Health Breaks down.—Professor Davis Shot by a Student.—His Death.—Funeral.—Note on the Sermon, by Rev. Dr. Dabney.—New Era in the Religious History of the University.—Anecdote about Dr. Speece.—Chaplain a Second Time (1844).—Rev. D. B. Ewing Secured as Assistant.—Health Fails again.—The "Aliquis Controversy."—List of his Publications.—Gov. T. W. Gilmer.—His Tragical Death.—Funeral.—Illustrative Incident.—A Cause of the Prevailing Deism in Virginia.—Prof. W. H. McGuffey.—Opposition to him because a Minister of the Gospel.—Anecdote.—Review of Dr. Cooper's "Life of Priestley," by Dr. John H. Rice.—Dr. White's Impress on Charlottesville and Albemarle County, by a Member of the Methodist Church ------------------------------------- 105

CHAPTER X.
1848-1861.

Accepts a Call to Lexington, Va.—"The Skinner War."—Dr. Skinner Suspended from the Ministry by the Presbytery.—Restored by the General Assembly.—The Pastoral Relation: his State of Mind in Dissolving and in Forming it.—The Lexington Congregation—Major (afterwards the renowned General) T. J. Jackson.—John B. Lyle.—Anecdote about him.—Method of Collections for the Church.—Anecdote about General T. J. Jackson.—A Model Deacon -------------------------------- 128

CHAPTER XI.
1848-1861.

Pentecostal Seasons.—Special Prayer for the Approaching Meeting of Synod.—Its Fervor an Indication of Approaching Revival, which Occurred in his Absence.—Effects of the Revival on the Church.—Another Revival, extending from November, 1853, to February, 1854.—Full Account of another in 1856.—Proposition in 1857 to Colonize.—The Church Building Enlarged.—Efforts for the Colored People.—Sabbath-school Founded by Gen. T. J. Jackson for their Benefit.—Work in behalf of Temperance.—Anecdote about his Preaching against a Military Ball.—Home Missionary Work.—Stems a Torrent of Indignant Opposition to a Public Lecturer.—Rev. W. J. Baird, D. D.—His Pulpit Power _____ 144

CHAPTER XII.
1861-1865.

A "Union Man" at the Secession of South Carolina.—What Changed his Mind and that of his State.—Abolitionism and Secessionism.—List of those in his Church and Congregation who Perished or were Disabled for Life in the War.—Depreciated Currency.—Peace in the Midst of War.—Extract from a Letter of his Son who Fell in Battle.—False Philanthropy of Abolitionists.—Their Agency in bringing on the War.—The Nat. Turner Insurrection.—John Brown's Diabolical Scheme.—The Southern People on the Defensive for Thirty Years prior to the War.—Gen. Hunter's Ruffianism in Lexington.—Shells, Burns and Sacks the Town.—Gen. Averill's Raid: a Thorough Gentleman.—Chaplains in the Northern Army.—The Gaiety among the People.—Sir Walter Scott's Review of the French Revolution.—"The Lost Cause."—Grace Triumphs _____ 167

CHAPTER XIII.
1861-1865.

The Strife before the War _____ 200

CHAPTER XIV.
1800-1871.

Health Fails.—Offers his Resignation to the Session; Declined, and an Offer of Support for an Assistant Made, provided his Health not Restored by Rest.—Corresponds for Assistant.—Health not being Restored, Insists on Resigning.—Action of the Congregation.—Becomes Principal of the Ann Smith Academy.—Letter to Rev. John S. Watt.—A Touching Sight.—The School Succeeds.—Resigns.—Letter of the Trustees Accepting, 208

CHAPTER XV.
1871-1873.

Retreats to the Home of his Daughter, Mrs. Harriet McCrum.—Serene and Cheerful Old Age.—How he Appeared to his Brethren; *e. g.*, Rev. G. W. Leyburn and Rev. Dr. Wm. S. Plumer. His Chief Desire in Prospect of Death.—Leads his Physician to Christ.—Impressive Interview with Judge J. W. Brockenrough.—Anecdote of his Patriotism 220

CHAPTER XVI.
MEMORIAL NOTICES OF DR. AND MRS. WHITE.

By the Session of the Church.—Lines by Mrs. M. J. Preston.—By the Synod of Virginia.—The Faculty of Washington and Lee University.—*The Central Presbyterian.*—Rev. John S. Grasty, D. D.—Rev. Dr. Balch.—Lines by Rev. Dr. J. A. Waddell.—Memorials of Mrs. White.—By the Session of the Church and Mrs. Preston 235

CHAPTER XVII.
LETTERS OF CONDOLENCE.

From Rev. Dr. Wm. Brown; Rev. Dr. Wm. S. Plumer; Rev. Dr. B. M. Smith; Rev. Dr. R. L. Dabney; Mrs. Margaret J. Preston 268

CHAPTER XVIII.

Estimates of his Character by Life-long Friends: Dr. R. L. Dabney; Dr. T. W. Sydnor; Dr. Theodorick Pryor 275

REV. WILLIAM S. WHITE, D. D.,
AND HIS TIMES.

CHAPTER I.
PLACE OF BIRTH AND ANCESTRY.
1800.

HANOVER COUNTY, FAMOUS IN THE ANNALS OF CHURCH AND STATE.—PATRICK HENRY.—HENRY CLAY.—SAMUEL DAVIES.—FIRST FORMAL MOVEMENT FOR RELIGIOUS LIBERTY.—DRS. B. M. SMITH, THEODORICK PRYOR, AND W. S. PLUMER ON DR. WHITE'S LIFE AND WORK.—THE RESIDENCE OF THE WHITE FAMILY.—HIS ANCESTRY.

"I am a part of all that I have met."

HANOVER COUNTY is famous in the annals of Virginia for her contribution both to the State and the Church. Patrick Henry, whose eloquence helped to inflame the popular heart with patriotic indignation against the tyranny of Great Britain and bring on the Revolution of 1776, was born and brought up on her soil. The old brick court-house, built A. D. 1735, in which his voice thundered in peals that reverberated through the land, is still used for the administration of justice.

In "the slashes of Hanover" Henry Clay was born, a fact which (he was wont to say humorously) all but himself were ashamed to confess. In the country home of Mr. J. G. Tinsley the parlor-corner is still pointed out in which the great statesman made his first appearance, when a blushing youth, shrinking out of sight, at a social party. He was then employed in the clerk's office in Richmond, and the party was in the home of the clerk. From this county he emigrated to Kentucky early in life, accompanied by an uncle of the subject of this memoir.

Among the distinguished and useful men in the Presbyterian Church of Virginia, and indeed of the United States, perhaps none will be remembered longer than the eloquent, laborious and devoted Samuel Davies. Patrick Henry said of him that "he was the greatest orator he had ever heard."[1] His influence in procuring religious toleration in Virginia was unsurpassed. He met and nearly overthrew Attorney-General Randolph in a great discussion of the construction of the Act of Toleration,[2] and "succeeded in procuring from the attorney-general in England a decision that the Act of Toleration was the law of Virginia, and the consequent licensing of the dissenting churches."[3] "If Francis Makemie was the first licensed minister of the Presbyterian faith (1699), Samuel Davies was the founder of the church in Virginia."[4] For when Mr. Davies arrived in Virginia (1748) there was not a single organized Presbyterian church anywhere to be found in the old, settled parts of the State."[5] There had been "a small Presbyterian congregation on the Elizabeth river, near where Norfolk now stands, over which the Rev. Mr. Mackey, from Ireland, presided as their minister. But soon after Makemie's death he was forced to fly from intolerant persecution, and we hear no more of him or his congregation afterwards."[6]

It was some years after the death of Makemie before a Presbyterian church was organized in the Old Dominion.[7] The two congregations in Accomack county, gathered by Makemie, were extinguished after his death by persecution at the hands of the establishment. He had been called the "Father of Hanover Presbytery," and Hanover Presbytery is the mother of Presbyteries in the South and West of the

---

[1] Cooke's *Virginia*, 1883, p. 338.   [2] *Ibid.*   [3] *Ibid.*   [4] *Ibid.*
[5] Davies' Sermons, Vol. I., Robert Carter & Bros., 1857, p. xviii.
[6] *Ibid.*, p. xviii.   [7] Foote's *Sketches of Virginia*, Vol. I., p. 98.

United States. Samuel Davies was the head and front of dissent in Virginia, for, as he declared, there were not, when he first came, "ten avowed dissenters within one hundred miles of him."[1] The combination of Quakers, Baptists and Presbyterians to procure religious toleration in Virginia was initiated in Hanover county by the Presbyterians.[2] The first protest of evangelical Christianity against formalism, in the shape of a public document, was made by the Presbyterians of Hanover. "The noble memorial from the Presbytery of Hanover, which may yet be seen on the yellow old sheet in the Virginia archives, sums up the whole case with admirable eloquence and force. It is trenchant and severe, but that was natural. It is the great protest of dissent in all the years."[3]

This venerable document, although written November 11, 1774, and forwarded at that time by the Presbytery of Hanover to the Virginia House of Burgesses, lay concealed in the archives of the State until May 7, 1888, when, for the first time it seems, it was put into print by Mr. Wm. Wirt Henry, in the columns of the *Central Presbyterian*, in Richmond, Va.

From this document it appears that the first formal movement for religious liberty in these United States, which is now the glory of our land, was made by the members of the Presbytery of Hanover. It is also evident that Mr. Jefferson derived his ideas on this subject, as Mr. Henry remarks, from this and similar documents from the same body, written in 1776 and 1777, which he incorporated in the Bill of Rights of Virginia, by which, in 1799, the separation between church and state for the first time was effected. And so it is proved that from the bosom of old Hanover Presbytery flashed the *vis vivida* by which the established church was overthrown and a way opened for religious liberty.

---

[1] Cooke's *Virginia*, 1883, p. 338.   [2] *Ibid.*, p. 339.   [3] *Ibid.*, p. 392.

Two large Presbyteries in the Synod of Virginia now bear the name of Hanover. The first Presbyterian church in Tidewater was organized in a private house in this county— that of John Morris.[1] The historical significance of the establishment of religious liberty in Virginia, as estimated by Mr. Jefferson, may be inferred from the fact that he had his authorship of the bill, by which it was granted, inscribed upon his tombstone, along with his authorship of the Declaration of Independence and his founding the University of Virginia. These he evidently considered the broad and lasting foundations of his fame. While his credit for this immortal document is not to be abated in the least, yet it is not extravagant to say that Mr. Davies exerted a more powerful influence than Mr. Jefferson in *preparing the popular mind* for its enactment as law.

These facts render old Hanover county the *classic ground* of Virginia Presbyterianism, and, may we not add, of American Presbyterianism?

We propose to write of another, who was born and reared to manhood on the soil of Hanover, one for whom we claim no such distinction for oratory or statesmanship as that of those just mentioned, yet one whose life, as a minister of the gospel, was fruitful of noble results, and who, by the concentration of all his powers upon a full and determined purpose to do what he could for his race, achieved great success, and made his life instructive to all who would do likewise. It is the opinion of some who knew his life thoroughly that, *in his way*, he did a work not unworthy of comparison with that of any of them.

The Rev. Dr. B. M. Smith, in a letter giving his estimate of the life-work of Dr. White, written for publication, says: "Your father certainly did *most wonderfully popularize Presbyterianism*. Dr. John H. Rice did more, in a different

---

[1] Cooke's *Virginia*, 1883, p. 336.

manner, to build up our church, but your father's personal ministry exceeded in success, of the kind indicated, that of any man I knew."

The Rev. Dr. Theodorick Pryor, whose acquaintance with him began in 1823, when they were both students at Hampden-Sidney College, who succeeded him in the Nottoway Church, and who knew him intimately from that time until his death, writes: "I cannot conceive of a man better qualified to do good. Wherever he lived and labored, his work testified to his worth. . . . I heartily wish the church were now blessed with a thousand William S. Whites."

The Rev. Dr. Wm. S. Plumer, who, as he says, "was much with him for forty-five years, and saw him variously and sorely tried," writes for publication, viz.: "Such a man was of course useful. He was useful in the pulpit, in the church courts, in the parlor, in the sick chamber, at the marriage, in the house of mourning, by example, by precept, by doctrine, by his pen, especially in his excellent letters, and almost in every way."

Hanover county, and those adjacent to it, were settled by an intelligent population of English descent, who maintained the manners and customs of the old country. High living and hospitality were universal. Well-bred gentlemen set the key-note of good manners; horse-racing, fox-hunting, fish-fries, bird-suppers, and whist-parties brought the people together and promoted good fellowship. The old Virginia gentleman was the *beau ideal* in the mind of every aspiring youth of that day.

Not to be able to make one's self agreeable in company was an unpardonable defect in education. The young people were not set to work or drilled in business, but were taught to be agreeable at home and in company. The manual labor was performed by slaves, whose management was entrusted to an overseer. This led to much wasteful dissipation.

Mr. White's ancestry were English, and went to the extreme

in pleasure seeking. His father, who owned Ellyson's Mill, about six miles east of Richmond, which gave the name to one of the great battles of "the war between the States," and who occupied the dwelling house that still stands on the hill above the mill, was devoted to company. We have heard him say that, when the family were assembling for dinner, his father often sent him to the mill to bring up to dine with them any neighbor who might be there. In this way he was accustomed to company from childhood, and this, together with an inherited fondness for it, made him a welcome guest through life in houses where ministers of the gospel were looked upon with aversion.

The life of every man, no less than that of every plant and animal, is the product of the combined influence of heredity and circumstances. Inherited tendencies, unconscious impressions from men and things, are so many tuitional influences, or "schools and schoolmasters," that determine infallibly and within the scope of divine sovereignty the character and life of us all. The plastic mind of childhood, inconceivably more plastic than the body, can never throw off impressions then received. We may all say:

"I am a part of all that I have met,"

especially that I met in childhood. The history of no man's life can be written without relating the race from which he sprung, the place where he was reared, the institutions, the social customs and educational forces which moulded his character and thus singled him out from his species, individualizing him for all time. For this reason emphasis is laid upon the foregoing facts as the directing influences of Mr. White's life in his youth. We shall see, as we watch its unfoldings, how much he was indebted to them for what he came to be.

On the Chickahominy river, east of Richmond, is a historic spot known as White Oak Swamp. Here, it is believed,

Capt. John Smith was captured by the Indians. His canoe grounding in the shallows, he attempted to escape through the swamp. By a misstep he sank into the marsh, and so fell an easy prey into their hands. His rescue from a bloody death by Pocahontas followed.[1]

On this same river, about six miles east of Richmond, is a mound of earth, unlike that of the swamp, and identical with the soil on the adjacent hills, called "Sugar Loaf Island," about an acre in size, which, in 1855, was covered with white-oak, beech and maple. This is the head of "canoe navigation" on the river, and, agreeably to tradition, was the spot where Capt. Smith left his canoe and fled on foot through the swamp. [Cooke locates the spot further east in the same swamp.]

The residence of the White family for many generations, and the birth-place of W. S. White, was at Beaver Dam— an estate about a half of a mile from this point, and a quarter of a mile from Ellyson's Mill (then called Ellerson's Mill). This is the tract of land which, he says in his "Notes," is "still in possession of a branch of my family, and has belonged to it ever since the year 1680, the same body of land belonging to the same family for one hundred and eighty-four years, and probably longer. It lies on the north bank of the Chickahominy river, about six miles from Richmond."

Of his ancestry Mr. White writes as follows: "My father, William White, was married to Mildred Ellis in 1799. Both were of Hanover county, Va. Both were descendants of the earliest settlers of that county, and connected with the Presbyterian congregation gathered there by Rev. Samuel Davies. I can trace my paternal ancestry back to the year 1680.... My own birth occurred July 30, 1800. I was the eldest of seven children, four sons and three daughters. Two of these children died in early infancy. The remaining five

---

[1] See Cooke's *Virginia*, p. 34.

attained to maturity, and all became consistent members of the church."

It is to be regretted that he did not leave more information on this subject, for his aptness at tracing relationships was remarkable. From other sources, deemed entirely reliable, we have gathered the following additional facts, which will be of interest to the family:

[The grandfather of W. S. White was Barrett White. In a family Bible, now in our possession, out of which we have heard him say the Rev. Samuel Davies sometimes preached, is the following entry: "Barrett White departed this life February 18, 1782, in the fifty-fifth year of his age. His death was much lamented by his friends and neighbors, being a good neighbor, a tender husband, a good father, and a kind master to his slaves." His wife was named Elizabeth. In the family Bible now owned by Rev. T. W. Sydnor, D. D., a first cousin of W. S. White, is this record: "Elizabeth White departed this life December 14, 1815, in the eighty-second year of her age." "She was, therefore," adds T. W. Sydnor, D. D., "at the time of the death of Barrett White forty-nine years old, and he fifty-five.

"They left three sons, viz., Philip, who moved to Kentucky, and from whom were three sons, *i. e.*, Jefferson, Joseph M., and Philip S., all men of note in their day.

"Thomas, who lived in the upper end of Hanover county, Va., near what is now Ashland. He left five sons and four daughters, viz., Joseph, who moved to Kentucky; Clement; Larkin, who frequently represented his county in the General Assembly of Virginia; John Preston, Thomas Mercer, Mrs. Beasly, Mrs. Tinsley, Mrs Glaizebrook, and Mrs Kimborough.

"William White, who was the father of Wm. S. White, had four sons and three daughters, viz., Wm. S., Thomas J., Philip Barrett, Harriet E., who married James McLaurin, of

Powhatan county, Va., and who died early; and Elizabeth, who never married. Two died in childhood.

"Barrett White and Elizabeth also had three daughters, viz, Mrs. Penny, Mrs. Blackwell, and Mrs. Sydnor. Mrs. Penny and Mrs. Blackwell moved to Kentucky and left families. Mrs. Sydnor, mother of Rev. T. W. Sydnor, brought up a family in Hanover, Va."

Two general characteristics of these different branches of the family are noted by Dr. Sydnor, *i. e.*, "Fondness for talking and pride of ancestry." He also notes the following special characteristics, *i. e.*, "Philip White's sons were very talented men, fond of politics and the highest social circles. Thomas White's sons were men of pleasure, fond of horse-racing and similar sports. Two of them, Larkin and Mercer, late in life became exemplary members of the church. William White's sons and daughters all in early life became pious, and all *their* sons and daughters, as far as I know, are pious."

It was Philip White, uncle of W. S. White, who moved to Kentucky, I think, with Henry Clay. Joseph White, who also moved to Kentucky, was first cousin of W. S. White, and the oldest son of Gen. Thomas White. Thomas White, who moved to Missouri, was brother of W. S. White. Joseph M. White, son of Philip White, who went to Kentucky, represented Florida many years in Congress when Florida was a territory. Philip S. White, a famous temperance lecturer, was his brother.]

CHAPTER II.

1800–1822.

PATERNAL GRANDMOTHER.—LEARNING THE ALPHABET.—WASHINGTON-HENRY ACADEMY.—"PARSON HUGHS."—A LEADER AMONG BOYS.—HIS FATHER.—HIS MOTHER.—VARIOUS SCHOOLMASTERS.—FIRST ATTEMPT AT TEACHING.—ENTERS HAMPDEN-SIDNEY COLLEGE.—ROOM-MATES.—HOW AWAKENED.—WRESTLING IN PRAYER IN THE WOODS.—(REV.) DANIEL A. PENICK.—STUDENTS' PRAYER MEETING.—RECEIVED INTO THE COLLEGE CHURCH.

" I will arise and go to my Father."

IN the "Notes" referred to, Dr. White writes as follows: "I was carefully trained from an early age to read the word of God. This training I received chiefly from my paternal grandmother, whose maiden name was Starke. She was a woman of vigorous intellect, and eminently pious. She died in great peace when I was in the sixteenth year of my age.

"I have always believed that her bright example and faithful instructions did more to lay the foundation of my character and life than all other instrumentalities combined. She taught me to read, using a large family Bible, which I still own, for this purpose. Her plan was to turn the leaves of this Bible and teach me the large letters at the beginning of the chapters. Thus the Bible was my "first book," my *only* primer, spelling and reading book. From two to eight years of age I slept in her room. At a period further back than I can recollect she taught me a form of prayer, and so impressed my mind with the solemnity of the act that it abode with me to manhood.

"At nine years of age I was sent to Washington-Henry

Academy, an institution established cotemporaneously with Pole Green Church, in Hanover, under the auspices of the Rev. Samuel Davies. This school had, at that time, been in operation half a century, and was still prosperous. The principal was the Rev. Mr. Hughs, and his assistant was Mr. Bowling Starke, first cousin to my father. Mr. Hughs was an Episcopal minister, rather of the colonial stamp, who dressed neatly and in the fashion of that day, wearing a coat with very broad skirts and enormous pockets, vest with flaps, small clothes, snow-white stockings, large knee and shoe buckles of pure silver, and a white flowing wig. Every day at noon the boys were assembled for prayers, when a portion of the Psalter and a prayer were read; this, too, in an academy that had been planned, endowed and built by Presbyterians!

"At this time neither my father nor mother was a professor of religion. The former was emphatically a man of the world. Possessing at the time of his marriage a very ample patrimony with which to commence life, being eminently social in his tastes and habits, possessing a warm and generous heart, having around him several young friends like himself, newly married, but, unlike himself, possessed of large fortunes, he was easily drawn into a style of living to which his own inheritance was not adequate. With these friends he took extensive journeys, to them he gave expensive dinners, adopting a style of life unfavorable both to his spiritual and temporal interests. He died when forty-seven years old, leaving his five children about as much property as he had inherited from his father. Although he never made a profession of religion, we were not without hope in his death.

"Shortly before his death my mother was received into the Presbyterian Church, and for about thirty years led the life of an exemplary Christian. She survived my father twenty-five years."

The Rev. Dr. Sydnor, of Nottoway, Va., who knew Mrs. White well, says: "Her funeral sermon was preached by Dr. W. S. Plumer, in Richmond, Va., on the text, 'Well done, thou good and faithful servant; thou hast been faithful over a few things, I will make thee ruler over many things; enter thou into the joy of thy Lord.' Her character was beautifully portrayed, but by no means overdrawn. She was an eminently godly woman, uniformly cheerful, never very much cast down, and of a remarkably affectionate spirit."

Dr. Plumer writes as follows: "One of the most prominent features of Dr. White's character was strong common sense. He came by this lawfully. It was the prominent trait of his mother's mind, whom I knew very well. His good sense seemed never to fail him. It was as marked in his sermons as in his daily intercourse with men."

When Dr. White was a mere boy, his first cousin, then a matured man—the Hon. Joseph M. White, member of Congress from Florida—visited Beaver Dam, the home of Wm. White, and, being impressed with the boy's mind and manners, said to him: "Don't vegetate here on the Chickahominy. Resolve to be something." This remark, enforced by the brilliant career of his cousin, proved to be a nail fastened in a sure place. From that hour his purpose was formed to obtain an education.

His father was the more ready to help him because of a lameness in one limb which could never be removed, because of which he always introduced him to visiting friends as his "unfortunate child." Notwithstanding this physical defect, such was the energy of his spirit that he was very fond of field sports of all kinds, and, "to the surprise of everybody, could outswim, outride, and outclimb any boy in the neighborhood."

About this time, as we have seen, when in his ninth year, he was sent off to school. But difficulties of one sort and another rendered his efforts almost abortive. He was sent to three different schools, viz., Washington and Henry, one in the slashes of Hanover, near the birth-place of Henry Clay, and the third in Manchester, Va., taught by the Rev. John Kirkpatrick.

At eighteen years of age, being without money, he determined to teach school and earn it. "Accordingly," he writes, "a log building was erected, with an earthen floor, in a dense grove, near the road leading from Richmond to Hanover court-house, about eight miles from the former place. Here I made my first effort as a teacher of youth. I was liberally patronized, did my best, and made money enough in one year to defray my expenses at college a year-and-a-half.

"In January, 1819, in my nineteenth year, I went to Hampden-Sidney College, introduced to Dr. Moses Hoge, then the president, by my very kind friend, the Rev. John Kirkpatrick. This letter drew their attention to me strongly, and enlisted them warmly in my favor. Indeed, he had written to them before I went that I had some good qualities; learned readily, but was not very studious; was extremely social and much influenced by company.

"He therefore begged that I might be placed, if possible, in a room with sedate and pious students. Ignorant of all this, which I afterwards learned from Mrs. Hoge, I was much surprised to be told, almost as soon as I reached Dr. Hoge's parlor, that my room, furniture, and other things were all ready for me.

"When I entered the room and saw that my room-mates were two of the plainest looking men, each nearly thirty years old, grave-looking, coarsely dressed, and that the furniture was rude and scant, my heart sank in me like lead in the waters. 'This,' I said to myself, 'is too bad; I can't endure it.'

"They received me politely and kindly. But oh! how dry, how dreadfully dry! The old building, too, was rickety and dismal. The walls of the room looked as if no lime had touched them for twenty years, and the floor as if it had never been scoured.

"But in all this the hand of God soon became distinctly visible. These room-mates, who, to a thoughtless youth like me, seemed so uncongenial at first, soon won my confidence and love. One of them died, I think, without being licensed to preach; the other lived out his three-score years and ten, and was very successful as a herald of the cross. I cherish, with the tenderest affection, the memory of Hugh Caldwell and Wm. Hammersley (although more than forty-five years have passed), and that of Mr. Kirkpatrick and Dr. Hoge for having put me at that critical age under their influence.

"Rev. Dr. Moses Hoge was the president of the College, professor of theology, and pastor of the church, and filled each chair with ability. He took his turn in conducting the morning and afternoon worship in the College chapel, preached every Sabbath morning, and lectured every Sabbath night in his own parlor. The laws of the College required me to attend chapel service, and, from a sense of duty rather than inclination, I attended regularly. I also went regularly on Sabbath morning, but night meetings were new to me, and, as we were free to go or stay away, I did not attend. Dr. Hoge's sermons were rich in matter, but his manner was by no means attractive. To me it was rather repulsive, and decidedly awkward. But, in spite of my own vitiated taste and dense ignorance, I was obliged to hear enough to be convinced of his warm heart and brilliant intellect, and learned to listen with lively interest. Although my heart was sometimes moved, my conscience slept.

"One Sabbath night, so thoughtless was I and ignorant, I took up my text-book to prepare my lesson for Monday. Good Mr. Hammersley was surprised and mortified at this;

spoke in plain but kind terms of its wickedness, and ended by begging me to go with him to the meeting in Dr. Hoge's parlor. My conscience smote me. Memory recalled my loved and faithful grandmother, now in heaven, and I went. Dr. Hoge lectured on Belshazzar's feast, and dwelt particularly on the mysterious handwriting on the wall: 'Thou art weighed in the balances and found wanting.' I was interested, convinced, and deeply affected. I strove hard to conceal my feelings.

"When the services ended I hastened from the parlor, spoke to nobody, but did not return to my room. I was afraid to see my room-mates, thinking that the sight of them, even if they should not speak to me, would increase my distress. I hastened to the forest, several hundred yards beyond the College, and there, in the night and dark and silent woods, I had the first clear conception of the difference between saying prayers and praying. The first I was familiarized to in childhood, the latter I had never attempted nor understood. Nor did I understand it then. I knelt at the root of a tree, both hands resting against the trunk. I could not pray. I knew not how. I was deeply sensible that, if weighed in the balances of God's law and justice, I must perish. I clearly saw that a large measure of my guilt consisted not only in my not praying, but in my inability to pray.

"I returned to my room far more wretched than I was when I left Dr. Hoge's parlor. It may seem strange, but it is nevertheless true, that I was rather gratified than otherwise, on reaching my room, to find both my room-mates abed and asleep. I felt a strong repugnance to speaking to any one or having any one to speak to me. I slept but little.

"At a very early hour the next morning I hastened to the woods again. As I slowly descended into a densely wooded ravine, my attention was attracted by the sound of a human voice, as of one in distress. I paused a moment, then slowly and cautiously advanced in the direction of the sound. I soon discovered its source. I saw the body of a man kneeling, with his hands resting on a rude seat built against the trunk of a tree. I soon recognized the person as that of my excellent friend, now the Rev. Daniel A. Penick, pastor of Rocky River Church, North Carolina. I caught some of his words, and even a sentence or two. I wept because I could not pray as he could. I desired greatly to speak to him and have him tell me how to pray. But I saw the impropriety of disturbing him then, passed on as quietly as possible to another part of the forest, and renewed my effort to pray. I recalled the parable of the prodigal son, in which I had been much interested in early childhood, without comprehending its spiritual import, and made the confession and the prayer of the prodigal to his father mine: 'Father, I have sinned against heaven and in thy sight, and am no more worthy to be called thy son; make me as one of thy hired servants.' These words abode with me. They dwelt in my mind and on my heart. What I had seen and heard in the morning inclined me strongly to make my condition known to Mr. Penick. This I did during the day, but I well remember that my embarrassment was such that I could say but little to him. What I said, however, was quite enough to open the way for him, and he spoke in a way greatly to instruct and comfort me. My state of mind was soon known through the College, and others kindly sought to give me all the help in their power.

"The pious students held a prayer meeting every Friday night in one of the rooms of the College. To gratify my friend Hammersley, I had, previous to this time, attended this meeting two or three times; but a wicked student, who had unfortunately acquired some influence over me, had rallied me for going, and said nobody but 'the divines' went to that meeting, and they only went to learn to pray when they became preachers. But when Friday night of this week came I went to that meeting gladly. And greatly was my soul refreshed. The Scriptures read and the hymns sung, though somewhat familiar to me in their letter, now seemed new. Indeed, it seemed as if I had never seen or heard them before.

"In the course of a week or two I sought an interview with Dr. Hoge. I was amazed and deeply affected to find one of his age and distinction so approachable, so condescending, and so kind. He followed me to his front door, took my hand in his, and said: 'I think you may safely apply for admission to the next communion, and feel a comfortable persuasion that this will not be with you as the morning cloud and early dew.' I did apply at the next communion, and was received into the College Church at Hampden-Sidney, where my membership has remained until this day, never having been dismissed to any other church. This occurred on the 19th of July, 1819."

This account of his conversion, written by Dr. White in his old age, calmly reviewing his past life, in the full possession of all his faculties, on the border of the world to come, and written for the instruction of his children, is certainly reliable testimony on a most important subject. This is a "religious experience," proved by a long and useful life, and, as far as such personal narratives can be relied on, very suggestive. Men of the world may say of it, as the great historian and essayist, Macaulay, once wrote, viz.:

"From Augustine downward, people strongly under religious impressions have written their confessions, or, in the cant phrase, their experiences; and very curious many of their narratives are. John Newton's, Bunyan's, Will Huntington's, Cowper's, Wesley's, Whitefield's, Scott's—there is no end of them. When worldly men have imitated these narratives, it has almost always been in a satirical and hostile spirit. Goethe is the single instance of an unbeliever who has attempted to put himself into the person of one of these pious autobiographers. He has tried to imitate them, just as he tried to imitate the Greek dramatists in his Iphigenia, and the Roman poets in his elegies. A vulgar artist would have multiplied texts and savory phrases. He has done nothing of the kind, but has tried to exhibit the spirit of piety in the highest exaltation; and a very singular performance he has produced." [1]

This confession will be *very curious* also to thoughtful men, who have never been strongly moved by the word and Spirit of God; but only to such.

The Rev. Dr. T. W. Sydnor, of Blackstone, Va., has drawn the following pen and ink portrait of young White at this time of his life:

"I know well the impression of him made early and indelibly on my mind. It was this: He was a youth of handsome features and pleasing manners, playful in his disposition, full of fun and frolic, but never vicious. He was kind and generous in all his impulses, gentle towards the weak, pitiful towards the unfortunate, forgiving towards the injurious—only sometimes a little precipitate and indiscreet in resenting insults, or wrongs against other persons than himself. True and steadfast to his friends, he would never, if he could prevent it by any means which seemed to him right and proper, allow them to be imposed upon. Far from being a bully, he was equally far from being a coward. His schoolmates and other associates regarded him as the very bravest of the brave. He was apt to learn, but not very studious. Still, being habitually respectful and dutiful to his teachers, he shared largely their confidence and affection. He was a great favorite with his fellow pupils, foremost in their schemes and sports—a leader among boys as he was afterwards a leader among men.

---

[1] *Life and Letters of Lord Macaulay*, Vol. II., p. 193. Leipsic. Lemmermann & Co.

"Very early in life he was piously disposed—like Timothy, knowing the Scriptures from a child; like David, glad when it was said unto him, 'Let us go into the house of the Lord'; like Samuel, attentive to the voice of God, and ready to minister in his service. My mother confidently predicted that he would become a preacher of the gospel."

The following letter from the Rev. Dr. Theodorick Pryor sketches young White at the same time of life:

"NOTTOWAY C. H., VA., *May* 11, 1886.

"REV. AND DEAR BROTHER: My acquaintance with your father, the late William S. White, D. D., began in June, 1823, when I entered Hampden-Sidney College. He was then a member of the Junior class. I occupied a room immediately above his, and was thus thrown into frequent and familiar intercourse with him. We belonged to the same debating society. I knew him well. My impression, is that he was the most popular man in College, universally loved and esteemed. He was among the best debaters in his society. Whilst he was not honored with a distinguished oration at graduation, my impression is that he *always* stood well in his class. Because of his genial disposition and his delight in familiar conversation, he probably lost some time which would better have been employed in study. His college life was without a blemish or censure, and he carried, when he entered the Theological Seminary, a character of eminent piety. My opinion is, that he studied better in the Seminary than in College."

CHAPTER III.

1820-1824.

TEACHING IN HIS FATHER'S FAMILY.—A PROFITABLE PRAYER MEETING.—GILBERT TENNENT SNOWDEN.—DEATH OF HIS FATHER.—SEEING HIS WAY INTO THE MINISTRY.—DR. JOHN H. RICE.—MRS. JOHN H. RICE.—THEIR HOME.—ANECDOTES ABOUT DR. RICE.—DR. RICE'S DEATH.—RE-ENTERS COLLEGE.—HOW HE GETS THROUGH COLLEGE.

> "Thou hast marked the slow rise of the tree,—how its stem trembled first
> Till it passed the kid's lips, the stag's antler—then safely outburst
> The fan branches all round."

WHEN Mr. White had completed six months of his Freshman year, he was compelled, by want of funds, to suspend his studies for a year. So he opened a school in his father's family, in Richmond, where they had moved a short time before. Here he made the acquaintance of a Mr. Gilbert Tennent Snowden, a native of New Jersey and lineal descendant of the Rev. Gilbert Tennent, of Log College. He was an intelligent and very earnest Christian, and took Mr. White to the "Young Men's Prayer Meeting," and showed an interest in him otherwise.

"On one occasion," Dr. White writes, "having sold me a small package of goods, as he handed it to me over the counter, he asked, in a low tone of voice: 'Do you think you have religion enough?'

"Somewhat startled, I replied promptly, 'By no means; indeed, I often doubt whether I have any.'

"'Well,' he said, 'suppose you and I meet at your school-room to-night, and spend an hour in reading the word of God, and prayer? We will have a prayer meeting all to ourselves.'

"I readily consented, and for several months we thus met three nights in each week, and I have ever believed that that was the most profitable prayer meeting I ever attended. There, for the first time, I prayed in the hearing of another, and there the question first rose in my mind as to preaching the gospel.

"I spent one year in Richmond, and then returned to college. Snowden left about the same time for Columbia, South Carolina, where he became a wise, active and generous ruling elder, and one of the most trusted and useful directors of the Theological Seminary at Columbia, and often represented his Presbytery in the General Assembly.

"When my Sophomore year in college ended, Snowden urged me to come to Columbia and make his house my home, offering me abundant pecuniary help. I was always strongly averse to leaving my native State, and to accepting gratuity in prosecuting my studies. But when every effort to raise money on my prospective inheritance failed, I agreed to go to Columbia and teach school, if a good situation could be gotten, as a last resort. Divine providence ordered otherwise, and so my life has been spent in Virginia instead of South Carolina.

"In September, 1820, my father died, and my mother returned to her farm in Hanover. Having to look for a home, my thoughts turned to the Rev. Dr. John H. Rice, then pastor of the First Presbyterian Church in Richmond. To my great joy, he consented to board me, and thus an acquaintance began, the benefits of which to myself can never be estimated. I was thus introduced into one of the best-modelled Christian families, and into the best society which the city or country afforded.

"I had not yet determined on a profession. Indeed, my mind was so engrossed with the purpose to get a good education, with little prospect of doing so, that my thoughts had never extended beyond it. Soon after I became a member of Dr. Rice's family, he placed in my hands the "Life of Cornelius Winter," by the Rev. William Jay. When I had read it, the Doctor asked me if that book had not awakened a desire in me to preach the gospel. I expressed a lively interest in the life and character of Mr. Winter, and a strong desire to become as good and useful a man, and added, 'But, Doctor Rice, I can't see my way into the ministry.'

"'How far can you see?' he asked.

"'With what I hope to make by my school this session, I can see one year ahead.'

"I have never forgotten his reply. It was in these words:

"'Very few persons can see a whole year before them at one time. Surely Moses could not when he stood with the Red Sea before him, the mountains on his right and left, and the Egyptians in his rear.'

"Thus ended this interview, but the impression it made has never been effaced.

"Soon after this, on entering the Doctor's study, I found him reading a new book. He raised his eyes and said, 'Here is one of the best books of the kind I have ever read. It is just from the press. One may profitably read it through every year of his life. I wish you to read it with prayer, saying, as you read, "Lord, what wilt thou have me to do?"' It was the "Life of Henry Martyn." I had no sooner finished it than my purpose was formed. The language now both of my tongue and heart was, 'Woe is me if I preach not the gospel.'

"Dr. Rice, even at this early period, had risen to great distinction. He had commenced the ministry an humble missionary to the negroes in Charlotte county, Virginia. Now he was the pastor of the First Presbyterian Church in Richmond, and editor of the *Southern Literary and Evangelical Magazine*, a monthly, conducted with great ability. Rev. Drs. Moses Hoge, Conrad Speece and John Matthews were his chief helpers among the ministry, while the Hon.

Wm. Wirt and Wm. Maxwell, Esq., were his chief helpers among the laity. The variety of matter, as well as the practical wisdom displayed in the conduct of this magazine, give it a value that will make it attractive and useful to the end of time. The twelve volumes, of which it consists, constitute one of the best portions of my library.

"To strangers, and especially to young men who did not know him, Dr. Rice seemed austere. His tall, majestic form, and thoughtful, solemn countenance, as he was seen on the street or in the pulpit, repelled rather than attracted persons of this description. It was so in a sad degree in my own case, until I met him in the social circle, and especially in his own delightful parlor. Here all austerity and sternness vanished, and a more approachable, more genial, more delightful companion could nowhere be found. Young men of good character, brought thus in contact with him, became passionately fond of him. During his pastorate at Richmond there was a large number of such who were familiarly designated as 'Dr. Rice's young men.' I had the good fortune to be of that number.

"The Doctor seemed to be aware of the difficulty of approaching strange young men directly, and hence his method was to do it indirectly. The following little incident will illustrate my meaning. On coming home from a visit of business to several stores, he said to me, 'I saw a young man just now in the store of Cotton & Clark, whose appearance impressed me very favorably, and I would be glad to make his acquaintance.' On his describing the personal appearance of the young man, I said to him, 'Doctor, I know him, but you would hardly like him, for he is a Socinian, from Boston.' He promptly replied, 'That only makes me the more anxious to know him. I wish you would bring him up to tea with you.' Soon after I told the young man that Dr. Rice had been so much pleased with his attention to customers that he desired me to bring him to his house to tea. The young man seemed surprised, but evidently gratified. He declined, however, at that time, but on further thought he determined to accept the Doctor's invitation, went with me to tea, was delighted with his visit, soon attended 'The Young Men's Prayer Meeting'—a meeting composed almost exclusively of 'Dr. Rice's young men'— and in a few months became a member of the Doctor's church, and a great favorite in his family.

"I must not fail to say that he was not the only attraction found in his parlor. He had no children, but he had a wife and a niece—an adopted daughter—who had no superiors in the art of polite entertainment. The Doctor did *the solid* and they *the beautiful*, so that both instruction and amusement could always be found in that parlor. Mrs. Rice possessed a very happy talent for dispelling from the minds of her visitors the thought that they were strangers. She did this by treating them very much as they were treated at their respective homes. Visitors were not invited to this hospitable house to eat and drink, but if eating and drinking came on during the visit, they partook of just what was on hand. Even if the tea ran short, as I have sometimes known it to do in consequence of an unusual number dropping in just at tea time, no sad looks, no dolorous apologies caused embarrassment. The company were supposed to have good sense enough fully to account for the failure.

"By the way, I have often been frightened away from the house of 'the best people' about meal time by knowing into what an agony of distress I should throw the lady of the house by catching her with a wash-day dinner, or a milk and bread supper. No visitor could ever distress the Doctor, nor even his kind, hospitable wife, in that way. It may be that this distinguished couple had, somehow, come to think that to people of taste and sense other sources of delightful entertainment might be expected in their house, even better than roast beef and plum pudding. They thought it quite as reputable and as useful to feed the mind and heart as to pamper the perishable body.

"But let none suppose that there was any lack of all that was necessary and agreeable on that hospitable board. But 'eat to live and not live to eat' was the sound and Christian-like maxim that ruled in that house, and, as a consequence of this, among higher influences, I am free to declare that in all my life I have never known so large an amount of good done to the soul through the proper culture of the social affections.

"Dr. Rice was too good, too strong, too faithful a man ever to have it said of him, as it is often foolishly said of the deceased minister of the gospel, 'he had not an enemy on earth.' I always regarded this as a virtual attempt to elevate the man above his Saviour. 'Woe be unto you when all men shall speak well of you.' And with equal truth may it be said, Woe be to him whose life is such as to provoke no ill-will, even from the devil or any of his emissaries. It may be said in truth, that the intelligent, the wise and the good only needed to know Dr. Rice in order to respect, admire and love him.

"On entering his study one morning he handed me a letter filled with vulgar abuse of him, and written by a bookseller of Richmond of no small pretensions. The reading of it filled me with indignation. I wondered how he could endure it, or what he would say in reply. But when I returned to him the letter, he handed me the reply already written, smiling good naturedly as he did so. It was couched in the well-known stanza of Wm. Cowper, with only the prefix 'sir'—

"'A pious, learned, or well-bred man
Will not insult me, and no other can.'

This, with his signature, abruptly appended, was the whole reply. There the matter ended.

"My brief residence in the family of Dr. Rice at Richmond brought me in contact with some of our most distinguished, as well as with many of our most intelligent citizens. Among the former were Frank Gilmer, Esq., Judge A. P. Upshur, Gov. J. P. Preston, and Hon. Wm. Wirt; among the latter were Morton Paine, Wm. Maxwell, Chas. Copland, Henry E. Watkins, Esqrs., and many others not now remembered. To be brought from time to time into the society of such men was a rich privilege to a youth like me. I have a vivid recollection of the cultivated, social intercourse which such men delighted to hold.

"At one time a youngster, with more impudence than brains, entered the Doctor's parlor when it was filled with the society of such as I have named. He had scarcely been seated when, with a very pompous manner and a voice loud enough to attract the attention of the whole room, he said: 'Dr. Rice, I have just read Lord Byron's last, splendid poem, "Don Juan." I would like to know your opinion of it.'

"The Doctor, with all the politeness of manner he could command, said: 'Well, sir, I do not know whether Satan can write poetry or not, but if he can, as far as the principles and spirit of the poem are concerned, it is just such an one as he would write.'

"With this 'Don Juan' was dismissed, and the pretentious young man soon took his departure.

"Dr. Rice had a favorite servant, named Charles, who had the confidence of his master to such an extent that he did all the marketing for the family, and transacted much other business. His sole charge in this way of work was to wait in the dining-room and attend to the visitors. On one occasion the family dined out. When they returned in the evening, Charles told his master that a gentleman had called that day to see him, but 'he neither left his name nor his card, sir, and I didn't like to be so impolite as to ask him.'

"'You do not know, then,' said the Doctor, 'who he was? But, Charles, can't you guess who he was?'

"To this Charles replied: 'I doesn't know, sir, but I rather 'spose he was a Yankee preacher.'

"'Why so, Charles?' said his master.

"'Well, sir,' said Charles, 'I has two reasons for 'sposin' he is a Yankee, and two for 'sposin' he is a preacher. I think, sir, he is a Yankee because so many of them comes here, and because he talks so percise; and I 'spose he is a preacher because he was dressed in black and wears spectacles.'

"Dr. Rice entertained a great deal of company, especially from the North. He had often travelled through that section of the country, and made many friends, and received liberal contributions there for the Seminary he had founded and for other objects. He was free from sectional prejudices, and trusted and loved those whom he considered good men wherever he found them. The scarcity of preachers in Virginia, caused in part by the want of a theological seminary, led to the coming of many from the North, and they invariably came to him to find for them a field of labor. The consequence was that he often had two or three together staying at his house for weeks at a time. Charles was right in supposing that the visitor spoken of above was a Yankee preacher. He reported himself as such the next morning, and he must have spent at least two months under Dr. Rice's roof. Indeed, it was very unusual to take a meal at his table without having one or more strangers present.

"The last journey of the Doctor to the North was taken in the summer of 1831. He came home with the disease upon him of which he died in September following. Settled then in Nottoway county, and hearing of his sickness, I rode up to the Seminary to see him. On every former occasion he had returned from the North in cheerful spirits. But at this time I was pained to find him much depressed. He spoke gloomily of the spirit he had discovered almost wherever he went. I well remember his saying: 'There is a fierceness in the utterances, looks, and even in the tones of voice in which the people indulge. Large portions of the country seem to have been burned over by spurious revivals. I fear there is a terrible storm ahead.' He was the first man I remember to have heard use the word 'fanaticism' as characteristic of large numbers at the North, and even of some whom he had hitherto regarded as wise and good men. The storm he predicted has come, but he was not permitted to witness it.

"My school in Richmond ended, and I returned to college. I entered where I stopped, Freshman, half-advanced, having of course new class-mates. I wish my sons to remember, three of whom graduated before they were nineteen and one before he was eighteen, that their father was only half through Freshman in the twenty-second year of his age. (Perhaps it may be wiser to call the attention of my grandsons to this.) I graduated on the 24th of September, 1824, when turned of twenty-four years of age, having as my classmates Dr. Peyton R. Berkley, Thomas T. Giles, John Clarke, Esq., Samuel V. Watkins, Esq., Hon. Wm. Ballard Preston.

[Dr. Theodorick Pryor, who was a student at the same time, is our authority for saying that among his fellow-students were Hugh A. Garland, Virginia; Alex. Rives, Virginia: Beverly Crawford, Georgia; Bishop Atkinson, North Carolina; Robert Carter, Virginia; Allen D. Metcalf, North Carolina; Dr. Jesse Armistead, Virginia; Robert Burwell, North Carolina; Robert T. Turnbull, Virginia. There were at that time about one hundred and fifty students at Hampden-Sidney. —— Cushing, an Episcopalian, was president. The University of Virginia, going into operation in 1825, drew off their patronage]

"For the encouragement of boys struggling for an education, I must state that, when my Sophomore year ended, the money I had made by teaching in Richmond was exhausted. I had an annual income, which, with close economy, would pay for my tuition and books, but not a penny had I with which to pay my board. I could have pressed for a division of the little estate which my father had left, but the administrator urged that I should not do this, as the estate was in debt and all the other children were minors; that by keeping it together a few years he could pay the debts and thus render it much more valuable, especially to those still at school. I felt the force of this, and yielded. I then said to him: 'As you are a moneyed man, and have all of my property in your own hands, and as I am competent to execute my bond, will you lend me money enough to pay my board at college for two years longer?'

"He replied, 'You have been too long at college, and wasted too much money there already.'

"Now, the old gentleman dealt a good deal in horses, and made much money thereby. Just at this time he had for sale a very handsome and highly-pampered, yet not very salable, horse, which he held at $200. He had vowed to take no less, and could not get it. As my vacation drew to a close, I began to feel a little desperate about the means of paying my board through my Junior and Senior years, so I went to the old gentleman and said: 'I have come down this morning to buy your fine dark roan horse. I will execute my bond to you for the price you ask, and you may be as sure of the pay as my property in your hands can make you.'

"'What on earth do you want with such a horse? What wild scheme have you in your head now?'

"'Never mind,' I said; 'will you accede to my proposal?'

"The bargain was soon closed, and I set out for college, hoping to 'ride through the course.' I was very indifferently equipped as to saddle, bridle, saddle-bags, and apparel, and had no sooner entered upon the journey than I commenced offering my fine roan for sale. Now, my anxiety to sell was so great and so obvious, my equipment so indifferent, and my horse so fine, that, although no one among the strangers whom I met ventured to hint such a thing, yet I was forced to believe that, in at least two or three instances, the suspicion was felt that I had stolen the horse. But sell him I could not, and I began to despair, when suddenly I fell into the following soliloquy: 'The price of board is just $100 per annum; two hundred dollars, then—the price of the horse—will take me through. My excellent friend, Colonel Armistead Burwell, now the steward of the College, is a great admirer of fine horses, and, in his better days, owned many of them. I'll try him.' So I reined up the roan and rode up as magisterially as possible. Fortunately, the Colonel was standing at his yard gate, and, although he was one of the politest men, I was glad to see that his attention was soon diverted from me to my horse. Having scanned him closely, and with evident satisfaction, he asked, with marked emotion:

"'Where did you get that fine horse, and what are you going to do with him?'

"The prompt reply was, 'I got him in Hanover, and I have brought him for you.'

"'I should be delighted to have him,' replied the Colonel, 'but I have not the money now to buy such a horse as that.'

"'Money!' I said. 'I don't want a cent of money for him. Just give me my board through my Junior and Senior years in college and you shall have him. This will be paying you in advance.'

"The bargain was closed before we entered the house, and I verily believe that it has been of no small service to my sons to know that their father got through college by *eating up a horse!*"

CHAPTER IV.

1822-1827.

GRADUATES.—TEACHERS' SCHOOL IN FARMVILLE.—TAKEN UNDER CARE OF PRESBYTERY.—OPENING OF UNION THEOLOGICAL SEMINARY.—STUDIES THERE WHILE TEACHING IN FARMVILLE.—ANECDOTE OF DR. B. H RICE.—LICENSED APRIL 30, 1827.—ANECDOTE OF DR. RICE, OR HOW TO TREAT OTHER DENOMINATIONS.—GOES AS HOME MISSIONARY TO NOTTOWAY.—LETTER OF ENCOURAGEMENT FROM DR. B. H. RICE.—SKETCHES AND ANECDOTES OF THE TWO RICES AND OF DR. WILLIAM S. REID.

"It's wiser being good than bad:
It's safer being meek than fierce;
It's fitter being sane than mad."

I HAD graduated, and, with a head very partially filled and a purse entirely empty, I engaged to teach a limited number of boys on a fixed salary in Farmville, Va. As I had but eight boys, and nearly all of them classical scholars of the same grade of scholarship, I had leisure to commence my theological studies I accordingly placed myself under the care of Hanover Presbytery as a candidate for the ministry of the gospel, and went once, and sometimes twice, a week to the Seminary for assistance in my studies. This school of the prophets was opened with three students just as I commenced my school at Farmville. The whole labor devolved at first on Dr. Rice, and the course of instruction was not fully developed until the autumn of 1825. By this time Dr. Rice had an assistant; eight or ten students were added to the original three, and at this time I entered systematically upon my studies. Two full years at the Seminary, with what little I had done while teaching in Farmville, was all the preparation I made for the work of the ministry.

On the 30th of April, 1827, I was licensed by Hanover Presbytery—not then divided into East and West Hanover—as a probationer for the gospel ministry. My preparation was by no means complete, a fact that has embarrassed and perplexed me through life. My licensure took place in the Tabb-street Church, Petersburg, of which the Rev. Dr. Benj. H. Rice was then the minister. This excellent man now became as a father to me. During the meeting of the Presbytery at which I was licensed, considerable religious interest was awakened in Dr. Rice's church, and, as he was chosen to represent the Presbytery in the General Assembly of that year, he left me to do the best I could for a couple of weeks in supplying his pulpit. He had an excellent session, well fitted to lead in prayer-meetings, and even in revivals, so that I was rather a learner than a teacher. Having spent a week or two with my friends in Richmond and Hanover, upon the advice of Dr. B. H. Rice, and sustained by the Young Men's Domestic Missionary Society of Petersburg, I went as a missionary to the county of Nottoway. I commenced my labors there early in June, 1827. All the Presbyterians that could be gathered in Nottoway and Amelia, with two or three in the upper part of Dinwiddie, and as many in the lower part of Lunenburg, constituted what was called the Nottoway Presbyterian Church. They amounted in all to eighteen, and lived over a region of country thirty miles long by twenty-five wide.

My indebtedness for much kindness to the Rev. Dr. Benjamin H. and his brother, the Rev. Dr. John H. Rice, renders it meet that I should give my impressions of these two great and good men. Between these two brothers there were points of resemblance and of contrast. The former was the younger of the two. They both possessed large and well-proportioned bodies, large and liberal views, vigorous minds, and warm hearts. Both commenced their ministry under many disadvantages, their earliest labors being performed in small and obscure congregations. One organized the first Presbyterian church ever existing in Richmond, commencing with only fourteen members, and worshipping, for the want of a house of worship, in the Mason's Hall; the other organized the first Presbyterian church in Petersburg, worshipping, for the same reason, in a tobacco warehouse, and commencing with only ten or twelve members. They settled in these important positions near the same time. There they grew, and the churches grew with them, until they became, for size and usefulness, the foremost churches of the State. Dr. J. H. Rice spent about twelve years in Richmond, and his brother about fifteen years in Petersburg.

The former was the more studious and learned man of the two. The latter was the more popular preacher. Dr. B. H. Rice made a more favorable impression on strangers at first sight. He was more fluent, both in the social circle and the pulpit. He formed his opinions quicker, and expressed them with less hesitation. He had more wit and humor. A man so eminent and yet so approachable is very rarely met with. My acquaintance with him commenced thus:

I had ridden fifty miles all alone to attend the Presbytery, at which I was to present my first two "trial pieces." The meeting was held in a small country church. On the morning of the meeting, before the hour for worship had arrived, I was standing a hundred yards from the church, near the road which approached from the direction of Petersburg, while several ministers and elders were about the door, conversing freely; but with none did I feel sufficiently acquainted to approach them, nor did one of them approach me. I felt lonely and low-spirited. My "trial pieces" were in my pocket, but I almost wished they were in the fire, for I felt heartily ashamed of them and quite sure they would not be approved.

While indulging these gloomy thoughts, my attention was attracted by an old-fashioned sulky, in which sat a large, dignified-looking man, coming from the direction of Petersburg. As he approached, he slackened his pace and said:

"Isn't that White?"

I replied very promptly, "Yes, sir." I knew who he was, for I had heard him preach several times.

"Well," said he, "I know what you are here for. Just come and help me with this horse, and I will help you with your trial pieces through Presbytery."

I went to his assistance with all promptitude, greatly cheered by his unostentatious and kind salutation. While we were taking the horse from the sulky and hitching him to the limb of a tree, he said:

"I expect you feel badly. Have you brought your 'exegesis' and 'critical exercises'?"

I told him I had.

"Well, now," he said, "don't be afraid of these preachers and elders; they don't know half as much as you think they do."

By this time gloom was gone, and from that hour I respected, loved and honored him with my whole mind and heart.

A year after this I was licensed to preach. The Presbytery that licensed me met in Dr. Rice's church, Petersburg. There I preached my first sermon. When this solemn service was over, as I stood in front of the church, Dr. Rice came up to me and said:

"Well, the Presbytery has opened your mouth, and now I'll tell you what to do. I am going to the General Assembly, and, as I wish to stop at Princeton, I shall start next week. Go over to Richmond, visit your friends, come back to this place, preach two or three Sabbaths to our people, get you a horse, and, when your time here expires, go to Dr. James Jones, of Nottoway. He will give you and horse your board, and, with three other gentlemen assisting, will pay you $200 in money. Then go to work with all your might. You will find a good many Baptists, a great many Methodists, and very few Presbyterians in that county. To other denominations be kind, fraternal, and strive only to *outpreach, outpray* and *outwork* them."

I promptly assented. The meeting of Presbytery at Petersburg had been followed by a blessing. A pleasant work of grace was enjoyed. Thus my ministry was literally begun in a revival. It is worthy of record that four young ladies from Nottoway, attending a boarding-school in Petersburg, were subjects of this work, but did not join the church until they returned to their homes. These were almost the first persons I admitted to the church of which I was pastor. And lovely wives, mothers and church members they all made. One of them became the wife of my successor in the pastorate of Nottoway Church—Rev. Dr. Theodorick Pryor.

As soon as Dr. Rice returned from the General Assembly he wrote me a long letter, replete with advice and encouragement. He charged me to attend to the poor. "Take care of Christ's poor," he said, "and he will take care of you. . . It is far better to suffer wrong than to do wrong. Don't complain. Don't talk of going away. You'll soon think that your preaching is like trying to batter down a stonewall with a cork hammer. But never mind. The walls of Jericho were thrown down by ram's horns. You'll find a famous race track and jockey club in Nottoway. *Don't abuse them.* Indeed, never allude to them in any public address. But so preach and so pray, so unfold the doctrines and provisions of the gospel, and so illustrate and enforce these by your whole deportment, that the people may be gradually brought to see that, as a source of present happiness, the gospel is infinitely preferable to racing horses." This is but a brief and very imperfect sample of the wise counsel he gave me.

A Presbytery was soon held for my ordination and installation. He and my venerated preceptor, Dr. J. H. Rice, both attended. It is not easy to express the gratification it gave me to have two such men to visit and cheer me at the commencement of my work. During my examination for ordination a little incident occurred, which illustrates in part the difference between these two distinguished brothers. Dr. John H. Rice was conducting the examination on church government. In the course of it, with that slow and solemn manner which was peculiar to him, he said:

"Mr. White, tell us, in the fewest words possible, what is the chief use of ruling elders in our church."

The demand for the fewest possible words caused me to hesitate. Embarrassment began to rise, when suddenly his brother, who was reclining in a remote part of the house and seemingly asleep, arose and said, with great distinctness:

"*Tell him, to watch the preachers.*"

This fully relieved my embarrassment, and raised a laugh all over the house. The examiner enjoyed the laugh quite as much as anybody else, and even apologized for framing the question as he did.

Wingfield Academy, in Dinwiddie, was one of the many places at which I preached during the first year of my ministry. The Fourth of July that year came on the Sabbath. My two excellent friends, Hatch and Atkinson, advised me to make a religious improvement of the day. I accordingly preached with that view. Some weeks afterwards, passing through Petersburg to Richmond, I called, as I always did in passing, on my valued friend, Dr. Rice. Soon after I entered his study he said: "I see from a Petersburg paper that you have been preaching a Fourth of July sermon. Knowing the ideas our writers for the newspapers generally hold of eloquence, I was somewhat grieved to find that they had spoken of your sermon as, in some parts, eloquent. But when I saw that they had not represented you as *praying eloquently,* I was better pleased. I hope I shall never hear of your praying eloquently, whatever other bad things I may hear of you."

I assured him that I knew nothing of any newspaper notice of my sermon, and that I had never supposed I should ever be accused of eloquence, in the popular sense of that term, either in my sermons or prayers.

Dr. Benjamin Rice was more successful than his brother in producing an immediate impression on his hearers. Hence his preaching was more productive of revivals of religion. It is hard, if not impossible, to discriminate in this matter. Larger accessions were made at a time to the Petersburg than to the Richmond church; but in a period of twelve years they increased very much alike. Both churches were about the same size when the two brothers left them. The sermons of the elder brother operated more silently and slowly, but no less surely. The younger was eminently instrumental in several extensive revivals, the fruits of which, after the lapse of many years, have proved that they were genuine works of the Holy Spirit. In 1822 he preached nine sermons in the Hampden-Sidney College Church consecutively, but adopted no measures to ascertain to what extent the word spoken had taken effect. After preaching the last sermon, he appointed a prayer-meeting to be held on the afternoon of the next day in the church, giving as a reason for appointing it in the church, and not at a private house or the College chapel, that no smaller building would hold the people who he thought would attend. To us who were familiar with the small assemblies that ordinarily met for prayer, this seeming prediction appeared surprising. He left early the following morning, and, at the hour appointed for the prayer-meeting, I left my room in College to attend it, expecting to find but a dozen or two present. Judge of my surprise when, coming out from the College building, I saw a large number of carriages and other vehicles surrounding the church, and, on looking back towards the College, it appeared as if the entire body of students were coming. The church was filled to its utmost capacity. There was no preacher present, the church being without a pastor. The worship was conducted by a pious student. This work continued and deepened for several months, resulting in the addition of over sixty members to the church.

Dr. Rice's views of the nature and best means of promoting revivals were eminently sound. He was accustomed to say that all feeling not produced by clear apprehensions of God's truth was more or less spurious, and that measures contrived to produce feeling were dangerous and hurtful. He was opposed to much singing in the presence of awakened sinners, maintaining that the state of mind of such was not suited to render praise to God. They must pray, repent, believe, and then they might sing. Nor did he favor very protracted meetings, especially in congregations blessed with preaching two or three times every week. He was urged to protract the meeting in Prince Edward, but he persistently refused, saying that, in the nine sermons he had preached, he had delivered his message, and had nothing more to say to that people at that time.

I shall go to my grave distinctly remembering and deeply feeling the impression of his wise counsels and invaluable life. May it please God, even at this late day, to give me more of his fidelity and success in Christ's cause.

Dr. Rice, like his brother in Richmond, kept open house, especially for preachers, generously entertaining all who called. Like him, too, he was blessed with a wife whose admirable manners, genial spirit, good sense, and fluent tongue added immensely to the attractions of his house. But, unlike him, he had a lovely group of sons and daughters. One of this group is now Rev. John H. Rice, D. D., of Mobile, Ala. One of the daughters became the wife of Rev. Mr. Foreman, of Kentucky, and another is now the wife of Rev. Drury Lacy, D. D., of North Carolina.

Of another of this group I must say a word. I refer to little Benjamin. He died at the early age of eight years. He was a child of rare endowments. From his third or fourth year he displayed a surprising aptitude to learn, and an uncommon taste and even reverence for the Bible.

I have heard his mother say that she could control him at that early age far more effectually with the Bible than with the rod. Under the latter he was turbulent and rebellious to the last. To the teachings of the former he bowed at once. She gave me an amusing illustration of this. On more than one occasion she had chastised him for striking his brother, but with no good effect. At length she resorted to the Bible. Turning to the sermon on the mount, and placing him on her knee, she said:

"Now, Ben, I am going to prove to you out of the Bible that it is wrong for you to strike your brother, even if he does strike you first."

She then read and explained to him these words: "Whosoever shall smite thee on thy right cheek, turn to him the other also."

Ben, then only six years old, listened with attention, and even solemnly. He was evidently much perplexed and absorbed in thought. When his mother had indulged him in this for two or three minutes, he looked up into her face, with a countenance beaming with new thought, and said:

"Well, mother, when I let Archie strike me on both cheeks, then I'll whip him."

The mother was now as much perplexed as her little boy had been at the first reading of the passage. But this early reverence for the Bible displayed itself before and at the time of his early death in a way to assure his parents of his abundant fitness for heaven.

The Presbytery which licensed me was moderated by the Rev. William S. Reid, D. D., of Lynchburg, Va. It has always given me pleasure to have his name appended to my license. Dr. Reid was a man of very prepossessing person, attractive manners, well cultivated mind, an amiable and devout heart. He spent a long and useful life in Lynchburg, much of the time connecting a school for young ladies with the duties of pastor. This school had a wide reputation, which was richly deserved. It was emphatically a Christian school. Pupils were sent to it from remote parts of the State, and many a germ of a Presbyterian church was planted by it. In the summer of 1835 I made a missionary tour through the county of Southampton. On going "down to Jerusalem," the county seat, a village of several hundred inhabitants, but in which I learned there was not one Presbyterian and, I think, but one Methodist, I put up at the hotel and commenced preaching daily, morning and evening, in the court-house. On the second day of the meeting a gentleman called to see me, gave his name and said:

"I reside one mile from the village, and have come in my carriage to take you out to my house. Neither my wife nor I make any pretensions to religion, but she has a great liking for your church, and says you must spend your time with us."

I accompanied him, and soon found that his wife was a very sincere Christian and a very firm Presbyterian in her principles. After satisfying myself on these points, I asked how she had become so decided a Presbyterian in a county in which there was no church, nor preacher, nor even a member of that church. She said:

"When I was a girl I went to school to Mr. Reid, of Lynchburg; and, although he never made an effort to make me a Presbyterian, his instructions and his life combined led to my conversion and my choice of this church."

A Presbyterian church was soon organized in that neighborhood, and this lady became one of its first and best members. I have reason to know that this was one of many cases more or less alike. When Dr. Reid's great age and bodily infirmities incapacitated him for any longer discharging the duties of pastor, the church retained him in that capacity and called the Rev. C. R. Vaughan, then just licensed, to serve as collegiate pastor. This arrangement continued for several years—as long, indeed, as the old man lived. Mr. Vaughan was popular and useful. The extent to which Dr. Reid esteemed and treated his young associate as a son, and to which the colleague regarded and treated the doctor as a father, was so lovely, so Christian-like, as to make it worthy of record. As long as his strength permitted, he went regularly to church, always sitting in the pew with his family, and listening to the sermons of his young brother, not only with the most fixed attention, but often with tears. He told me once that he loved Mr. Vaughan as he did his own sons, for, he added, "he has been to me all that a son could be to his father."

Dr. Reid was one of the men who contributed so largely to give to the Presbyterian Church its distinctive type, which, I am thankful to believe, it retains to the present time. May the impress of those fathers ever abide!

CHAPTER V.

1827-1832.

SHILOH CHURCH BUILT.--FRUITS OF FIVE YEARS' WORK IN NOTTOWAY, LUNENBURG, AMELIA AND DINWIDDIE.—JETER'S RACE-TRACK.—DR. RICE'S WISE COUNSEL TO HIM IN DESPONDENCY.—BAPTISTS AND METHODISTS.—MARRIAGE.—GENEROSITY OF DR. JAMES JONES.— UNCLE JACK, "THE AFRICAN PREACHER."—ANECDOTES OF HIM.— THE DYING INFIDEL.—ENCOMIUM BY DR. PRYOR.

"My own hope is, a sun will pierce
The thickest cloud earth ever stretched;
That, after last, returns the first,
Though a wide compass round be fetched;
That what began best, can't end worst,
Nor what God blest once, prove accurst."

IN Nottoway I preached on two Sabbaths of the month at a new church, commenced, but not completed, in the upper part of the county—one Sabbath in Amelia, and one at Wingfield Academy, in Dinwiddie. When a fifth Sabbath occurred, I spent it in Lunenburg or elsewhere, as best for the cause. This was my plan through the first year of my ministry. At the close of that year, the Rev. John Barksdale, a man of great worth, one year behind me in the Seminary, took a commission to labor in Amelia. There were then only five or six Presbyterians in that county. These were organized into a church, very small to be sure, but, under Barksdale, it grew rapidly.

I now confined myself to Nottoway. Shiloh Church was built, and I alternated between that in the lower and the Republican Church in the upper part of the county. [This church was built by the energy and influence of Mr. White, and is still in constant use by the Rev. Dr. Pryor. It stands four miles east of Blackstone, on the Norfolk and Western railroad, ten miles east of the courthouse, and five miles from the Dinwiddie line.] During three-fourths of the year I preached on the afternoon of the day on which worship was held at "the Republican," at Little Creek, and in the afternoon of the day at Shiloh I preached at the "mouth of Cocke's lane." These places for afternoon worship were each eleven miles from the place of the morning service. While this arrangement continued, I frequently took my dinner in my pocket, and ate it as I rode. The labor was severe, but healthful, and, I hope, useful. The church grew slowly, but surely. During the five years of my ministry in Nottoway that church increased to sixty members. A church had been organized in Lunenburg of twelve members, which had increased to forty or more; and the little church gathered in Amelia had increased to about the same number. In Dinwiddie nothing of consequence was done.

My life in Nottoway may be characterized as one of incessant, but delightful, labor. That county had long been celebrated for the politeness, refinement, and hospitality of its inhabitants. But they were deplorably irreligious. They had been afflicted with some of the worst specimens of the old English clergy—men who were leaders in fashionable dissipation. One had the misfortune to be visited by the wife he had left in England, after he had married in this country. The influence of such men on the cause of true religion, and even of sound morality, was bad. Card-playing, horse-racing and wine-drinking were almost universal among the higher classes.

Within a few hundred yards of Shiloh Church, where Mr. White preached statedly, was Jeter's race-track. This famous institution was laid off about A. D. 1822. The wealth, style and beauty of old Virginia assembled here from time to time. All the distinguished racers in Virginia attended, coming from the Blue Ridge on the west to the

Chesapeake Bay on the east, and North Carolina line on the south. Wm. R. Johnston, "king of the turf," often attended. Jimmie Junkin Harrison, from Brunswick county, used to bring a very fine stable of horses. All the surrounding counties poured out their wit and beauty to the races. Many days were spent in the most exciting forms of fashionable dissipation, such as cards, wine, balls, and betting on the races. From 1822 to 1842 its influence was immense upon the morals of the land. It began to decline under the force of the truth preached by the ministers of the different churches "*who wisely abstained from abusing it in public.*" Its owner, Mr. Richard Jones, was converted and received into the church by Mr. White. Three of the presidents of the jockey club were converted and joined the church. Major Hezekiah R. Anderson, one of them, was received into the Presbyterian Church by Rev. Dr. Pryor. In 1838 a revival of religion in the Methodist and Presbyterian churches gave it the death-blow. It survived about four years, when a *tactum de cœlo* destroyed the judges' stand. After this, it was reduced to cultivation, and became a thing of the past.

For fifty years, ending with the year 1825, the Presbyterians almost wholly neglected the county. Except an occasional sermon by some such distinguished itinerant as Rev. Dr. Hill or Dr. Archibald Alexander, the gospel, as held by that church, was wholly unknown. The popular mind was filled with mistaken views and prejudices against this church. When I began my ministry there, these met me at every turn, and for some months such was my want of success, and such the discouragement, I felt that, had it not been for the strong and salutary influence exerted over me by my excellent friend, Dr. B. H. Rice, I should have left the field in utter despondency before the first year had closed. But in his plain, blunt style he would say to me:

"Did the Presbytery license you that you might seek your ease and convenience, or that you might play the coward when difficulties or dangers threatened you? Abandon this field, and you will have to confess that you have failed to answer the expectations of friends and brethren. One failure always leads to another, and you will soon get the name of an unsuccessful man, and your life will end in failure. Remember that the good farmer prefers any sort of a horse to one given to backing."

Deeply impressed by these thoughts, I resolved, by the help of God, to succeed in my first charge or perish in the attempt. I carefully concealed from the people the discouragement I felt, and never so much as hinted at a desire or purpose to go elsewhere. Even when on the point of going away, I conversed, preached and labored as if I expected to spend my whole life with them.

The Baptists had gathered a church in that part of the county which borders on Prince Edward and Lunenburg; but through the centre and lower portions they had done nothing. The Episcopalians never made an effort. Old Parson Wilkinson, of matrimonial memory, had left behind him an odor so unsavory that, with the downfall of "Green's church," every vestige of that sect disappeared. I never met with man or woman in the entire county who even professed to belong to "the church." The service was not so much as once read in public during my residence there.

The Methodists were the efficient and successful pioneers in the work of planting the gospel. They had spread and were numerous over the entire county. There was not a neighborhood that had not its chapel and class-meeting. Many of the most wealthy and intelligent people of the county, whose early prepossessions would have inclined them to join some other church, had joined the Methodists. Among these I found some of my warmest personal friends. Although they made no change in their church relations, they became constant attendants on my ministry when our meetings and theirs did not conflict, and extended to me and my family the most refined and generous hospitality.

The sons and daughters of some of these good Methodists were among the earliest additions to my church. One of them became a valuable Presbyterian minister. To such an extent did this proceed that in a few years it became very common to find the old people of a family Methodists and their descendants Presbyterians. This commenced with four young ladies—daughters of the wealthiest and most intelligent Methodists of the country—who had been educated at Petersburg, and received their bias to our church chiefly through their connection with some of Dr. B. H. Rice's church. But these things occasioned no ill-feeling. No proselyting was practiced on our part, and no offence taken on the other side, and hence all went peaceably on.

In the beginning my congregations were very small, and, as some thought, very cold, while those of the Methodists were very large, and, as all thought, (for it was impossible to think otherwise) very warm. During the first year my congregation, in the best weather, rarely amounted to fifty; while their houses, close by me, were overflowing. I had an occasional addition of one or two, while they at the same time would receive from fifteen to twenty. They had periodical excitements of great violence, called revivals, which gathered many into the church, followed by a reaction which ordinarily scattered as many from the church. They had neither Bible-classes nor Sunday-schools. At the outset we gathered one of the latter, numbering about twenty, and one of the former, numbering eight or ten scholars. In a few years the two churches became numerically equal, and ours in other respects greatly superior. In truth, considering the sparseness of the population, the Nottoway Church became one of the strongest and most generous churches in our entire connection in Eastern Virginia.

Here we met with those best of friends, Dr. and Mrs.

James Jones, With them we lived at the time of the birth of our first child, named, at the special request of Mrs. Jones, after her husband. Language fails to express the debt of gratitude we owe to those generous and disinterested friends. Without any extravagance, I may say they were both father and mother to us.

They were among the most highly-cultivated persons in this or any other country. Their beautiful home was literally the abode of the most refined, intelligent piety, and the resort of many visitors likeminded with themselves.

I failed to mention in the proper place the most auspicious event of my life, except my conversion to God and my consecration to the work of the ministry—viz., my marriage to Miss Jane Isabella, third daughter of Mr. and Mrs. George and Margaret Watt, of the city of Richmond, Va. This event took place on the third of October, 1827, about four months after my labors commenced in Nottoway. The marriage ceremony was solemnized by Rev. Wm. J. Armstrong, then pastor of the First Presbyterian Church of Richmond. Mr. and Mrs. Watt were among the first members enrolled by Dr. John H. Rice when he organized this church, and were always regarded by him with deep affection.

[Hugh Watt, father of George, died in Glenarm, Antrim county, in the North of Ireland, July 24, 1787. His daughter Elizabeth had sailed for Philadelphia, May 15, 1784. George Watt sailed for Richmond, July 14, 1790. Afterwards he returned and brought his mother and family. His betrothed, Margaret Dunn, came with the party. The Presbyterians in the North of Ireland were then suffering persecution from the English government. Mrs. White's grandmother was buried in the old church-yard of St. John's, on Church Hill. Her father and mother were also buried there.]

When I returned to Mountain Hall, after my marriage, and presented my wife to Dr. and Mrs. Jones, a stranger might have supposed, from the reception given to her, that I was their own son bringing to his father's house a daughter-in-law. And as she was received so she was treated until these excellent friends ended their earthly pilgrimage. Dr. Jones died in the spring of 1848, and Mrs. Jones in the autumn of 1860.

To mention but one of many instances of the generous kindness received from Dr. Jones, I will state that, soon after my removal from Nottoway, I received a letter from him containing these words: "The amount I contributed to your support during your residence with us was given for the sake of your ministrations in the gospel. I doubt not you are as actively employed in this work now as you were when here. I wish, therefore, to contribute to your support in your new field the amount I gave to you as our pastor. I have accordingly placed to your credit in the Farmer's Bank of Virginia, at Richmond, $1,000, the dividends on which will yield what I have been accustomed to pay you." Thus, to this day, is this faithful friend, though long since dead, generously contributing to my support.

Here, too, I met with that remarkable man, familiarly called "Uncle Jack," the African preacher, a native of the benighted continent of Africa. In 1848 I published a biography of this man, which was examined and endorsed by Mr. and Mrs. Dr. Jones, who had known him intimately for more than forty years. Having published already what I deemed it proper to say of him, I only add that, as I draw nearer to the end of my own earthly pilgrimage, I am ready to reaffirm all that I then said, and to express the firm and ever-strengthening conviction that he was, in many respects, the most remarkable man I ever knew.

The Rev. Dr. Theodorick Pryor relates the two following anecdotes of this African preacher.

"Talking with the Rev. John S. Watt on religious experience, and lamenting the want of satisfactory evidence of his own conversion in a very melancholy vein, he said: 'How can I hope, when I see no fruit in myself?'

"Mr. Watt replied: 'That cherry tree has no fruit, not even leaf or flower, and yet we know it lives, for it has borne fruit.'

"'Ah! yes,' responded the African preacher, 'but I know it has a *live root;* if I could only know that of myself!'"

Suffering for Christ.

"A band of 'lewd fellows of the baser sort' once arrested the African preacher to punish him by whipping for preaching the gospel. They charged him with many and various crimes, and asked what he had to say for himself, when he replied:

"'The great Apostle to the Gentiles says, "Five times received I forty stripes save one." I have never had the honor of even one stripe for my Master. You can lay on when it pleases you.'

"They were so impressed with his evident sincerity that they let him go."

[*The African Preacher.* This little book, a 16mo. of 129 pages, is still for sale by the Presbyterian Board of Publication, in Philadelphia, and being fresh, entertaining and wholesome, will be an addition to any Sunday-school library. Its wide diffusion among the freedmen of the South could not fail to produce the happiest results.]

Incidents in the life of a minister, at first view apparently too insignificant for remembrance, in course of time are seen to have been connected with results of great importance. When my ministry commenced in Nottoway there was not a comfortable house of worship in the county. The few Presbyterians had commenced one in the northern part of the county, but for want of funds it had not been completed; indeed, it was scarcely fitted for occupancy. In the southwestern section there was a large old church edifice, built prior to the Revolution, for the use of the Established or Episcopal Church. It had been utterly abandoned for many years, and was almost in ruins. Still, it contained a large amount of valuable building material. By removing rubbish and trees, which had grown up so as to obstruct entrance through the doors, we made it practicable to begin stated worship there in June, 1827. The pews were of various shapes, but all of immense depth, rising above the heads of all whose stature did not reach six feet. The ten commandments and the Apostles' Creed, in yellow letters, on boards painted black, still hung on one end of the old edifice. The pulpit stood in one side, octagonal in form, so small that only two gentlemen could occupy it, and that with difficulty, and so high that the preacher saw only the tops of the heads of those whose pews were nearest to it. There was a projection over the head of the preacher, commonly called "a sounding board." This approached so near to the head of the preacher that the sensation produced somewhat resembled the feelings of one who, enclosed in a hogshead, was attempting to preach through the bung.

The question was soon started, "Shall we repair old Green's Church, or move some four miles lower down and build a new house?" The descendants of the old revolutionary people strongly contended for repairing. They were the aristocracy of the region. They held much the larger portion of the money. "Their fathers and grandfathers had worshipped in old Green's Church." For this reason they would not consent to abandon it. Many of the plainer and poorer people lived below, and were for building anew. They plead that around them there was a dense population who had no means of riding, and for this reason could not attend the old church. Besides, it would cost more money to repair the old than to build a new house. I agreed cordially with the latter, and exerted myself to the utmost in support of their views. But I had been a preacher only some three or four months, and had acquired but little influence. And, then, among those who contended for repairing there was scarcely one professor of religion of any name. Moral and religious considerations, therefore, had no weight with them, so that, when I said to them, you have good carriages and horses, and can easily attend at the place selected for the new house, while the people there have no means of riding, and must be left wholly without preaching, they expressed surprise that I should urge such a motive.

Meantime the summer had ended, and the weather became too cold for comfort in the old church. It was impossible to build without the money of our opponents. The whole matter was dropped, and I was deeply discouraged.

But man's extremity is God's opportunity. I made a visit that fall to Richmond. On my return, and when within a few miles of home, I met a plain man in the road, of whom I enquired the news of the neighborhood. He said: "All the news I know is, that old Green's Church is burned down."

Without reflecting, I promptly replied, "I am glad of it."

"You'd better not say that," said the man, "for a good many people say that you hired some one to do it, and then went away to keep from being caught."

This surprised me. To be charged with burning a church was a serious matter to one of my age, profession and condition.

But my comfort sprang from the hope that the leading people of the county had confidence in my veracity, if they had no respect for my talents or religion, and would accept my denial of the charge as sufficient. With a large majority of the people this hope proved to be well-founded, and the result was that we soon had the new church in the new place. This was Shiloh Church, near the Belmont racecourse, of which I shall have more to say presently.

THE MYSTERY CLEARED.

It may amuse, if it does not instruct the reader, to add, that after several years had passed, the burning of the old church was fully explained. Within the long period in which the church had not been used by the congregation, an old woman, by no means noted for her intelligence, amiability, or piety, had gotten exclusive possession of that spring, and was greatly annoyed at the use of it by the people. She became ill, and, in her alarm at the prospect of death, sent for a Methodist minister, to whom she confessed, among other sins, that of having burned Green's Church, pleading however, in extenuation of her guilt in the matter, that she "*had not been able to keep a water-gourd at that spring* since that young man had commenced preaching there."

I have already stated, that after the burning of this old church, we commenced our efforts to secure the means of building a new one several miles to the east. The Bellemont Jockey Club was in vigorous operation. Indeed, it was the great institution of the county. The owner of the race-field kept a large and attractive house of entertainment. One mile below him there was a much older house of the same kind, which had long been liberally sustained by the travelling public. There was no little rivalry and jealousy between these two applicants for public patronage. The keeper of the older and plainer establishment was not a religious man, but he did not sell spirituous liquors, and he hated horse-racing and card-playing.

I called on this old man for help in building our contemplated house of worship.

"Well," said he, "on that part of my land which borders on J——'s race-track, there is a beautiful site for a church. If you will place your building there, I will give you an acre of ground, covered with a beautiful grove of oaks. And I will give you besides $50 in money."

This astonished and delighted me; for, small as this contribution may seem now, it was great then. It gave quite an impetus to my enterprise. It became the subject of conversation in all companies, and some were uncharitable enough to insinuate that "Old Capt. M—— only wanted to break down his hated rival, Col. J——, and knew that the most effectual way to do it was to build a church as near as possible to his door." With the motive, however, we had no concern, but thankfully accepted the offer, and located the church in accordance with the old Captain's wish.

Not many years rolled round before the Bellemont racetrack and hotel were in the possession of a former member of the jockey club, but now a member of the Presbyterian Church; the race-field converted into a cornfield; and the large hotel into a seminary for young ladies. Such is a brief history of Shiloh Church, in the eastern part of Nottoway county.

WORKING FOR TEMPERANCE.

My active labors in the temperance cause commenced in the county of Nottoway, in 1828. The extent to which drinking intoxicants was carried on in this county was fearful. Wine-toddy and grog were almost in as universal use as bread and bacon. The people were generous livers, hospitable to a fault.

I was long in determining how to commence operations. After many conferences with about half a dozen who favored my purpose—among whom were Dr. James Jones and Dr. Archibald Campbell—I determined on calling a public meeting. These gentlemen promised to attend and address the meeting. For wealth, intelligence and piety, they were among the foremost men in the county. The former was a leading Presbyterian and the latter a leading Methodist. I suggested to them the propriety of keeping the real design of the contemplated meeting as much of a secret as possible. I resolved on making the notice as enigmatical as I could; so, after the preaching, I said.

"There is an enemy ranging through our land, robbing and slaying our people at a fearful rate; and so artful and insidious are his movements that many are robbed and even slain by him without once suspecting his designs or realizing his power. Now, as neither the State Legislature nor the National Congress will, or possibly can, take any steps to arrest the progress of this enemy, I give notice that a meeting of the people, male and female, young and old, will be held on next Saturday, at Cellar Creek Meeting-house, to take this matter into their own hands. With a promise of the assistance of two of the most distinguished physicians and politicians in the country, I will then and there make fully known the character and designs of this invader, and suggest the best means of resisting him."

Some, of course, knew what all this meant; but many did not. Public curiosity was greatly excited, and when the appointed day came a prodigious audience met. The ladies alone filled the house, while the gentlemen filled the yard. My two friends and I did our best in the way of speech-making. Good behavior and good attention characterized the audience, but after all a beggarly dozen were all who could be prevailed on "to sign the pledge."

A detail of my efforts in this cause for more than thirty years would fill a volume. Scores of incidents, of illustrative facts, might be given, which would now excite laughter and then tears; but I forbear. Long before "temperance societies" were known, Rev. Drs. John H. and B. H. Rice did immense good in reclaiming drunkards, and saving young men from the demon of drunkenness. This they did by voluntarily abstaining from the habitual use of intoxicants, and often making gospel calls in their sermons to the same habit. I never heard the bitter consequences of intemperance, both in this life and the next, presented in as impressive terms by any professed temperance lecturer as in the sermons of these great men.

Dr. Theodorick Pryor's Estimate.

During my residence in Nottoway nothing like a general revival of religion occurred among our people. But there was an obvious and steady increase in the knowledge and activity of the members of the church, and at almost every communion some additions or profession of their faith. But one case of apostacy occurred, and when I left there was not one member of whose piety I had reason to doubt. I am convinced that, during the five years I labored there, our permanent increase was greater than that of our good Methodist brethren, whose system of measures was so different from ours.

[Rev. Dr. Theodorick Pryor writes of him at this period of his life, viz.:

"He married in the fall of 1827, and, with his wife, resided at the Mountain Hall—the then elegant homestead of Dr. James Jones. Whilst pastor of the church in Nottoway . . . his labors covered the entire county, and extended into Amelia and Dinwiddie. No man could have been more acceptable to the community. Possessed of a highly cultivated mind, of a genial disposition, he was a welcome guest in every household. His pulpit work was of a high order, very attractive and deeply impressive. When he commenced preaching in Nottoway county, he found but few Presbyterians. When, in the providence of God, he was called away, he left a strong church, constituted of the very best elements in the community. Personally, your father was one of my very best friends. It was through his influence that I succeeded him in charge of the Nottoway Church. Wherever I went I found and felt the savor of his blessed work. My impression of your father is, that, practically, he was one of the wisest men I have ever known. Whilst firm and decided in his convictions and maintenance of the truth, he was pre-eminently conciliatory in manner. When called away from the county, I do not suppose he left an enemy in it, or any one who was not kind and respectful in feeling toward him.

He conciliated in the very highest degree the affectionate esteem and love of Dr. James Jones and family, and, indeed, of all the families with which he was intimate. I cannot conceive of a man better qualified to do good. Wherever he lived and labored, his work testified to his worth. In conclusion, my dear young brother, I have only to say, that I heartily wish the church were now blessed with a thousand William S. Whites.

"Yours, in the precious faith of the gospel,
"THEODORICK PRYOR."]

CHAPTER VI.

PASTORAL SKETCHES.

INFIDELITY IN PROSPECT OF DEATH.—"CAUGHT WITH GUILE."—INTERESTED HEARERS.—ANTI-PRESBYTERIANISM CURED.—"THE DEVIL THREW HIM DOWN AND TORE HIM."—EARLY CONVERSION; E. F. P.; E. W. W.; A. R.; A. H.; E. S.; A. A. B.

RICHARD HARDAWAY, Esq., was one of the leading citizens of Nottoway county when I went there in 1827. He married the daughter of John Rutherford, Esq., of Richmond. She was a member of the Presbyterian Church; he a gentleman, but a skeptic. Through the connection of his wife with my church I made his acquaintance. He received and treated me hospitably whenever I visited him, but always seemed reserved and even embarrassed in my presence. I readily perceived the cause of this, and by degrees succeeded in convincing him that a preacher of the gospel *might be a gentleman*. In the summer of 1829 I held a meeting in a grove, near his residence, where there was no house of worship. His attention was soon arrested and fixed, but he exhibited no depth of feeling until the congregation sang, at the conclusion of the last service, Hymn 552 of our collection—

"The day of wrath, that dreadful day," etc.

He wept freely, but I purposely avoided speaking to him. I knew his disposition, and thought I knew the treatment his case demanded. The first intelligence I had respecting him was that he was very sick, desired to see me, but his physicians objected to my being sent for. His disease, however, soon became so violent, and his distress of mind so great, that the doctors changed their minds, and, infidels as they all were, of their own accord, sent for me. When I arrived I found three in consultation. They said, "You must do something to quiet his mind, or medicine will do him no good."

As I entered his room he looked wildly at me and said, "You have come too late. Did you ever read Dr. Young's account of young Altamont? My case is precisely like his." I replied, "How do you know it is too late?" He answered, "The devil tells me so, and I have yielded to him so long that I must yield now. I know there is no mercy for such a sinner as I am." "You are a great sinner," I replied, "but not so great as Saul of Tarsus. He was a persecutor and a blasphemer, and yet he found mercy. You are not a persecutor; you have been friendly and polite to me as a minister of the gospel." Here he stopped me abruptly, saying, "Not as a minister of the gospel; I had no respect for you as such; I treated you as I did merely to gratify my wife, and because it would have been disgraceful not to do so. Had I lived when Saul of Tarsus did, I should have been far worse than he was. His case affords me no comfort." I then said to him, "Remember the case of the penitent thief. Even he found mercy, and why may not you?" He answered, "I find no encouragement from his case. True, I am not a thief in the popular sense of the term; but I have stolen, yes, *stolen* my neighbors' money at cards and on the racefield, and, what is worse, I have *robbed God;* yes, sir, robbed my Maker. And then my birth, education and opportunities have been greatly superior to those of that thief. He probably never heard of Christ until they met on the cross; he embraced the first offer he ever had, while I have heard of and rejected him all my life."

He then became greatly excited, avowing there was no mercy for him; that he must perish, for he deserved it. I then said, "There is one thing you can and must do: you can pray." "No, no!" he replied; "prayer in me now would be blasphemy." Then said I, "May I pray for you?" He answered very promptly, "No, sir; even your prayers could not avail for me now."

I then said, "You say you have been an infidel. Are you one still?" He answered, "By no means. If I had but one breath to draw, I would spend that breath in renouncing it. I firmly believe that the Bible is the word of God, and that I must suffer all it threatens." I replied, "You said just now that the devil told you that there was no mercy for you; that it was too late for you to pray, etc. Now, listen to me for a moment. The Bible says 'the devil is a liar.' It also says, 'Ask, and ye shall receive.' Which will you believe, God or the devil?" After a very solemn pause he said, "I will believe God and pray." He then closed his eyes and clasped his hands, and offered audibly a brief, but earnest and most appropriate prayer. When he closed, I said, "Shall we now pray for you?" Several of his near relatives were present. He replied, "If you please." We knelt and prayed. He was very calm. I left the room in search of his physicians. They had remained under the magnificent elms which shaded the yard. They plead, as an apology for doing so, the intense heat of the weather. They saw him, and expressed gratification at his composure. I remained through the day, and from time to time had brief interviews with him. He now received the teachings of the gospel as a little child. I spent much time with him during the three following weeks. Even his doctors said that, if his mind could have been thus quieted a few days sooner, he would have recovered. He died in three weeks, giving as full proof of conversion as a sick and dying man could. One of these physicians, a young man, abandoned the practice of medicine and became a preacher of the gospel.

"CAUGHT WITH GUILE."

Mrs. Dr. E. S., of N., was the wife of a young and rising physician, and had been reared and educated with great care, and held a high social position in one of the best communities in the State.

Unfortunately, neither Mrs. S., nor her husband, was a professor of religion. Both, however, were constant and most respectful attendants on my ministry, and among my most generous supporters. So far as she had enjoyed any religious training, it had been of a sort to fill the mind with erroneous views of the Calvinistic in contradistinction to the Arminian creed. Her extreme politeness, however, restrained her from any expression of those views in my presence. But, after our acquaintance had continued for several months, she one day addressed a mutual friend of ours substantially thus: "I like Mr. and Mrs. White very much, and shall take great pleasure in hearing him preach so long as he refrains from the discussion of predestination; but if he ever introduces those topics with a view to propagate them, I shall cease to attend his church."

On being told this, I gave some evasive, but kindly, reply, but at the same time set my wits to work to determine on the wisest course to be taken on such a subject with such a lady. The judgment must not only be convinced, but prejudice must be removed and kind feeling preserved. To do this an expedient was adopted which some may think of doubtful propriety.

The Rev. Dr. Matthews had published in *The Southern Religious Telegraph* a series of letters on "The Divine Purpose," which, I knew, Mrs. S. had never seen. These letters had been recently republished in a small volume. Now, I thought that this little book was the very thing for my Arminian friend; but how to approach her was the question. She had carefully refrained from making her sentiments known to me, and could have no suspicion that I had heard what she said to our mutual friend. I suspected that something more than politeness had led to her reticence; for she was a lady of uncommon candor, expressing her opinions on all other subjects with great freedom. My course soon appeared plain. I said to my wife, "Suppose we go and spend the night with our good friends, Dr. and Mrs. S." She consented, and I armed myself with a copy of Dr. Matthews' little book. We were received with great cordiality, and treated with elegant hospitality. The evening was passed in free and pleasant conversation on general topics, social, literary, and even religious; but I carefully avoided any allusion to the hated doctrines. When the hour arrived for leaving, on the next day, I went to our room, took my little book from the trunk, and thus soliloquized:

"If I go away without some honest, earnest effort to remove from the mind of this good friend the prejudices which now exclude from it the truth of God, I shall be very culpable; but, then, in seeking to remove prejudices of one sort, I may implant others. If she suspects me of a purpose to make her a Calvinist, I may lose the influence God has evidently given me over her. I must approach her indirectly."

Now, Mrs. S. was not only a highly-cultivated and refined lady, but a care-taking, skillful housekeeper, and I felt sure that, as soon as we left, she would go to our room, to see if we had forgotten anything; so I opened my little book, and, turning it down upon a table so as to make the impression on her mind that I had read just to that place, *I purposely forgot it*, and, breathing a prayer that God would own the expedient, we returned home.

This was early in the week. On the following Sabbath I preached Christ the only Saviour as fully and faithfully as I could. I had not proceeded far with my discourse when I made the discovery that my friend, Mrs. S., was giving unusual attention, and before I closed she wept freely. She was not given to weeping, and this fact increased my encouragement. Strange, and even censurable, as it may seem to some, when the worship was over, I avoided speaking with her, but hurried out of the church by one door as I saw her passing through another. She was a lady of too much intelligence and too much commendable pride to be willing to be made a gazing stock for others; and then I knew that I could say nothing more appropriate to her than much I had already said in the sermon. All she now needed was time and opportunity to think and pray alone.

My purpose was to visit her early on Monday. Accordingly, I had no sooner taken my breakfast than I set out for this purpose. She met me in the porch, and said:

"I had just called a servant to send for you as I saw you alight from your horse. I am a miserable sinner."

As we entered the house together, I asked her how she had made the discovery. She said in reply:

"You remember the last visit you and Mrs. White paid us. When you left, *you forgot* the book you had been reading, and, being interested in the title, I commenced reading where you had finished. My attention was at once arrested, and I determined to begin at the beginning and read the book through. This I have done twice from the beginning to the end, and portions I have read three or four times. It not only removed my objections to the doctrine of election, but, when this was done, I at once, and distinctly, saw that I was a lost sinner. The sermon yesterday only deepened this conviction."

I need only add that she soon became a member of the church, and lived and died a firm Presbyterian and a consistent Christian.

INTERESTED HEARERS.

In the summer of 1829 I went as one of a committee of Presbytery to take part in the organization of a Presbyterian church in the county of L. There was no house of worship at all adequate to the accommodation of the large congregation—especially on the Sabbath. Accordingly we preached in a grove. It devolved on me to preach on Sabbath morning. The congregation was immense. The wind blew freely in my face, and the tramping and neighing of the horses tied to the trees made it very doubtful whether I could be heard. To determine this question I fixed my eyes upon a man who stood leaning against a tree more remote from where I stood than any other hearer, and concluded that if I kept his attention I might be satisfied that the rest heard me. He seemed so attentive that I was not only convinced that he heard me, but hoped that he heard to some good purpose. When the worship was over, it so happened that in riding away I fell in with this very man. I had no acquaintance with him, but recognizing him as the man who leant against the tree, I asked him if he were not the man. He replied that he was. "I am glad to meet you," I said, "especially as I desire to know whether, standing so far off, you heard me." "Oh, yes," he said, "I heard every word, and I'll tell you what I was thinking about." I replied:

"I shall be glad to know what your thoughts were," hoping to discover that some good impression had been made on him; and added, "do tell me candidly just what you were thinking about."

"Well," he said, "I was thinking all the time you were preaching that *your lungs must be made of white-oak.*"

"My dear sir," I replied, "I am deeply grieved to find that you were thinking of my *lungs* and not of *your own soul.*"

Some further conversation convinced me that the tree against which he leaned had as wakeful a conscience as he had. And yet he seemed not to lose one word of the sermon.

Young preachers are often sadly mistaken in the judgment they form of the interest manifested by their hearers in their preaching.

Anti-Presbyterianism Cured.

Another incident, which occurred at the same meeting, may be worth relating.

Just as I had mounted my horse to leave the ground, my attention was attracted by a group of gentlemen, whose dress and manners convinced me that they belonged to the best class of citizens—I mean the wealthiest, most intelligent and influential. In the centre of the group one stood who seemed to be addressing the rest in a very earnest and impassioned style. He smote the palm of one hand with the fist of the other, accompanying the action with words I could not hear, but which evidently expressed much earnestness and some anger. This gentleman was W. O., Esq., a prominent lawyer and a man of great influence.

A few days after, I met, in the house of a friend, one of the gentlemen to whom he was speaking. I said to him pleasantly, "Our friend, Mr. O., seemed to be preaching at the close of our late meeting almost as earnestly as I had done during its progress. I do not wish to be impertinent nor to tempt you to violate the rules of good breeding, but if you do not object, I should be gratified to know what interested him so deeply."

"There is no impropriety," he replied, "in telling you. To be perfectly candid, I think he would be pleased for me to tell you. The substance of his speech was this:

"'I am resolved to spare neither time, effort, nor money, to keep these Presbyterians from getting a foothold in L. For this, among others, I have two reasons—viz.: 1. They are shrewd, smart, meddlesome people. Their preachers especially are educated men, and on this account they aspire to be the equals of the first gentlemen in the community, and accordingly they meddle with the opinions and claim the right of rebuking the social habits of all classes of people. 2. If they once become established here, you will never be able to dislodge them.'"

I simply replied, "Tell my good friend, Mr. O., that I live in the adjoining county where he practices law; that I live very near to the court-house, and when he comes to N. court I shall be very glad to see him at my house."

A missionary was sent to take charge of this newly organized church, and within less than twelve months my friend, Mr. O., became a member, and in less than twelve months more a ruling elder in the church, the organization of which had so provoked him. He lived to serve the church with great fidelity for many years, and died deeply lamented by an extensive circle of friends and brethren.

As young ministers should not readily be elated by favorable, so they should not be readily discouraged by unfavorable appearances. Indeed, the manifestation of opposition is often the way in which an awakened conscience first displays itself. It is nothing but a desperate effort to silence by violence the first whisperings of conscience. Mr. O. confessed that this was the case with him, and that his own speech did more that day to convince him of the native depravity of his heart than the preaching.

"The Devil Threw him Down and Tare him."

Mrs. M. P. was the wife of a physician in the county of A. She was young, accomplished, and beautiful. Neither she nor her husband was a professor of religion. He was well-bred, intelligent, and skillful in his profession, but was an undisguised skeptic, and, on some occasions, a scoffer. She had been reared under religious influences, but was, to all appearances, wholly unconcerned as to her spiritual interests, and extravagantly gay. On one occasion I preached at night to a small audience in a private house near their residence. Mrs. P. attended this service, accompanied by two gay young ladies who were visiting her. The doctor declined going, although urged by ladies. They plead their want of an escort, but he, in reply, plead that the distance was short, and the carriage-driver everyway trustworthy.

I closed my sermon with an earnest request that each of my hearers would consent to spend, on their return home, fifteen minutes in secret meditation and prayer. I urged that this was a very small portion of the entire day and night thus to devote to God.

As the three ladies rode home, Mrs. P. asked her two young friends if they intended to comply with my request. They answered promptly in the negative, and laughed heartily at her asking them such a question. She replied, with much solemnity, "I think the request very reasonable, and intend to comply with it." On reaching home, Mrs. P. at once withdrew to a room in a remote part of the house, and kneeling, attempted to pray. The attempt greatly increased her concern. In a few days she rested peacefully on Christ, and avowed her purpose to consecrate herself to his service. I visited her in the earlier stage of her awakening, and was highly gratified with her intelligence and firmness. She then very modestly intimated her fear that her husband would be offended at her course. She said he had thus far exhibited no ill-temper, but only sought, as he expressed it, to "laugh her out of her fanaticism."

After a few weeks I received a note from her, desiring me to visit her, stating that she was in the deepest distress. I hastened to her house and, to my great surprise, found her closely confined to her chamber, with her first and only child—some ten months old—in her arms. As I entered the room she wept profusely, and said, "O Mr. White, I am a ruined woman." She said no more, but continued to utter cries that pierced the heart like daggers.

After a few words of instruction, followed by prayer, she became calm, and told me her story.

She said: "My dear husband first tried to shake my faith by ridicule, then argument, and then—I am afraid to utter it—he tried violence. Two nights ago he retired early, and when I came to the chamber I thought he was soundly asleep. Having read my accustomed portion of Scripture, I knelt at my chair to offer prayer. I was soon startled by his voice, and still more so by his springing out of bed, and seizing me around the waist, placed me on my feet directly before him. Then, looking at me sternly, as I trembled and wept, he said, '*You must quit this nonsense, or I will quit you.*' I at once felt as if I were sustained in a way I could not explain, and said, 'You are my husband; as such I love you dearly, and if you will give me the opportunity, I think I can convince you that my becoming a Christian will not cause me to love you less, but help me to love you a great deal more. *But Jesus Christ is my Saviour, and if you force upon me the alternative, I cannot deny him.*' He then left the room abruptly, ordered his horse and sulky, packed his trunk, and left. I have neither seen nor heard from him since. Oh! my friend and pastor, tell me what to do."

Her statement affected me deeply, and yet I could not refrain from answering hopefully, and, almost humorously, said: "I know Dr. P. very well. He is a gentleman and a fond husband and father, and he had a very pious mother, and is the child of many prayers. Rest assured that he will not go far nor remain long absent." Having again joined her in prayer, I left her much more tranquil and hopeful.

I heard nothing from her during the remnant of that week. But on the ensuing Sabbath, as I went to the pulpit, I saw Mrs. P. sitting near the centre of the church, and, as I arose to commence worship, I saw him sitting very near the door. His countenance, at that distance, seemed to indicate rage rather than repentance, and strange emotions were awakened by the apprehension that he had come for some bad purpose. It was impossible to refrain from looking at him often during the sermon.

My text, I well remember, was, "How shall we escape if we *neglect* so great salvation?" In the course of the sermon I said, if *mere neglect* may prove fatal to the soul, then who can conceive, much less describe, the doom of those who make open and even violent opposition to the gospel. Just then I purposely averted my eyes from him for obvious reasons. Nor did I observe him again until the benediction was pronounced and the people had commenced slowly leaving the house.

Then I saw him approaching the pulpit, with a countenance which, to me, seemed terrific. I descended, and placed myself in front of the pulpit, resolved to meet the issue, whatever it might be, with the utmost coolness. When he had approached very near he raised both arms, then, bringing them down slowly, rested one on each of my shoulders and sunk to the floor, exclaiming, with a loud voice, as he fell, "Oh! tell me, sir, if there is one drop of mercy in all heaven for such a sinner as I am."

This was heard in the yard, and the people came hastening back into the house. A highly intelligent and excellent Methodist lady, Mrs. F., commenced shouting, and we were on the borders of a terrific storm. Raising my voice to its utmost pitch, I called on all to be silent; and there was at once perfect silence, save suppressed sighs and groans that came from every part of the house.

I then called two of the elders by name to come to me. They did so promptly, and we raised the Doctor from the floor and seated him on a bench. He made no noise, but his face was livid, and his whole frame shook with emotion. I sat beside him and said, "My dear friend, get home as soon as you can, and I will go with you." With a tremulous voice he said, with peculiar emphasis, "Will *you* go home with *me?*" "Assuredly I will, and with the utmost pleasure." Each of the two elders supported him out of the house. We found his wife awaiting us at the door, bathed in tears and attended by several ladies, who had wisely kept her from coming to us at the pulpit, and were kindly endeavoring to quiet her nerves and compose her mind. I accompanied them home and spent the night.

I shall not attempt any recital of what then transpired, further than to say that he found no peace of mind for several days. But at length his peace became like a river, and in a few weeks both he and his wife appeared before the session together, were received into the church, and became exemplary and useful servants of Christ.

Early Conversion.

E. F. P. died at the age of ten years and seven months. She lost her mother at the early age of three years. Her parents, being members of the Presbyterian Church, she was dedicated in baptism to Christ while an infant. Her father was faithful in doing what he could to supply the loss occasioned by her mother's death. This greatly endeared him to the child, and the child to him. Her fondness for her father was extreme. She studied his comfort, not only obeying all his commands promptly and cheerfully, but in contriving whatever she could to make him happy. She read her Bible a great deal, and never seemed happier than when reading it to him. She also read her Sabbath-school books with much eagerness, and, after reading them, would repeat their contents to her father. This she could do with much accuracy. She was tenderly attached to her Sabbath-school teacher. When she became ill, she asked that this teacher should be sent for, and said, "If she does not get here before I die, give her my love, bid her farewell, and tell her to meet me in heaven." She sent a similar message to her classmates. She expressed a wish to see her pastor. He hastened to her bedside, and is free to declare that her state of mind and heart evinced itself in expressions that were wonderful. She spoke in most appropriate language of Christ's great love for her, and of her love for and reliance upon him. She was confident that she would die and go to heaven. When asked why she felt so confident, she said: "Christ is in heaven. When he was on earth he said, 'Suffer little children to come unto me'; and I am sure that I want to go to him more than anything else."

So considerate was she of the comfort of her father and others, that she would often decline even necessary services to avoid giving them trouble.

Looking round upon those in the room, she said, "If I have done wrong to any of you, I hope you will forgive me." She made a careful distribution of certain little articles belonging to her among her brothers and sisters, and bade them all a calm and affectionate farewell.

Her disease was very violent, and her bodily sufferings very great; yet she not only never uttered a murmuring word, nor exhibited the least restlessness, but seemed throughout perfectly happy.

I received this little girl's parents into the church, buried her mother, baptized and then buried her. She was truly a precious lamb of the great and good Shepherd. Borne in his arms along the banks of the river of life and beneath the shade of that tree whose leaves are for the healing of the nations, she is safe and happy forever.

Instead of being surprised that children are converted so early, if the covenant was duly considered and duty duly performed, the surprise should be that many more are not thus converted.

E. W. W. seemed to be pious at nine years of age. At that early age her father found her alone in her mother's chamber reading the Bible with great apparent interest. He said to her, "My daughter, do you love to read the

Bible?" "Yes, sir; very much," was her reply. He added, "Can you tell me why you love it?" She paused awhile and said, "Because there are so many pretty prayers in it." She was reading the Psalms.

When eleven years of age, she went to her father's study on Saturday morning preceding a communion Sabbath, sat on his knee, rested her head on his shoulder, and commenced weeping. He asked her very tenderly why she wept; but, for some time, she could make no reply. At length, with apparent effort, she merely said, "The communion is to be to-morrow," and then wept more freely. On inquiry, her father discovered that she greatly desired to participate in the sacred ordinance. On questioning her closely, he found that her ideas on the subject were clear and scriptural. But he proposed that she would wait until she was older and more confirmed in her experience. She seemed to understand very clearly the meaning and force of her father's reasons, and yielded.

This scene, with very slight variation, was reënacted at each communion for the ensuing twelve months. All this time she read carefully books fitted to explain the scriptural experience of the true Christian. At the close of that year, when she was just twelve years of age, she appeared before the session, gave very satisfactory answers to the questions asked her, and was admitted to the communion of the church. She was consistent as a religious child, then as a well-educated young lady, and still lives, adorning her profession as a pious wife and mother of a large family of children.

A. R. was much such a child as the foregoing. At the same early age she seemed pious, but made no profession of religion, nor had she ever expressed any desire to be connected with the church. When about twelve years old she was attacked with a lingering disease, of which she died after a confinement of two months. At an early stage of her sickness she communicated freely with her godly mother as to her religious ideas and feelings. She gave the most satisfactory evidence of a thorough change of heart, spoke confidently of dying, and expressed the utmost willingness to die. On one occasion, after speaking of the reasons she had for being happy in the prospect of death, in a way to satisfy the most incredulous, she paused for a while and commenced weeping. Her fond and anxious mother inquired for the cause of her distress, to which she replied, "Mother, I was only distressed at thinking that I should have been so foolish and wicked as to put off giving my heart to Christ so long."

This ebullition of grief passed away; her peace again became as a river; and, at the early age of twelve, she died happily, never having ceased to regret that she had not given her heart to Christ sooner.

A. H. was the son of an intelligent, rich and pious father. He applied for church-membership at the early age of fourteen years. So satisfactory was the examination he sustained that the session did not hesitate to admit him. He held fast his profession as a boy, a young man and a minister of the gospel—which sacred office he still holds.

E. S. was a little girl, whose mind and heart seemed imbued with love to her Saviour at the age of eight years. This was evinced in all the ordinary ways, which need not be repeated. When just at the early age mentioned above, her father found her reading the Bible and weeping freely as she read. On inquiring into the cause of her grief, and taking her Testament in his hand as he talked with her, he discovered that she had been reading the nineteenth chapter of the Gospel by John. He said to her, "My child, what is there in this chapter to make you weep?"

"Why, father," she said, "don't you see that near the beginning of the chapter they said, 'we find no fault in him,' and yet, before the chapter ends, it tells us that they crucified him? How can I help crying to think of that?"

Two days after this touching incident, this child's clothes took fire from standing too near the fire-place, and, as there was no one with her in the room to extinguish the flames, she was so badly burned that she survived only about twenty-four hours. During this time of intense suffering her mind was clear, calm, and peaceful. She spoke of her Saviour with great propriety and warmth of affection, and several times referred to the fact that they declared him innocent, and yet crucified him. She never referred to this without weeping bitterly. She died very happily.

A. A. B. was the daughter of E. B., Esq., one of the wealthiest, most intelligent, but yet one of the most irreligious men in the congregation to which I ministered when first licensed to preach. Mr. B. was a lawyer who, though irreligious, was not profane nor dissipated. He might have been considered a man of good moral character, but whose views of religious questions were in open conflict with the teachings of the word of God. He had a large and gay family. He lived freely and entertained generously. His children were trained in the ways of the world. To gratify their natural love of worldly pleasure he spared neither pains nor expense. A. A. was his third daughter. The eldest was married, and the second grown and much admired. The whole family was utterly destitute of all knowledge of, or interest in, evangelical religion.

Soon after my settlement I preached in a school-house, to a very small audience. This school-house was within a few hundred yards of Mr. B.'s house. Yet the only member of his large family who attended was the subject of this sketch—then just thirteen years of age. She was large for her age, not very handsome, but of an engaging person and attractive manners for a child. She was awakened at this meeting to a sense of her sin and misery, and, when the small audience dispersed, she remained of her own accord, to converse with me on the subject. Her knowledge of religion was very limited, for she had enjoyed no religious training. Still, her convictions of personal guilt and danger were deep and scriptural. I gave her such counsel as I deemed appropriate. Her impressions were abiding. She soon visited me at my house. She seemed to have accepted Christ as he is offered in the gospel. She gave very satisfactory reasons for the hope that was in her, and expressed a desire to be admitted to the church. I advised her to wait, in consideration of her youth and the probable opposition her family, and especially her father, would make to this step. She yielded readily, but sadly, especially when I told her that I hoped God designed to make her the first fruits of religion in the large and gay family to which she belonged

About two months after her first visit to me, her second sister was married. The wedding was extravagantly gay. A very large company was invited. Musicians were brought from Petersburg, and for two or three days and nights the large house resounded with music and dancing, and every form of fashionable revelry.

Through these gay scenes A. A. bore herself with Christian propriety. She was modest, good-humored, and polite to everybody, yet firmly refrained from direct participation in the dance Her father observed this, and spoke very kindly to her (for he was a very affectionate father), urging her to do as her sisters and young friends were doing, and not make herself an object of ridicule and disgust. She modestly and firmly declined. Her father then took her on his knee and told her that, if she would only conform to the customs of the party, he would give her fifty dollars. To this she very meekly replied, "Papa, I am sure you would not have me to violate my conscience for money. I cannot do it." This provoked him, and he told her to go to the kitchen and associate with the cook, as she was the only Christian in his family. This so distressed her that she left the room in tears; but she controlled her feelings and soon returned, only to persist in the course she had adopted.

More than a year passed away, during which she often visited me, improved in knowledge, and grew in grace. During this time she said little about joining the church; still it was evident that she desired to do so.

At length she made me a visit, during the week preceding a stated communion, expressly to make application for membership. She prefaced her application by saying that she had recently heard her father say to a prominent member of the church, who was trying to convince him of his errors, "Sir, it is useless to endeavor to change my opinions, for I adopted them when I was fourteen years old, and they have continued to strengthen ever since."

Now, thought the dear girl, I will ask papa's permission to join the church, and, if he objects because of my age, I will remind him of what he said to Captain Jones about making up his mind at fourteen; and, as that is my age, he certainly cannot object to my doing as he did. "But," she added, "I wished to see you before I made my wishes known to him." I encouraged her to ask for her father's consent, assuring her that, if she obtained it, she should be received to full membership in the church.

She met me at church on Saturday preceding the communion, and gave me the following account of her interview with her father. She said:

"I went into his office, and, standing at his side, laid my arm on his shoulder, but said nothing. He laid down his pen, looked at me very kindly, and said, 'My daughter, what do you want?' But my heart failed me. I could say nothing, but walked quietly out of the room. When I had returned to my chamber, I remembered that I had not prayed before I went to the office, and then understood why I failed to make my errand known. So I locked my door, knelt and prayed for God to help me to do what I wanted, and to do it in the right way. I then returned to the office, had no difficulty in making my errand known, and at once received my father's permission to do as I pleased in the matter."

She accordingly appeared before the session, was cordially welcomed to the communion of the church, and made ever afterwards one of our most useful members. Such was her good sense, prudence, and piety, that she soon acquired great influence over her whole family. Their gaiety continued, but her feelings were respected. Nor did she ever swerve in the least from the line of strict Christian propriety. The whole family became constant attendants at church and generous supporters of the ministry.

In about a year after A. A. joined the church, her father became ill. She conversed with him freely about his future prospects. He listened to her respectfully, and finally asked that I be sent for. I saw him several times. He spoke freely on the subject of religion, but his views were indistinct and confused. They certainly afforded him no comfort. He died without any discoverable saving change. But from that time, a work of grace went forward in the family. The mother, two sisters, and a brother, soon became members of the church. The latter still lives, and has for many years been one of the best ruling elders in the church.

Meantime, A. A. grew to womanhood, married one of our best ministers, and made one of the best minister's wives I have ever known. She died recently, leaving one daughter, the wife of a minister, and other children, a blessing to their father and the church.

These are a few, and only a few, out of many instances of early piety which have occurred under my own observation.

These are, perhaps, the most striking; but many others might be stated, well-fitted to convince every candid mind that the children are often the most interesting and promising portion of a minister's charge. It has been pertinently said, that "the shepherd who does not look well to the lambs of his flock will soon have no flock to look after."

But I must not leave this subject until I have specifically stated that the greatest caution must be observed, and the greatest skill displayed, in dealing with the religious convictions and feelings of children. They must be taught to restrain mere animal feeling. They must be guarded against those excitements in which some ministers so delight, and to create which such unreasonable and unscriptural measures are often adopted. No class of persons so much need the ballast which only saving truth can give to the mind.

The reader is referred to the account I have elsewhere given of revivals in Charlottesville Female Academy.

CHAPTER VII.

1832-1836.

LEAVES NOTTOWAY FOR SCOTTSVILLE, VA.—MR. (AFTERWARDS REV. DR.) PEYTON HARRISON BUILDS A PARSONAGE FOR HIM AT HIS OWN CHARGES.—REVIVAL —REV. DANIEL BAKER.—ACCEPTS AGENCY FOR AMERICAN TRACT SOCIETY.—OBSERVATIONS ON HIS AGENCY AND SIMILAR ENTERPRISES AUXILIARY TO THE CHURCH.

"Rejoice that man is hurled
From change to change unceasingly,
His soul's wings never furled."

IN April, 1832, our Presbytery met at Providence Church, in Louisa county, Va. I was invited by the session of the church in Scottsville, Albemarle county, then vacant, to visit them on my way to the meeting. I did so, and the result was a unanimous call to become their pastor. With great difficulty, and after much reflection, I accepted this call, and prepared to leave my much-loved people in Nottoway.

They made strenuous opposition to my leaving them; but, when they discovered that I was clear in my judgment as to my duty, they yielded.

[Mr. Cralle Jones, a ruling elder at the time, gave us, in May, 1886, a touching account of the congregational meeting, called to unite with Mr. White in his application to Presbytery for permission to take charge of the Scottsville Church. The vote of the congregation was silent—not a voice was heard. The Rev. Mr. Pryor, who was to succeed him, was on the floor, in the vigor and beauty of his youth.]

Every feeling of my heart was opposed to this step, but judgment and conscience impelled me to go. With many tears I bade them farewell on the second Sabbath in June, 1832.

Scottsville was then a small village on James river, but rapidly increasing in size and importance. A turnpike had recently been constructed, extending to Rockfish Gap, and inviting the trade of the Valley of Virginia in that direction. The result was that so small a village rarely ever commanded so active a trade. A hundred large Valley wagons have been seen unloading their rich freight of flour, bacon, venison hams, butter, cheese, beeswax, etc, in one day; and this when the population did not exceed five hundred persons of all ages and conditions. Small as the population was, it was far too large to find comfortable habitations. A small, but neat, Presbyterian church was the only house of worship, and this incomplete when I arrived. The church contained about forty members, with four highly intelligent and active ruling elders. My predecessor, the Rev. Samuel Hurd, a man of blessed memory, had gathered and organized this little church. His work was well and faithfully done. He left them in so healthful a state that it was pleasant to succeed him. A Sabbath-school, Bible-class, and a congregational prayer-meeting were in successful operation.

But only the half of my time could be given to this people. The other half was given to a little church in Buckingham, eight miles from Scottsville, called "Mars' Hill." Here were a few Presbyterians, intelligent and excellent people. Among these was Mrs. Martha Nicholas, of "The Seven Islands," a lady of large estate, yet larger heart. She was, to a great extent, to my little family, what Mrs. Dr. Jones had been in Nottoway. She was a widow, over three-score years of age, with three grown sons still living with her. Her hospitality was unbounded. She loved and labored for her church. She loved and sustained her pastor and his family.

It was put into the call that I should reside in the village of Scottsville; but so rapidly had it increased in population, and so straitened were the people for house-room, that it was impossible to find a home for my family, either as housekeeper or boarder. In this extremity, Mrs. Nicholas proposed that we should reside with her, free of charge, until some arrangement could be made for our accommodation at Scottsville. We accepted her kind offer for a few weeks.

But Peyton Harrison, Esq., then a ruling elder in the Scottsville Church, now the Rev. Dr. Peyton Harrison, of Baltimore, determined to build a parsonage at his own charges, and, meantime, procured boarding for us in the family of Mr. Edward Tompkins, who lived about four miles from Scottsville.

With this very kind family we boarded through the summer and into the autumn of 1832. During the following winter we boarded with Mr. Peter White, a ruling elder in Scottsville, and an uncommonly good man. In the spring of 1833 we took possession of the plain, but neat house built for us by Mr. Harrison.

During the following summer we were visited by the Rev. Daniel Baker, whose preaching was owned and blessed of God to the increase of the church. Now, for the first time in a ministry of six years, it was my privilege to enjoy a general and genuine revival of religion. Now, for the first time, I had to guide about thirty anxious inquirers all at once. This was new and difficult, but delightful, work. About twenty-five were added to the church, including some of the most prominent persons of the village and surrounding country. They ran well, and added much to the strength of the church. One of the fruits of this revival was the bringing of Mr. Peyton Harrison into the ministry. He was a ruling elder and a lawyer. He had thought of the ministry before, but the obstacles seemed insurmountable.

He had a family, a large landed estate, and many servants. The difficulty of deciding what disposition to make of these had hitherto held him back. But the active effort and prayer, called forth by this revival, so increased his own faith and so inflamed his own zeal that he hesitated no longer.

Mrs. Harrison cheerfully consented to take her children and go with him to the seminary. His brother, Carter H. Harrison, readily consented to purchase his entire estate—land, stock, farming implements, and servants—on his own terms. In this way the servants were not disturbed in their domestic relations. Thus Providence opened up the way; he entered it, and in due time became a minister of the gospel. Two valuable additions were made to the session as other fruits of this revival.

My ministry now became very pleasant; but within a year from that time it ended, and, at what seemed like a call of Providence, we left our pleasant home for a widely different field of labor. This happened thus: Up to this time the American Tract Society had published only unbound tracts. Several leading ministers in Petersburg and Richmond had resolved to seek, through the Virginia Tract Society, the enlargement of the parent society's plans. The result was that a number of the best books on practical theology were published, and a scheme inaugurated, technically termed "The volume enterprise of the Virginia Tract Society," and I was chosen to take in hand the prosecution of the scheme as the general agent for the State of Virginia.

It was extremely difficult to decide what was my duty. I had been pastor at Scottsville only two years. God had graciously granted us an outpouring of his Spirit, which had revived and strengthened the church. I was yet a young man, scarcely beyond the infancy of my ministry. The church warmly and unanimously opposed the resignation of my pastoral charge. Still, the arguments employed by those who sought my services, with what then seemed the will of God, determined me to yield to the proposal, and enter upon this very new and untried field. This, with the reluctant consent of the church and Presbytery, I did. We had now four children.

It has been, for a long time, clear to my mind that I seriously mistook my duty in taking such a family from their home, exchanging such a pastoral charge for any migratory agency whatsoever. Of this I became fully convinced before the second year of my agency was half expired; and at the end of the second year, in the spring of 1836, I joyfully resigned. Still, my most judicious and candid friends expressed the opinion that God had enabled me to accomplish a great and good work.

True, I became something of a traveller; made a great many off-hand speeches; preached a few sermons a great many times; explored almost every part of Virginia, and many parts many times. I went beyond the limits of Virginia; attended "the anniversaries" in New York and in Boston; made quite a number of the sort of speeches common and popular in that day, especially in that Northern region; touched for a night and day at New Haven; about as long at Hartford and Providence, R. I. I put an immense number of books in circulation, the solid and excellent "bound volumes of the Tract Society."

But then there were scores of excellent laymen in the church who could have done all that I did, save the preaching of a few thread-bare sermons, even better than I did. They could have travelled more easily, more expeditiously, and less expensively. They could have excelled me in making the sort of speeches I made, and, as to the filling and sending abroad boxes of books, they could have surpassed me greatly.

But, above all, Presbytery did not license and ordain me to do this sort of semi-secular work, but to gather together the lost sheep of the house of Israel by the oral preaching of the gospel, and by faithful pastoral visitation from house to house. And then, God had blessed me in making me a husband and a father, thus placing me at the head of another institution as really of divine appointment as is the church itself. This, of course, I almost wholly neglected, at least so far as their religious instruction and training were concerned; and, but for the fidelity and skill of the mother of those four children, they would probably have suffered irreparable injury through my neglect.

If a man enters the ministry, as I fear many do, through mistake as to his adaptedness to the work, and, hence, after proper exertions faithfully made, fails to secure a useful position in a pastoral charge, then he must do the next best thing he can. In other words, if on full experiment, he fails to meet the just demands of the church in the pastoral work, yet can preach a tolerable sermon as stated supply of some feeble church and has aptness to teach a classical school, why let him serve God as stated supply and schoolmaster. If another, with similar disqualifications as to the pastoral work, can commit to memory the story of some benevolent association; can tell that story fluently; is fond of a migratory life; possesses some ease of manner, which much intercourse with all sorts of people, blended with some impudence, will give him; has a wife well fitted for the duties of a mother, and is himself good for nothing as a father, why let him become an agent.

And yet the best of pastors may, in certain emergencies, and for the immediate furtherance of some great cause, get leave of absence from his church for a short time to set in motion or urge forward this cause; or, when incapacitated by age or some infirmity unfitting him for the full work of the ministry, he may turn teacher, or farmer, or even agent, by and with the consent of his pastoral charge and Presbytery. Presidencies and professorships of colleges can be undertaken with propriety by ordained ministers of the gospel only under similar limitations.

The extent to which, especially in the North, the ministry of the gospel is "*tacked on*" to some presidency or professorship, merely to add dignity and sacredness to a far inferior calling, has had a deplorable tendency to elevate the inferior at the expense of the superior profession. It has greatly helped to secularize and degrade, and even to corrupt the ministry, until, in many, very many cases, the preachers in the United States have become the wildest and most narrow-minded politicians and agitators in all the land.

So much I have deemed it proper to say of my two years' agency, chiefly for my two sons who are now, and for my grandsons who may become, ministers.

[Dr. White has left a diary of his experience while on this agency. It abounds in entertaining incidents, and would be published in this memoir but for fear of making the book too large.]

CHAPTER VIII

1836-1838.

HIS FIELD IN AND ABOUT CHARLOTTESVILLE.—ABANDONS SOUTH PLAINS AND BETHEL.—REV. JOSEPH F. BAXTER CALLED TO THEM.—CONFINES HIS WORK TO CHARLOTTESVILLE.—OPENS A SCHOOL FOR YOUNG LADIES.—THE SCHOOL A NURSERY TO THE CHURCH.—DECLINES ENTERTAINING A CALL TO A VALLEY CHURCH.

*"This is not a world of finalities of any kind;
But one of broken arcs, and not of perfect rounds."*

THE church at Charlottesville, Va., made vacant by the resignation and removal to Georgia of the Rev. Francis Bowman, invited me to become their pastor. This church had been united, under Mr. Bowman, with that of Bethel, and now united in their call to me. There was a third place of worship embraced in the limits, called South Plains. These three houses of worship, with their intervening lines, formed almost an equilateral triangle, whose lines were from six to eight miles long. Mr. Bowman had resided first in the bounds of Bethel, where his labors had been much blessed. A religious awakening had occurred at an early period of his ministry, and there sprang up a small but vigorous country church. His success at South Plains had been encouraging also. But certain influences in, and especially around, Charlottesville had greatly retarded and counteracted his work at that place. Still a few noble spirits were found there, who, though defrauded of their interest in a house of worship which they had unwisely built in connection with another denomination, relinquished their right in that church, and forthwith built another of their own.

Mr. Bowman's ill health, which at length compelled him to seek a more southern clime, had, for a long time, seriously interrupted his labors, and the little churches suffered on this account. When, in the early spring of 1836, I visited them with a view to a more full and satisfactory consideration of their call, the field, especially at Charlottesville, exhibited so unpromising an appearance that I was exceedingly reluctant to undertake it. The Rev. George A. Baxter, D. D., who had succeeded my honored preceptor, Rev. Dr. John H. Rice, as professor of theology in Union Seminary, Virginia, urged me to accept, and presented considerations which, with God's guidance I trust, prevailed with me to do so.

Accordingly, on the 17th of May, 1836, I commenced my work. The arrangement for the first year was the following: I preached on one Sabbath in the month at Charlottesville, one at South Plains, and two at Bethel. I met with warm and generous friends in the church, but outsiders were distant and cold. Altogether the prospect was very dreary, and at Charlottesville it became more and more so as the year rolled by. It could hardly be otherwise. The Episcopal, Methodist, Baptist and Campbellite churches all had the start of the Presbyterian. They made good use of the advantage thus secured. Most or all of these had service every Sabbath, and I but one Sabbath in the month. On many a fair and lovely day I preached to twenty, or at most to thirty people. As to service in the week, and especially at night, that was a thing unknown. (See the *Life of Sampson*, by Dr. Dabney, pp. 18, 19.)

At the end of the first year I succeeded in prevailing on the South Plains people, among whom were some of my most generous friends and supporters, to relinquish their claim on me for Sabbath services, and to consent to take a Saturday service once in two weeks. Then I spent two Sabbaths in Charlottesville, two at Bethel, two Saturdays a month at South Plains, and two Thursdays a month at Mount Tabor, a vacant church some twelve miles west of Charlottesville.

These scattered labors extended my acquaintance among the people, and friends outside the church began to gather around me. But still I clearly saw that we must have worship every Sabbath in Charlottesville, or next to nothing could be done. But how could this be done? The two churches to which I ministered on the Sabbath paid for my support $350 each, and thought and said they could pay more. I had now five children, and three of these were at school. My expenses were increasing rapidly, and my salary was stationary. From the time I became a father I resolved on two things: First, that I would never attempt to make a fortune for my children; second, that I would spare no expense of time, effort or money to give them a good education. But how was this to be done? Only in one way, and that I brought about thus:

About the time my second year ended, in the spring of 1838, my venerable friend, Dr. George A. Baxter, wrote to me that his son, Joseph, expected to be licensed at the approaching meeting of Presbytery, and that if I could find a field of labor for him somewhere in my neighborhood, he would be gratified. I at once concluded to ask the Bethel and South Plains churches to release me from my obligation to preach to them, and unite in calling young Baxter into their service.

To this they at first objected strongly. Bethel pleaded that they had as many members, and could give as much as Charlottesville and South Plains together; that they had first moved to call me there; that but for them I would never have come; that they would purchase a parsonage, and settle me permanently among themselves.

To this I replied that, feeble as the church in Charlottesville is, nevertheless it is the county-seat, and as such is the heart of the county; excellent schools are there; and there especially is the University of Virginia. I *must* educate my children, and however generous you may be, you cannot afford to them the advantages of those schools at this distance; but living there I may hope to give them those advantages.

Their reply to all this was: There are only about twenty members of that church, and they give you only $350, and we doubt whether they will ever give you more. You cannot accomplish your purpose on means so limited.

My answer was: I can easily attend to so small and compact a church and teach a female school; and as they give me less than half a support, I shall feel bound to serve them only the half of my time; the other half I can give to a school conducted on thoroughly Christian privileges.

At length they yielded. The union between Bethel and South Plains was formed. Mr. Joseph F. Baxter was called to be their pastor, and duly installed as such.

Now I started afresh, with a church of less than twenty members, a congregation of fifty hearers, on a salary of $350, and this in the eleventh year of my ministry. This seemed like receding, instead of advancing.

The little church increased my salary to $500, five gentlemen giving me their joint bond for this amount. This amount was duly paid.

I had now been preaching eleven years, and was just eleven hundred dollars poorer that when I commenced. As far as I was known at all in the church, I was known to be a strenuous advocate for ministers giving themselves wholly to the work of the ministry. Up to this time I had never added one dollar to my income by any secular calling. I had also said much and written something in opposition to ministers serving their churches for less than an adequate support. Now I was about to do what seemed to militate against all this. But I viewed the case thus:

I considered Charlottesville (as wiser men than I did) as one of the most important positions in the State. I had been brought there much against my own wishes, and obviously by the leadings of Providence. I enjoyed, to an extent far beyond my merits, not only the confidence and love of the little church, but also of a constantly widening circle not belonging to the church. I was convinced that, if I left, no one whom the people would approve would be willing to go there. Such a salary as they could give would not command the services of such a man as they ought to have.

After I had gone there, and before I had accepted their call, having only promised to stay for a short time, I was assured by a committee of the session of one of the largest and best churches in the Valley of Virginia, that the church would give me a call if only I would say that I had declined the call to Charlottesville. This committee visited me to press the subject. Had I encouraged them I would have furnished the church and the world with another instance, already too common, of consulting my ease and reputation rather than my duty. I accordingly determined, while this committee were with me, to remain in Charlottesville, and told them so.

As to the other point—the secular school teaching—I have this to say: So small a church, and one so compact, could not demand more than half my time, leaving the other half to be employed in any way which might promise to promote directly the proper work of the ministry. The school would call before me, and bring directly under my influence every day, a large number of the girls of my own congregation and of others; for, while the school was to be strictly Christian, it would not be sectarian. A school might be made, without offence to any right-minded men, an *every day congregation*, to which the gospel might be fully dispensed, omitting a few points about which the true people of God differ. Accordingly, it was commenced on these principles. All denominations patronized it. The Scriptures were diligently studied, and the God of the Scriptures worshipped.

[Dr. White felt his responsibility for the conversion and growth in grace of every pupil in his school, as he did for every member of his congregation. He was not content with setting them a godly example, but made direct and affectionately earnest appeals to them individually on the subject of personal salvation. As they were usually reticent, and had difficulty in expressing their feelings orally, he encouraged them to write him letters asking questions about religion, and stating all their feelings on the subject. Many of these letters are now in our possession, carefully preserved by Dr. White throughout his life. His interest in his scholars lasted while he lived.

Is it any wonder that a large boarding-school, conducted in this way, should be visited with revival after revival, and that the scholars under his care, should imbibe religious principles that would mould their character and shape their life forever?]

This, to a great extent, was the discipline of the school. I soon became satisfied that I was as legitimately, and even more successfully, employed in the work of the ministry than I had ever been. Ministers of the gospel who aided me in my sacramental meetings would frequently go to the academy on Monday morning to join in the devotional exercises held at the opening of the school. They often said, when these services ended, "Why, this has been the best and most promising meeting we have yet had."

The Rev. Dr. Arch. Alexander spent several days with me during his last visit to Virginia. He was present more than once, addressed the school, spent an hour or two in walking through the rooms, and at the close of his visit said: "If you should be called to another pastoral charge, your chief difficulty would be in parting with this school. It is a powerful handmaid to your ministry."

The school was commenced with twelve pupils, in a small and inconvenient building. I was old-fashioned enough in my views to think that the true plan was to begin with a few scholars, and so teach and govern them as to gain the confidence of the public, and make the impression that a larger and better building was needed, and also to have such able and ample instruction provided that the public might see there was to be no lack of teaching of the best sort. A consequence of this was that, as the school did not exceed, during the first term, thirty pupils, I paid more for assistants than the whole income amounted to. In this way I lost, the first year, about $200.

Another purpose was that, as I was fully determined this school should not hinder but help my ministry, I would have competent teachers in sufficient numbers to carry it on in my absence about as well as when I was present. Thus, I was enabled to attend protracted meetings in other congregations, meetings of Presbytery and Synod and of the directors of Union Theological Seminary, as regularly as if I had had no school. This detracted greatly from my pecuniary profits; but to this I cheerfully consented.

The house in which I commenced became too small. The people all saw and felt this. My purpose was accomplished. We *must* have a larger building; the size of the school demanded it. The requisite funds were soon raised, a lot and plan agreed upon, and a suitable building erected. The school grew steadily until it reached nearly an hundred pupils. I had charge of it just ten years. The average, during these years, was seventy pupils, thirty-five of whom were boarders.

God was pleased to own and bless this school greatly. A gratifying religious interest continued almost without interruption during the ten years. Many were truly converted to God, and have made bright ornaments in the church of Christ. An account of my method of conducting religious awakenings in this school may be found in a small work, entitled *The Gospel Ministry*, composed of letters to two of my sons. This need not be repeated here.

I had therefore no trouble with conscience, either for taking less than an adequate support from the little church, nor for supplementing my salary by founding this school.

To the church I preached twice every Sabbath, and held one stated meeting during the week. I did fully as much pastoral visitation as I honestly thought was profitable to them, and found my labors among those people pleasant and useful. We enjoyed two or three seasons of revival, and a goodly number of valuable members were added to the church. Meantime, I secured the means of furnishing my children with the best literary advantages which that highly favored place afforded. My two oldest sons graduated at the University of Virginia, and my oldest daughter completed the entire course of my own seminary. The three younger children had all made a very favorable beginning with their education when I removed to another field.

CHAPTER IX.

1836-1848.

UNIVERSITY OF VIRGINIA,—MR. JEFFERSON SEES HIS MISTAKE.—POPULAR DEMAND FOR RELIGIOUS INSTRUCTION.—DENOMINATIONAL ROTATION IN THE CHAPLAINCY.—HIMSELF CHAPLAIN IN 1840.—HEALTH BREAKS DOWN.—PROF. DAVIS SHOT BY A STUDENT.—HIS DEATH.—FUNERAL.—NOTE ON THE SERMON BY REV. DR. DABNEY.—NEW ERA IN THE RELIGIOUS HISTORY OF THE UNIVERSITY.—ANECDOTE ABOUT DR. SPEECE.—CHAPLAIN A SECOND TIME (1844).—REV. D. B. EWING SECURED AS ASSISTANT.—HEALTH FAILS AGAIN.—THE "ALIQUIS CONTROVERSY."—LIST OF HIS PUBLICATIONS.—GOV. T. W. GILMER.—HIS TRAGICAL DEATH.—FUNERAL—ILLUSTRATIVE INCIDENT.—A CAUSE OF THE PREVAILING DEISM IN VIRGINIA—PROF. W. H. McGUFFEY—OPPOSITION TO HIM BECAUSE A MINISTER OF THE GOSPEL.—ANECDOTE.—REVIEW OF DR. COOPER'S "LIFE OF PRIESTLY," BY DR. JNO. H. RICE.—DR. WHITE'S IMPRESS ON CHARLOTTESVILLE AND ALBEMARLE COUNTY, BY A MEMBER OF THE METHODIST CHURCH.

> "A healthy and well-toned spiritual life
> Is with him the furthest removed from asceticism."

THE University of Virginia was opened in 1824. Mr. Jefferson brought over from Europe professors of some literary distinction, but of loose religious principles. In the beginning they allowed no form of religious worship within the precincts of the University. The discipline was extremely defective The confidence reposed in it, and the patronage extended to it, were almost wholly confined to a limited portion of the people. They chiefly belonged to the deistical aristocracy of Virginia, a party then, I am sorry to say, large and influential. But the whole thing worked so badly that, in less than two years after it opened, Mr. Jefferson had to revise the whole system of discipline, and propose to the Board of Visitors, which met about the time of his death, in 1826, a very unexceptionable system of by-laws. He also proposed that each denomination of Christians should be invited to establish a professorship of theology in connection with the University. He did not live to carry this measure through, and it failed.

But not many years after his death—three, I think—the necessity for some religious influence became so great, and the demand for it from Christian people of every denomination so clamorous, that the faculty and students were authorized to elect a chaplain. The plan agreed upon was to select one from each of the prevailing denominations—the Methodists, Baptists, Episcopalians, and Presbyterians—who should serve one year each in rotation. For two or three years this plan worked indifferently; but at length it got into successful operation. One of the medical professors, Dr. Magill, and the professor of law, Mr. Davis, became earnest and active Christian men. The former was a Presbyterian, and the latter an Episcopalian. This was soon followed by the conversion of Dr. Harrison, Professor of Ancient Languages. He became a Methodist. A great change began to appear at once. They succeeded in getting, about the year 1834, a talented and efficient chaplain. He was followed by others, for several years, from other branches of the church, like minded with himself. There began to appear, among the students, young men of decided Christian character. Most of the English professors left. The Board of Visitors adopted the wise policy of selecting young Virginians of promise, and by degrees the religious element in the faculty became strong. The confidence of the public generally was gradually secured, and the number of students increased.

In the summer of 1840, when my academy had been in operation two years, it was again the turn of the Presbyterian Church to furnish a chaplain. I was greatly surprised to receive, from the faculty and students, the offer of this position. It seemed impossible for me to add to my pastoral charge and the superintendence of the academy this office. But as the two former were permanent and the chaplaincy temporary—extending only through a single session—I could not think of resigning either of those for the sake of this; and to assume the labor and responsibility of all three seemed unwise, and even foolish. But my congregation favored, and I accepted it. Now came an amount of labor that had well-nigh put an end to my life. I preached every Sabbath morning at the University and every Sabbath afternoon in town. I held a lecture one evening in the week at each place; taught in the academy laboriously six hours on each of five days in the week; and as the New and Old School controversy was then in full blast, I carried on an extensive correspondence, and wrote a good deal for the press. To accomplish this, I slept but little, and took very little exercise. Near the end of this session my health failed. I was compelled, as soon as the University term expired, to suspend labor of every sort. Two months' rest nearly restored my health, and I resumed my work in my church and school.

On the 12th of November, 1840, about two months after my service as chaplain to the University commenced, the excellent Professor Davis was shot by a turbulent student. On Friday night of that date, Professor Davis was interrupted at his family worship by the firing of pistols on the lawn, just in front of his residence. When the worship was ended, he stepped out to see the occasion of the disturbance, and near his front door discovered a student, masked and otherwise disguised, with a pistol in his hand. On advancing to apprehend him, the student fired, and he fell. He survived until Saturday afternoon, when, at five o'clock, he expired. I was with him in his last moments, heard his last words, and saw him draw his last breath. With great clearness he reaffirmed his faith in the Lord Jesus Christ as the only ground of his hope of salvation, then gave his dying blessing to his two eldest sons, both of whom were kneeling at the side of his bed. He requested me to lead in prayer; then asked, "Where are my colleagues?" So many as could be collected were soon present. He evidently desired to speak to them at some length, but the powers of nature were too far exhausted. He could say but little, and that little was in broken sentences. Taking one of them by the hand, he said, "*Through Christ—die happy—you all too.*"

All were in tears. Dr. Harrison, whose hand he held, said, "Do you mean that through the Lord Jesus Christ you now die happy, and through him we may all die in the same way?"

"Yes, yes; that is my meaning; so may it be." He spoke no more, and in a few moments he slept quietly in Jesus.

The impression made by the cause and manner of this death cannot be described. Intellectually, socially, and religiously, Professor Davis was one of the first men of his age and country. He had been one of a committee of three who had edited and published *The Life and Correspondence of Thomas Jefferson.* At that time he sympathized with the well known deistical sentiments of the great statesman. He had even favored, in opposition to the opinion of one of the committee, the insertion of those letters, and especially the one to John Adams, that gave such offence to the whole Christian church. But soon after this, a sermon by the Rev. Daniel Baker, D. D., on popular objections to Christianity, arrested his attention, and led ultimately to the utter renunciation of his former creed, and to as cordial a reception of the gospel. In a word, he became a thoroughly converted man, a member of the Episcopal Church, and to the hour of his death illustrated his faith by a lovely and useful Christian life. Although he belonged to a different branch of the church from my own, when I became chaplain his abounding kindness to me could not have been surpassed had I been a minister of his own denomination.

His was the first house of a professor in the University of Virginia ever opened for a social prayer-meeting. The excellent Dr. Magill had died just before I was chosen chaplain, and hence there was no professor belonging to my own church there. But Professor Davis' warm piety and enlightened liberality made amends for this. In my many visits to his delightful family, and in my free and frequent interviews with him on religious subjects, it rarely occurred to me that he belonged to one branch of the church and I to another.

On the Monday succeeding his death, his funeral was held in the rotunda of the University. It devolved upon me to preach on the occasion; and it was such an occasion as rarely occurs in this world. The crowd was immense, and the grief almost uncontrollable. Not only children and ladies, but the sternest men, from the learned professor to the humblest peasant, were bathed in tears from the commencement to the close of the service.

The Rev. Dr. R. L. Dabney has a note on this funeral, which will be read with interest:

"The startling occasion, the unique nature of the calamity, the distinction of the victim, and the place, all conspired to excite the people to an intense pitch. The notice allowed the chaplain for the preparation of a discourse was brief. He felt much embarrassed about a suitable topic. He had concluded to take up the doctrine of the *divine providence*, and endeavor to improve the occasion, to enforce it argumentatively, and he was experiencing that inexpressible embarrassment and pain which the literary man knows so sadly, when he forces himself to a line of thought out of harmony with the instincts of his soul. When almost in a state of desperation about his composition, he received a visit from Professor P. Powers (now a clergyman of the Episcopal

Church, then principal of a classical seminary in Charlottesville), who asked him what subject he had adopted. When Dr. White told him he said, 'Now, that is all wrong; the people are feeling intensely, and will be in no mood for abstract discussion. There is a providence, as you and I know, and such dispensations of his plans as this are themselves the only demonstration needed. Let me advise you to change your plan; take a simpler view of truth, and merely aim to give expression to the emotions which now flood every mind.' Dr. White at once acceded to this advice. He threw his incipient preparation away, and adopted a text which suggested the contrast between the blessedness of the righteous in the extreme hour and the misery of sin. The result was one of the happiest efforts of his life. He spoke in a strain of noble, evangelical eloquence, with inimitable pathos, which swayed all hearts, 'as the trees of the forest are bent by the wind.' The learned and cultivated professors were as completely borne away by his unction as the impulsive youth. The whole audience was bathed in tears. The angry excitement and fierce tension of the public mind were replaced by Christian sympathy and tenderness."

The University had lost, by the hand of violence, one of its brightest ornaments, the poor one of their most generous benefactors, and the church of Christ one of its firmest pillars.

One of the last petitions he uttered, as he died, was, "God bless my family." There were seven children, four sons and three daughters. The eldest was about seventeen years, and the youngest about six months old. God's blessing has rested upon them in a most remarkable degree. Two of the sons became ministers of the gospel in the Episcopal Church, and all the children consistent and useful members of the same.

The life and death of Professor Davis mark a new era in the religious history of the University. Soon after, Professor and Mrs. Cabell became earnest Christians. The attendance on divine worship became larger and more solemn, and during the term several students professed faith in Christ. A Sabbath-school, composed chiefly of the children of the professors and the hotel keepers, and a Bible-class, composed of students, were well sustained; and the religious influence diffused through the institution became strong and controlling. This went on to increase from year to year, until parents throughout the country were brought to see that the moral and religious character of their sons was as safe there as anywhere.

The village and neighborhood of Charlottesville had, almost from time immemorial, been, not only as irreligious, but as anti-religious as any community in the State. As late as 1824, or near that time, there was not a house of worship in the village or its immediate vicinity. The number of professing Christians was very small. Dissipation of a certain genteel sort was very common. Deistical sentiments were widely diffused and unblushingly avowed. Dr. Conrad Speece, in passing through the town about the year 1818, attempted to preach one night in the courthouse, but well-nigh failed because of the insufficient light and the rudeness of the boys. He spent the night at the hotel, and such were the sentiments uttered in his hearing by prominent gentlemen, and such the ill-conduct of the young men frequenting the tavern, that he said, in the house of a friend the next day, "When Satan promised all the kingdoms of the world to Christ, *he laid his thumb on Charlottesville,* and whispered, 'Except this place, which I reserve for my own special use.'"

Early in the year 1826, about the time I went there, the Rev. Richard K. Meade, son of the excellent Bishop Wm. Meade, took charge of the Episcopal Church; the Rev. Mr. Poindexter, a man of decided talent and undoubted piety, became pastor of the Baptist Church; the Methodists erected a neat and commodious house of worship, and had for their first stationed minister the Rev. Mr. Riddick, an excellent and able man. The Spirit of Christ dwelt in these servants of our Lord, and the work of reformation went forward, not rapidly, but steadily and efficiently. All these churches grew so that, within thirty years from the time of Dr. Speece's visit—that is to say, in 1848—the Christian religion, as held by these four denominations, was as widely diffused and exerted as controlling an influence in and around Charlottesville as in any part of the country with which I was acquainted. There were not more than two or three gentlemen who did not habitually attend some place of worship, and who did not consider themselves identified with some congregation. Even such as were not communicants attended church regularly, and sustained the ministry of the gospel liberally.

In 1844 I was again appointed chaplain of the University of Virginia. Fearing to attempt what I had undertaken before, with the cordial consent of my church and Presbytery, I engaged the services of Rev. Daniel B. Ewing, then just licensed as a probationer for the gospel ministry, to take temporary charge of the church, while I confined myself to the academy and University. Notwithstanding the fact that this greatly lightened my labor, and proved to be both agreeable and useful to myself and the church, yet my health began to decline. In quick succession I had two attacks of illness which seriously threatened my life. My physicians began to fear that my constitution was undermined, and to intimate that, if I persisted in being both pastor and teacher, I must soon die. But I secured the services of another assistant teacher, reduced my correspondence, and wrote less for the newspapers, went to bed earlier and rose later, and thus regained my health in part.

I would remark, in passing, for the sake of my children, that if they have any curiosity on the subject, and can get

HIS PUBLICATIONS. 113

access to the files of the *Southern Religious Telegraph* from 1834 to 1837, they will find, over the signature of "Observer," articles having more or less reference to what was then widely known as the "Aliquis Controversy," and sometimes occasional articles over one or more of my initials, on subjects not now remembered. In the files of *The Watchman of the South*, from 1837 to 1848, they will find a series of articles on the sin of gambling, another on the evils of promiscuous dancing, another on the life and character of Uncle Jack, the African preacher, another on "*so* preaching that many may believe," signed "Iota." They will also find quite a number of biographical sketches of friends recently dead, besides many obituaries. Of the biographical sketches, the most extended they will find about the close of 1844, consisting of nine articles on "The Social and Religious Character of Governor Thomas W. Gilmer, late Secretary of the Navy."

This reference is made chiefly because scarcely any of these articles are now in my possession, either in manuscript or in print. They will also find scattered through these pages, usually over my initials, accounts of church meetings, revivals, and other religious news of local interest. I have published but two sermons—one on the evils of drunkenness, and another on the necessity of intelligence and piety to the perpetuity of republican government. These have long since perished. I did not think them worthy of preservation. In this the public seems to have agreed with me, although they were both published at the earnest solicitation and at the expense of the public. I also published "A Plea for Sympathy on the Part of the Church for her Ministers." A series of letters to "A Son in the Ministry," and to "A Son out of the Seminary," published in *The Central Presbyterian* of a more recent date, have been published in a small volume. I have doubtless failed to remember many isolated fugitive pieces. But no matter, what is not worth remembering is not worth knowing. Much the greater part of my life has been too much of an out-door life. I have spent too much of my time in the society of men, and too little in that of books, for success as a writer; but necessity seemed laid upon me.

GOVERNOR T. W. GILMER.

Returning from this digression, I would remark that, early in the same year, 1844, occurred a tragedy much like that of the death of Professor Davis. I refer to the death of the late Governor Thomas W. Gilmer. This gentleman was born and educated in Albemarle county. His ancestors and connections were among the most reputable in the State. Entering professional life prior to the opening of the University of Virginia, his early literary advantages were not of the best sort. This defect, however, was supplied in part by the vigor of his intellect, the amiability of his temper, the attractions of a very engaging person, and the energy of unwearied self-culture. It is sufficient here to say that he rose rapidly from the editorship of a small village newspaper to the profession of the law, to a seat in the Legislature of his State, to the speakership of that body, and to the office of Governor of the Commonwealth, before he was thirty-eight years old. When his services as Governor ended, he was chosen to a seat in Congress, and then to the Secretaryship of the Navy. Rarely, if ever, has so young a man reached a position of such influence and distinction.

"Shortly after Mr. Polk became President, in consequence of the death of William Henry Harrison, the Oregon boundary dispute with England led to the development of a war spirit throughout this country, which, to some extent, was shared by members of Congress and executive officials at Washington. Two large guns were manufactured, called the 'Oregon' and 'Peacemaker,' of which the military authorities were very proud, and swelling boasts were indulged in of the effects of which these weapons were capable if

called into actual service. On the 28th of February, 1844, at the invitation of Captain Stockton, a large company of officials and persons of distinction from Washington went on board the *Princeton* at Alexandria, it having been arranged that a demonstration should be given of the power of the new guns, with which the vessel had been equipped. The party included the President of the United States, and the heads of the several departments, with their families. After the vessel had gone down the Potomac, past Fort Washington, to a point where the river was wide enough to afford scope for the desired experiments, the gun, 'Peacemaker,' was fired several times with entire satisfaction. A dinner was then given, at which many toasts were honored, the President proposing 'the Oregon,' 'the Peacemaker,' and 'Captain Stockton'; Miss Wickliffe, daughter of the Postmaster-general, proposed '*the American flag, the only thing American that will bear stripes,*' which was received with great enthusiasm. A portion of the party returned to the deck, and it was agreed that one more shot should be fired from the 'Peacemaker.' The gun, however, on this occasion exploded with terrific force, the pieces flying among the adjacent spectators. Five of these were killed instantly, or so badly wounded that they soon expired: Judge Abel P. Upshur, Secretary of State; Thomas W. Gilmer, Secretary of the Navy, previously Governor of Virginia; Commodore Kennon, of the Navy; Virgil Maxcy, a diplomat; and Mr. Gardner, of New York. Seventeen seamen were wounded, several mortally. President Polk had but a few moments before been standing where Secretary Gilmer received his death-blow, but having gone aft was uninjured."
—*New York Observer, March* 6, 1844.

Governor Gilmer had held the office of Secretary of the Navy but two weeks when this accident happened. Mrs. Gilmer accompanied him on the excursion. He never breathed or spoke after the explosion of the gun; for his body was torn into two parts, barely held together by a small portion of flesh. His remains, attended by a large committee, who went on for them from Albemarle, and another from Washington, were brought for burial to Mount Air, his native place, fifteen miles south of Charlottesville. As his pastor I was requested to meet and bury the body at that place. I did so. His body, in a metallic coffin, with a glass exhibiting his head and breast, was placed in the passage of the venerable homestead.

The immense crowd that had assembled from the surrounding country was admitted, a few at a time, to this passage. Entering at the front door, they passed in silence, yet with many tears, pausing to gaze in mute sadness on the face, which was distinctly visible through the glass, and which, being wholly uninjured by the explosion and in a state of remarkable preservation, still seemed to be that of one in calm, sweet sleep. Having looked for a moment on the scene, they passed out through the back door, and others were admitted. The crowd was so immense that much time was spent in this ceremony. When all had looked, and wept that they should see his face no more, he was carried to the grave, and, with a few words and a prayer, laid to rest until the morning of the resurrection.

On the following Sabbath a funeral service was held in the Presbyterian Church in Charlottesville. My text on the occasion was Psalm xcvii. 2: "Clouds and darkness are round about him; righteousness and judgment are the habitation of his throne." The crowd of attendants was immense. Every house of worship in the place, except the Presbyterian, was closed, and the ministers of the Methodist, Baptist and Episcopal churches sat in the pulpit with me. Each took a part in the devotional exercises of the morning. Notwithstanding it was the 10th of March, and the weather very wintry, the windows were all raised and the doors opened to give the crowd who could not enter an opportunity to hear.

GOVERNOR GILMER'S DEEP PIETY. 117

After filling the yard, they filled the streets in front and on the western side of the church. Not only did the ladies fill the house completely, but many sat in their carriages and others stood through the whole service in the yard. In the course of the sermon I read a letter to Mrs. Gilmer by her husband, written a few months before his death. During the reading of this letter the feelings of the immense audience became uncontrollable, and very many wept aloud.

Governor Gilmer was one of only five male members whom I found in the Charlottesville Church. He had then been a member of the church three or four years. He received me with great cordiality, and gave me the full benefit of his great influence. No minister ever enjoyed more delightful intercourse with a member of his church than I did with him. His social qualities were of the highest order, and his piety unquestionable.

An illustrative incident, not mentioned for prudential reasons in the sketches of his life I published, may be stated here. Just before he left home to assume the duties of Governor he had the misfortune to differ in opinion with a ruling elder of the church, a Christian gentleman of most exemplary character, and one with whom he had been on terms of great intimacy from his early youth. This difference ended in such ill-feeling that they parted without speaking. Soon after reaching Richmond, he wrote to me thus: "I am neither a better nor happier man for the office to which I have been promoted. Much of the unhappiness I feel results from the alienation which has arisen between R—— and myself. Cannot you adjust this difficulty?"

Before I had time to do anything in the matter, he came to C——. He arrived on Saturday night before a communion Sabbath. I did not know he had come until I took my seat in the pulpit and saw him in the congregation. I at once remembered the unfriendly relations between him and the elder just about to assist in celebrating the Lord's Supper.

It was so painful that I at first thought of leaving the pulpit and requesting him not to commune; but this thought was soon dismissed. By prayer and supplication I left the issue to God. When I closed my sermon and called the communicants to the seats assigned them, Mr. Gilmer arose, came forward, and took his seat on a bench nearest the pulpit and immediately fronting me and the table on which the elements were spread. He sat with his arms folded and his eyes closed, so that, when this elder with whom he had had trouble approached him with the plate of sacramental bread, he had to touch him gently to attract his attention. The moment their eyes met across the plate, Governor Gilmer drew forth his right hand, and, passing it over the bread, seized that of the elder with the deepest emotion. The feelings of Mr. R—— so overcame him that he handed the plate to another.

Occurring, as it did, in the face of the congregation, the impression was great and very happy. As I walked from church, falling in with him, I said, "Governor, I want to settle that difficulty between you and R——." He replied, "You are too late. It is all settled. *The Lord settled it to-day.*"

Like Professor Davis, he left a large, young and interesting family—a fond wife with four sons and four daughters, the eldest about eighteen years, and the youngest only a few months old. The infant died in a few months after its father. The rest lived to be grown. Two of the sons are ministers of the gospel in the Presbyterian Church.

I think it was in the year 1844 that Professor George Tucker, who had filled the chair of Moral Philosophy in the University for twenty years, resigned. A successor was to be chosen. Notwithstanding the great and gratifying change that had taken place in this institution, and notwithstanding the popular mind of the State had become so much more favorable to Christianity, there still lingered one sentiment in both. The untold evils that had accrued both to true religion and sound morality from the dissolute lives of the English parsons prior to the first great American Revolution, had created in the public mind many and strong prejudices against the whole clerical profession, and had intensified the just abhorrence almost universally felt for a church establishment.

These parsons were so strongly attached to such an establishment and to a monarchical form of government that, on the breaking out of the Revolution of 1776, nearly all who could at once fled to England. Charity constrains me to ascribe much of the deism of the educated classes in Virginia of that day to this cause. And as these parsons, though destitute of true religion, and often very immoral men, were nevertheless well educated, from this arose the strong opposition to an educated ministry, which the Rev. Devereux Jarrett of the Episcopal and the founders of the Presbyterian Church had to encounter. Mr. Jarrett lived after the Revolution was over, and, I think, was the first member of his church who commenced the work of giving a new and spiritual life to that communion, which efforts were subsequently so successfully seconded by the late Bishop Meade.

Our efforts commenced some thirty-five years before the Revolution, and we had to contend with the opposition of the educated classes to an evangelical and those of the illiterate to an educated ministry. But into all this I should go no further. These remarks are made to account in part for what occurred at the University of Virginia in electing a successor to Mr. Tucker.

Professor W. H. McGuffey.

Mr. Dew, Professor of Moral Philosophy in William and Mary College, was the candidate of one party, and the Rev. Wm. H. McGuffey, D. D., of Ohio, of the other. There were then seven visitors, only five of whom attended the meeting at which the election took place. Upon the nomination of Dr. McGuffey, by the Hon. Wm. C. Rives, the question was at once asked, Is he not a minister of the gospel? On being told that he was, strong opposition was at once made to him on that ground. Thus far it had been thought altogether wrong to permit one of that hated class to hold a place in that seat of learning. It was conceded that they were good enough in their place, but a university chair was not that place. For a long time the vote stood two for Dew and two for McGuffey. The presiding officer hesitated anxiously as to the casting vote. Finally he gave it for McGuffey, and he was accordingly declared elected. Now arose a considerable amount of clamor on the part of the old party who had been defeated. One of them, a man of consideration, said to me, "Have not you Christian people gained enough in getting a religious man into that chair? Don't you see how mischievous it will be for this new professor to be known as a preacher? As he is to draw his salary from the State, *the people, not I, but the people*, will say that this is but the first step to a reunion of church and state."

To which I replied as follows: "If Dr. McGuffey should prove neglectful of or incompetent to his duties as professor, or if he should seek to disseminate his peculiar sentiments as a Presbyterian, and to proselyte the young men to his distinctive faith as an officer in a State institution, his course would be censurable. But if he is both faithful and able, as I doubt not he will be, and if he claims the privilege of addressing the people who may be inclined to hear him on religious subjects, and that in a way not to offend any branch of the church, he should exercise the right to do so." I then asked, "Is your opposition to his preaching based on the fact that he is a Presbyterian?" "By no means," was the prompt and emphatic reply. "It would be the same were he a Methodist, Baptist, or Episcopalian."

"Very well," I said, "make war on Dr. McGuffey on such grounds, and all the opposition hitherto made to the University will be as a summer breeze to the tornado. Every church in the land will combine as one man against you; and no institution, however richly endowed, can resist such a combination. Did not *your grandfather* become sensible of this before he died? Nay, did he not, with the Visitors, ascertain that they must secure the confidence of the Christian people of the country, or make no headway? You have been accustomed to look at the public through one sort of a medium, and I through another and widely different one. You have studied men as a politician, and I as an humble, but somewhat observant, preacher of the gospel. It is not surprising, therefore, that I should know rather more than you do of the extent to which the people of Virginia have become a Christian people." I then went briefly into a specification of facts designed to confirm this statement. He listened with respectful attention, reaffirmed in a very earnest manner that he had no objection to Dr. McGuffey's preaching, that he designed only to express his fears as to its influence on the public mind, but now hoped that these fears were groundless, and concluded by saying, with a smile, "Let me know when Dr. McGuffey is to preach for you, and I will come and hear him." This distinguished gentleman did become a warm friend and admirer of Dr. McGuffey, both as a professor and a preacher, from that time.

The clamor subsided, and the University, with the town and surrounding country, took a higher stand than ever before, both in morals and religion. The University now made rapid strides in every qualification fitted to render a great institution of learning a great blessing both to the country and the church of Christ. In a few years the number of her students ranged from five to six hundred, under a system of discipline which fully met every just demand,

and fully answered every wise and good purpose. The opposition referred to grew out of a mistaken judgment as to the state of public sentiment throughout the country. The truth is, that Christianity, as held and taught by the Methodists, Baptists, Episcopalians and Presbyterians, had made such silent, but efficient progress, had so gradually, but successfully undermined the Tom-Paineism of a former generation, that none but close and interested observers were aware of the extent to which this blessed work had been carried forward.

It is curious to recall the incidents occurring during the transition state of the University to which I have referred, some of them apparently trivial, yet each having its place and contributing its effect to the general result. Take the following as one of many:

The proposition was distinctly made and pressed, as this institution was about to be inaugurated, that there should be no definite system of discipline established, but that the students should be left to "their sense of honor" to make them studious and well-behaved. This senseless proposition was much discussed. On one occasion, a very plain, but sensible man, who had brought a load of potatoes to market, was a silent listener to one of these discussions held by some of the more intelligent and prominent citizens. Observing the fixed attention the countryman was giving to their conversation, they asked him what he thought of the question under consideration. He very promptly replied, "It seems very plain to me. For my part, I would as soon turn a parcel of hogs into my potato-patch, and trust to their sense of honor not to root, as I would bring a large number of boys together into one school, from all parts of the country, and trust to their sense of honor not to misbehave."

This little incident, I think it probable, helped on the good cause quite as much as some of the arguments of the learned.

In looking back to the men and measures contributing to this important revolution, none seem more considerable than the Rev. Dr. John H. Rice and the magazine he published.

Mr. Jefferson contemplated at first the establishment only of "the Central College." His success with the Legislature, however, was such that he felt warranted in enlarging his plans, until a great university was the result. This important movement arrested the attention and engaged the pen of Dr. Rice from the beginning. The *Literary and Evangelical Magazine*, which he edited for many years, may be consulted for his sentiments on this subject. In the volumes from 1818 to 1824 the reader will find the proposed plans discussed. The course of instruction, the standard for admission and graduation, the relations it should sustain to the colleges, and its religious character, are all discussed in these volumes. A most suggestive fact is, that, as early as 1820, the Visitors elected Dr. Thomas Cooper *their first professor*. This gentleman was of Philadelphia, had become distinguished in the natural sciences, but was perhaps as unscrupulous an enemy to evangelical Christianity as anywhere existed. He had published the *Life of Dr. Joseph Priestly*, in which he expresses his anti-religious sentiments with the utmost boldness. We repeat, this man, elected to this professorship several years before the University went into operation, came on at least one year before, made his home at Monticello, and received one year's salary without delivering a lecture.

As yet there were neither buildings nor students. Dr. Rice reviewed his *Life of Priestly*, and did it so ably and with such effect that, on the advice of Mr. Jefferson, he did not wait for the institution to open, but went on to South Carolina, where he was made President of their University, and where he remained long enough to smother the life out of it. A near relative of Mr. Jefferson, and a frequent visitor at Monticello, told me that he knew the great statesman read these articles of Dr. Rice, and especially his review of Cooper, and that it was under the influence of these writings he was dismissed. This was enough of itself to give a new form to the institution from the beginning.

All Dr. Rice's views in reference to it prevailed except one. He expresses the fear that it may become the mere rival of the colleges; that, to use his own words, it may be made a great academy, to which any who please may go when they please, study what they please, and leave when they please. This I conceive to be almost, if not altogether, the only defect in the system to this day. It has been too much—and is still so—a mere city of refuge for idle boys, who fail to pass regularly from class to class in college. Still, I maintain all I have previously said of its great worth in the cause of letters—an honor to its founders and a blessing to the world.

During my residence in Charlottesville there was always one or more classical and mathematical schools, admirably conducted and liberally supported. The teachers of these schools were usually graduates of the University. A number of such schools were erected through the county of Albemarle, until it far exceeded any other county in the State in its literary advantages.

The impression made by the life of Dr. White on the town of Charlottesville and county of Albemarle, and the secret of his great usefulness there, are well stated in the following publication, copied from a newspaper which was owned and managed by one who belonged to the Methodist Church. It must inspire the breast of the reader with a noble impulse, to read such words of commendation from an impartial writer:

Extract from the "Virginia Advocate."

"Rev. W. S. White.

"It is with sincere regret we learn that this gentleman, so long the pastor of the Presbyterian church in this place, has accepted a call from the church in Lexington, and will leave us in a few weeks for his new home. We think we express a sentiment which is common, not only to this immediate community, but to the entire county, when we say that in parting with Mr. White, we are losing one of the most efficient friends and supporters of *every good work*, whose influence it has been the privilege of our county to enjoy. Of his zeal and fidelity as a Christian minister and pastor, it is not for us to speak. These are attested by the growth, and the peace and harmony of the church here, during his twelve years' connection with it; and by the sorrow of its members in view of his removal from among them—a sorrow (we think we may in truth say) which is shared by every friend of religion among us, who has a heart to appreciate the principles of tolerance and universal benevolence, which have ever characterized the course of Mr. White, devoted, as he doubtless is, to the peculiar tenets of his own denomination. But in other spheres his usefulness has been exemplified in a degree which has won for him the love, and entitle him to the gratitude of our entire county. Always among the first and foremost in every benevolent enterprise, his labors have been as untiring as they have been eminently judicious and free from the slightest taint of that fanaticism which so frequently mars the efforts even of the well-meaning and sincere. But it is as Principal of the Female Academy, which he founded, and has raised to an eminence of usefulness unsurpassed by that of any similar institution, that the public, we believe, have been most indebted to Mr. White. With a heart full of affection for youth, and sensitively alive to the importance of their proper mental and moral culture, as connected with their own happiness and the well-being of society, he has given himself to the work of education with a zeal and self-denial which nothing short of Christian benevolence could have sustained, and with a measure of success which could only have been secured by qualifications of the highest order. Nor has the influence of Mr. White in the cause of education been confined to the institution over which he has presided. All who, like ourselves, regard the University of Virginia as an honor and a blessing to our State and country will admit, we presume, that he is a public benefactor, who has contributed to make known the truth touching the character of that institution. Few men, in our opinion, have done more to accomplish this than Mr. White. Having, from his long residence in the immediate neighborhood, and his connection with the institution for two years, as its chaplain, enjoyed the best opportunity of forming a correct judgment of its *men and measures*, his candid and discriminating mind could not fail to be favorably impressed; and hence, for years past, he has availed himself of every proper occasion for bearing his earnest testimony in behalf of the University, as in every way worthy of the confidence of those who desire that the promotion of solid learning, and the cultivation of sound principles of virtue and religion, untrammelled by sectarianism, should go hand in hand. We think it may be asserted without danger of doing injustice to any, that in years gone by, the Presbyterians, as a denomination, were, of all others, most prejudiced against the University. But it is certainly true that these prejudices have long since yielded to the light of truth; and we speak what we know, when we say that among no class of men has the institution at this time more ardent friends and admirers than are to be found in the ranks of this same denomination in Virginia. Nor do we hesitate to award to Mr. White a large share of the credit due to this remarkable change.

"But we have written much more than we intended. Whilst we regret to lose Mr. White from Albemarle, we rejoice that it is only to a sister and neighboring county that his labors and his influence are to be transferred. We congratulate those who are to constitute his new charge upon their good fortune in securing the services of so good and so useful a man; and we heartily wish him and them uninterrupted peace, prosperity, and happiness."

CHAPTER X.

1848-1861.

ACCEPTS A CALL TO LEXINGTON, VA.—"THE SKINNER WAR."—DR. SKINNER SUSPENDED FROM THE MINISTRY BY THE PRESBYTERY.—RESTORED BY THE GENERAL ASSEMBLY.—THE PASTORAL RELATION: HIS STATE OF MIND IN DISSOLVING AND IN FORMING IT.—THE LEXINGTON CONGREGATION.—MAJOR (AFTERWARDS THE RENOWNED GENERAL) T. J. JACKSON.—JOHN B. LYLE.—ANECDOTE ABOUT HIM.—METHOD OF COLLECTIONS FOR THE CHURCH —ANECDOTE ABOUT GENERAL T. J. JACKSON.—A MODEL DEACON.

"We shall never learn to feel and respect our real calling and destiny unless we have taught ourselves to consider everything as moonshine *compared with the education of the heart.*"—*Sir Walter Scott.*

"IN the summer of 1848 my social and professional life was comfortable; my school and church together afforded me a very ample support. I had purchased, enlarged and paid for a comfortable house and lot. My wife had beautified these premises with a rich variety of shrubbery. My school and congregation were full, and encouraging additions from time to time were made to the church; my friends kind, indulgent and generous; my children were progressing well with their studies. The two eldest sons were doing well at the University. Our two daughters were in my academy, and the two younger sons in a good preparatory school. The only other child, just three years old, made it the sole business of his life to seek his own and our amusement. I had abundant cause for contentment and gratitude. True, my labors were still heavy; my health feeble. The doctors still gave it as their opinion that I could not endure much longer the strain imposed by both preaching and teaching.

Still I got through the labors with a good degree of comfort. God had graciously given me a wonderfully recuperative constitution. The rest of the vacation and a short excursion through the mountains generally reinstated me. I had no desire to change either my home or employment. I had gone to that place in 1836, when I was just thirty-six years years of age. I had passed the period of early youth, when friendships are readily formed, and as readily broken. I had not reached that period of induration when new acquaintances are made with reluctance and friendships formed with difficulty. The state of the congregation, the diversity of my employments, an unusual succession of startling afflictions, more or less like those which befell the Davis and Gilmer families, with which I was brought in close professional contact; these things all conspired to connect me with the community, and to awaken mutual confidence and love to no ordinary degree.

"One hundred and forty had been added to the little church during my pastorate, and only ten remained who were members when I went there. Many seemed to me as my own children, and I found much comfort in their love.

"Such was the state of things when a call from the church in Lexington, Va., was unanimously made for my pastoral services. This was unexpected, surprising and painful. The decision instantly reached in my own mind was that I did not desire to go; nay, I was strongly averse to going; it seemed to me that I could not go.

"They promised me a salary on which I might hope to live without teaching, and this would be favorable to my health. But then I not only loved my church, but I loved my school. Indeed, it was a very important part of my church. I was truly fond of teaching, and I had good reason to think my pupils loved to be taught by me. So soon as it was known that I had received this call, the members of the church and other friends expressed their sorrow, and avowed their purpose to oppose my leaving by every justifiable means. Brethren in the ministry of my own Presbytery came to see me, or else wrote, dissuading me from accepting the call. It was easy for me to say in all sincerity, I have not only no desire to go, but personally am resolved not to go.

"But I had not sought this call, either directly or indirectly. Statements made to me by members of the Lexington Church and of Lexington Presbytery gave to the whole matter the appearance of a special providence. I did fear lest haply I might fight against God. I knew that it would have been just as sinful for Jonah to remain where he was when ordered to go to Nineveh as to go to Tarshish. My income was so ample and my condition so comfortable that I feared my desire and purpose to remain might be the result of a self-indulgent or avaricious spirit. Neither my wife nor children ever interfered in such questions. Even when called, as I was, to succeed Rev. Dr. Wilson in Fredericksburg, with the promise of an ample salary, they said nothing, and I found it easy to decline. But now the difficulty grew until I resolved to submit the question to my Presbytery.

"The Lexington Church had for seven years been under the ministry of the Rev. John Skinner, D. D., a Scotchman. The church was not unanimous in calling him, and instead of lessening, his course increased the minority against him. For five or six years no direct effort was made for his removal. But, in the summer of 1847, the attempt was made, and an excited controversy arose. The church was agitated to its deepest foundations. The struggle lasted for twelve months, and resulted in the dissolution of the pastoral relation, and his deposition from the ministry.

"A pretty strong minority adhered to him in the church, and so embittered had the two parties become against each other that it was supposed they could never unite in calling another pastor. Indeed, to us who were at a distance, the church seemed hopelessly divided, if not incurably ruined. Every member of Lexington Presbytery had taken an active part for or against Dr. Skinner, and hence, however anxious either party might be to call its favorite of the Presbytery, this was impossible. Neither would vote for the favorite of the other. They were forced to look beyond their bounds for a minister."

Being anxious to understand why the rancor in the church should be so strong as Dr. White describes it, and not having access to the Minutes of the General Assembly that tried this case on appeal, we wrote to Dr. Samuel J. Baird, author of the *Digest of the General Assembly*, for reliable information. From him we received the following reply:

"RONCEVERTE, W. VA., *Nov.* 15, 1887.

"DEAR BROTHER: . . . Dr. Skinner was tried by the Presbytery of Lexington upon charges made by certain parties, under the name of common fame of having slandered them and others. The testimony, taken by a commission, is all before me, together with the whole proceedings. The trial commenced on March 22, 1848, and was closed on the 3rd of April, when the charges were sustained by a majority of the Presbytery, and it was '*Resolved*, that the said Rev. John Skinner, D. D., be, and he hereby is, suspended from all the functions of the ministry of the gospel, until he make suitable confession of his sins, and give satisfactory evidence of repentance.'

"Against this decision Dr. Skinner gave notice of appeal to the Assembly, and the Rev. Wm. Calhoun, for himself and others, gave notice of complaint.

"In the Assembly, the same year, the appeal was 'sustained *pro forma*,' and the complaint dismissed. Dr. Skinner was 'restored to all the functions of the ministry of the gospel,' and all parties solemnly admonished.

"He was suspended by the Presbytery in April, and restored by the Assembly in May of the same year. Of course, therefore, it did not come before the Synod.

"Truly yours,   SAMUEL J. BAIRD."

From this statement of the case it is easy to see how the passions of the people of Lexington would be roused to such an extent as to render it doubtful whether they could ever "unite in calling another pastor." Their pastor had been tried by his Presbytery for *slander*, and the highest sentence of ecclesiastical law had been pronounced upon him—"suspension from all the functions of the ministry of the gospel," until he repent and confess his sins. The General Assembly had reversed the sentence of the Presbytery, and restored their pastor to his office. As we learn from other sources, the trial before the Presbytery had been conducted in the Lexington Church, in the very midst of the congregation; and officers and members of the church had been parties to the case in one way and another—nay, the community at large had been drawn into it by family ties and local jealousies, until those in and those out of the church felt themselves thoroughly identified either with the pastor or with his accusers; added to all these facts was the voluntary resignation of the pastor, after his restoration by the supreme court, and removal of his family, not only out of the State, but out of the United States, and his settlement for life a voluntary exile in Canada. It was, therefore, not without reason that Dr. White, and others at a distance, thought the church "hopelessly divided, if not incurably ruined." Such a case as that could not fail to leave a burning in the heart of the church that nothing but length of time and the almighty Spirit of God could extinguish.

"In July, 1848, two months after the final decision of Dr. Skinner's case, a proposition was made to call a meeting for the purpose of electing a pastor. The meeting was accordingly called, but scarcely any one supposed that any effective

effort would be made to choose one. The meeting was full.
Rev. W. W. Trimble had been duly invited to preside.
Great hesitancy appeared on the part of all. Each party
was reluctant to nominate one of its own friends, feeling
sure of the opposition of the other. At last some one proposed that they should unite in special prayer for the blessing and guidance of God. This was unanimously agreed
to. It was then proposed that each person entitled to vote
should at once proceed to prepare a ballot for the man of his
choice, without any nomination. This was carried. The
ballots were prepared, collected and counted, when it was
discovered that every vote except three or four had been
cast for myself. The minority readily avowed their willingness to acquiesce with the majority, and thus the vote was
made unanimous. The call was sent to West Hanover Presbytery, which met in August, at Rough Creek Church, in
Charlotte county, by the hands of Dr. Alfred Leyburn and
Mr. Wm. G. White, commissioners from the church. The
Charlottesville Church deputed E. R. Watson and L. R.
Railey, Esqrs., commissioners on their part to resist the call.

"Previous to the meeting of the Presbytery I had ascer-
tained that a large majority intended to vote against placing
it in my hands, as they honestly thought I ought not to go.
But hearing a brief speech from Dr. Leyburn, stating some
of the foregoing facts relative to the manner in which the
call had been made, and others not now remembered, they
voted almost unanimously to place the call in my hands, and
advised me to accept it. Notwithstanding a long and impassioned speech in opposition by my excellent friend and
brother, Capt. L. R. Railey, one of the commissioners from
Charlottesville, I accepted the call, and, with great sorrow
of heart, asked a dismission from the Presbytery which had
licensed and ordained me, and to which I had belonged for
twenty years. This was surely one of the saddest events of
my life. I returned home with a heavy heart.

"It is needless to consume time in detailing the circumstances under which I tore myself away from a people among whom I had lived and labored so pleasantly for twelve years and four months. It may be enough to say that, in bidding them farewell, as one by one I shook their hands, I was in no instance able to utter a word. The heart was too full and too heavy for speech. Tearfully and silently I grasped the hand and turned away. To my latest breath the best of my poor prayers shall ascend for such of them and their children as still survive. Many, very many, of the best of them have already gone to the 'rest that remaineth for the people of God.' And among the brightest visions of that 'happy land' which cheer my weary spirit, now that I am approaching my three-score years and ten, is the prospect of meeting them there.

"Next to the relation of husband and wife, parent and child, there is none on earth so tender and so sacred as that of pastor and people. Four times I have enjoyed the institution of this relation, and three times have I wept, literally wept, over its dissolution. I have to weep once more from the same cause, and then sorrow and sighing will flee away for ever. 'There's no weeping there.'

> ''O glorious hour, O blest abode,
> I shall be near and like my God,
> And flesh and sin no more control
> The sacred pleasures of the soul.'

"Not having heard the testimony taken by the General Assembly in the case of Dr. Skinner, and not having read the published proceedings of Lexington Presbytery, I knew nothing but what reached me at Charlottesville by rumor, and also what I had read in a pamphlet he had published in his own defence. I had learned enough to fill my mind with gloomy apprehensions of trouble in my new charge.

"Before going to Lexington I attended a meeting of Lexington Presbytery, at Hebron Church, in Augusta county, to connect myself with that body, and to have arrangements made for my installation. There I met Mr. Wm. G. White, a ruling elder and one of the commissioners who had recently met me at Rough Creek, and such was the state of my mind that, when he asked me, 'When are you coming to take charge of us?' my heart sank like lead in the waters. 'To take charge of us!' A fearful undertaking for such an one as I. How shall I ever succeed in healing wounds so deep? —in harmonizing elements so discordant? But, then, they had harmonized in calling a pastor, and this may be permanent. Hope revived, and I talked cheerfully with Mr. White.

"The manse at Lexington was not completed, nor could I complete my arrangements for removing my family at once. But my work at Charlottesville was over, and they greatly needed a pastor at Lexington. Major (now Col.) Preston had kindly sent by Mr. White an invitation to make my home at his house until my family could join me. I accepted this invitation, and about the middle of September, 1848, reached Lexington, entered on my work, and found a comfortable home for several weeks with my good friends the Prestons.

"There are some subjects about which ignorance is bliss, and about which it is folly to be wise. This was true, when I came to Lexington, of my predecessor and his fierce and protracted conflict with the church. Some of the better informed people of the church had taken this view of the subject before I arrived, and had agreed among themselves, and enjoined upon their children, that these were to be ignored as subjects of conversation. When persons of less intelligence and discretion brought it up, I declined to talk, because of my ignorance, and declined to listen, because of all such matters I preferred to remain in ignorance.

"But the truth is, the church had become, to a great extent, harmonious before I arrived. I account for this in the following way: the great body of the church, including those who were leaders on each side, were truly pious, and loved their church better than they loved any man or any pastor. God had signally blessed this church from the beginning with seasons of revival. Indeed, it had its birth in a revival. The leaders in both parties had passed happily together through more than one general revival. Hence, when Dr. Skinner pushed matters to such extravagant lengths, with so violent a spirit as to awaken in many minds the fear that the permanent division and probable ruin of the church would be the result, although his friends adhered tenaciously to him until the General Assembly of May, 1848, gave the final decision in the case, yet the moment that was done they dropped him and his cause at once, and never, I presume, in the history of the church was so deep a wound so thoroughly healed in so short a time. Here and there a case of personal alienation existed for a few months, but a few words kindly and prayerfully spoken to each of the individuals readily produced thorough reconciliation. With those alienations I really had no trouble whatever.

"The church and congregation gave me a very cordial reception. The church, in the double sense of house of worship and membership, was much larger than either of those to which I had been used. The manse, just completed and never before occupied, was beautiful for situation, spacious and convenient. Leaving our two eldest at the University of Virginia, the five younger children, with their mother, now joined me here, and nothing that any people could supply seemed wanting for our happiness. Still, for several months both my wife and myself spent many anxious and unhappy hours. Old trees do not bear transplanting as do saplings. We had almost reached that period of life when persons of very strong local attachments, fond of home and neighbors, find it extremely painful to move. And there was to be a great change in my manner of life. A comparatively small church, composed almost exclusively, when I left them, of persons I had received into the church, the large majority of whom were young, ardent and confiding; a school of about one hundred girls, with five assistant teachers, all affectionate and trustworthy—this was the charge I had left for a large, intelligent church, embracing some of the most venerable and well-informed ruling elders and members in our whole church. Here, too, I found two doctors of divinity and five other resident Presbyterian ministers of the gospel, only two of whom had any stated professional engagement, and all of whom were among my stated hearers. Unused as I had been to preach in my own pulpit with a brother minister in the congregation, this was a very severe ordeal for what modesty I possessed.

"But these brethren were all indulgent, forbearing and affectionate in a remarkable degree. They were the Rev. Henry Ruffner, D. D., who had resigned the presidency of Washington College, but was kept here for many months by the protracted illness of Mrs. Ruffner; Mr. William H. Ruffner, son of the Doctor, recently licensed, but kept by the affliction which kept his father; Rev. Geo. Junkin, D. D., just arrived as successor to Dr. Ruffner in the presidency of the College, and who for some months could not find employment in the country as a preacher; Rev. Messrs. Calhoun and Armstrong, professors in the College; Rev. Mr. Turner, son-in-law and assistant of Mrs. Nottingham, the principal of Ann Smith Academy; and Rev. James Kerr, whose failing health incapacitated him for preaching, and had come with his family to spend the winter here.

"It was very pleasant to have these brethren preach for me, as they occasionally did, and to enjoy their society at my house or at theirs, but it was a sore trial to have them sitting ostensibly as learners at my feet. But surely preachers are, or ought to be, the most indulgent hearers.

"My labors were soon distributed as follows: I preached

twice on the Sabbath, attended one congregational prayer-meeting and a young men's prayer-meeting during the week, attended a Bible-class in the lecture-room and one at the Academy during the week. In addition to my two stated sermons on the Sabbath, morning and evening, I frequently preached in the afternoon to the colored people. For the congregational Bible-class I subsequently substituted a class for the study of Dr. Green's Lectures on the Shorter Catechism.

"The congregation was much larger than I had been accustomed to and far less homogeneous. To a body of communicants numbering over two hundred and fifty there was a mixed assembly composed of people of the town and vicinage, members of the academy for young ladies, students of Washington College, cadets of the Virginia Military Institute, and a few colored people. On abandoning the old and erecting a tasteful and commodious house of worship, which was done a year or two before I became their pastor, the pews below were so engrossed by the white congregation, and the galleries so divided between the College students and cadets, that little room was left for the servants. This was soon found to be an evil, and some addition was made to the accommodations for worshippers by erecting a few pews in the open space around the pulpit. But this was very inadequate. In a few years a large addition was made to the building, a full portion of which was allotted to the servants. This additional room was soon filled, every new pew was taken, and the size of the congregation greatly increased.

"There were five trustees, twelve ruling elders, but no deacons. The duties of deacons were performed by the ruling elders and trustees jointly. This defect, however, was soon remedied by the election of a board of five deacons, of whom General Thomas J. Jackson was one.

"It is due to the memory of this great and good man to say that he was the animating and guiding spirit of that body. Mainly through his influence its meetings were held with a regularity, and its duties performed with a fidelity, that made it not only a blessing to our church and congregation, but to the whole community. Indeed, it was a source of encouragement and comfort to his pastor to have the co-operation of a man who prayed and labored as he did not to be expressed in words. Regarding that pastor, officially, as his superior officer, he reported to him and applied for orders with that soldierly fidelity which distinguished him subsequently as the greatest general of his time.

"The attempt was made to call the ruling elders into more active service. A stated meeting for official business was appointed to be held once a month. This has been kept up to the present day. The congregation was divided into six districts; two of the twelve elders were assigned to each district, to be the 'helps' of the minister in shepherding the flock, and another monthly meeting appointed, at which these elders were to report what they had done during the month, and what they thought should be done by the pastor. These reports were not to be confined to the stated meeting, but, as necessity arose and the opportunity occurred, they were to communicate with the pastor, that he might know where and for what purpose his presence was needed.

"For a time this scheme worked admirably well. How could one so accordant with our system of church government and polity and characterized by so much wisdom fail thus to work? But it was new, and many of the session were now getting old. Their habits had been formed under the ministry of those men of blessed memory, George A. Baxter, D. D., and the Rev. James W. Douglass. They had not pressed such service on them, and by degrees the whole scheme fell into utter disuse. This sad result may have been due in part to the fact that there was one member of the session who was himself a host. This was Mr. John B.

Lyle, then one of the younger members of the session, recently elected and ordained to his office, a man who, like Jackson, prayed and labored—laboring as he prayed and praying as he labored. In season and out of season, through evil report and good report, he gave a full portion of every day to the service of that church whose purity, peace and prosperity he had vowed to seek, both when he was received into its communion and when he was ordained to his office. These vows he faithfully performed, not confining himself to any one district. He was always posted as to the state of the congregation. He was especially faithful and successful in finding cases of religious concern. No man was freer from 'fashionable religious cant,' or possessed less austerity. He could speak to any one on personal religion in a way so affable and gentle as never to give offence, and yet so pointed as to learn just what he wanted to know. I have reason to believe that he conversed and prayed with more young men when partially or deeply awakened than any man not in the ministry I ever knew, and with far more than many ministers ever did.

"Such cases he always reported to me, and many such he brought to my study. His habit was simply to bring them in and then retire, leaving me to discover their state of mind as best I could. It was by him that I was first made acquainted with the case of General Jackson, and also that of two of my own sons. I have reason to regard him as, in a great degree, the spiritual father of these two sons, one of whom is now a preacher of the gospel and the other is in heaven. It is not surprising that on such a man the whole session should lean, and to him all would look to an unjustifiable extent. It was natural, if not wise, to say, as I apprehend was often said, 'Lyle will do this, and Lyle will do that; why trouble myself about it?'

"Mr. Lyle's pecuniary means were very limited, and yet they 'abounded to the riches of liberality.' His generous spirit diffused itself through the church and was felt even throughout the Presbytery. In the course of a few years three calls were made on the Lexington Church to complete the endowment of Union Theological Seminary in Prince Edward county. When the third application came, some complained that these calls were too frequent. The question was asked of several gentlemen, 'What do you think the church will give now?' One said,. 'I am willing to give what I gave before.' Another said, 'I cannot give anything, and I do not think the church ought to give anything.' Mr. Lyle, who was commonly the last man to speak on such occasions, answered, 'I am willing to double my last subscription. I think the church ought to do the same, and that they will do it.' The effect of this answer was visible in every face, and the result was precisely as he said—the church doubled their second subscription.

"Astonished at his liberality, I asked him the question, 'Lyle, how do you expect to pay this subscription?' He replied, with a smile, 'By making and selling brushes of peacock feathers, which I can get from Timber Ridge. You know, that part of the county abounds in peacocks, and it will do me real good to make their tails contribute to the education of young men for the ministry.' True to his word, he paid his subscription in that way.

"He not only had an ear but a soul for music. His voice, both for compass and melody, was inferior to none I had ever heard. For many years he led the church choir. He occupied the centre seat in the choir gallery, directly in front of the pulpit. The sound of his far-reaching yet melodious voice, and the sight of his broad, full face, radiant with devout emotion, kindled by the sacred truth embodied in the psalm or hymn, often led me to think that his singing was as helpful to me as my preaching could be to him. His spirit too in this regard was diffused through the congregation, so that, in his day, the singing of God's praise was a real and delightful part of social and public worship.

"The true source of the divine life this good man led was his faith. He could truthfully and habitually say, 'I believed, and therefore have I spoken.' His acceptance of every jot and tittle of the word of God, his reliance upon the scheme of salvation revealed in the gospel, were literally unqualified and unwavering. His understanding and his will bowed to the authority, and his desires and affections found their highest and purest gratification in the lessons of inspiration. Neither the speculations of the fanciful nor the cavils of the skeptic weighed a feather with him. 'Thus saith the Lord' was the end of all controversy, and 'Lord, what wilt thou have me to do?' resolved every question of duty with him. This faith gave him unwavering confidence in prayer. 'Ask, and ye shall receive; seek, and ye shall find,' was accepted and quoted by him in its most obvious meaning, and pleaded at the mercy-seat in the confident expectation of an answer. And many, very many, were the direct answers granted to his prayers. *He habitually went from his closet to the prayer-meeting, the church, and even on visits to his friends.*

"This excellent man was attacked with paralysis during public worship, and was borne out of the house of God on the arms of his friends. After lingering about twelve months, he died on the 20th of July, 1858. His powers of speech were spared him until very near his end. His sick-room was frequented by large numbers of warmly attached friends. His intercourse with such was characterized by what I must call a sanctified cheerfulness which made his room like the vestibule of heaven. Truly it was good to be there. His sun went down almost at noon, brightening to the last. He was a great reader of books on practical divinity, and especially of the word of God. His knowledge of the Scriptures was astonishing. He died as he lived, the fearless, faithful servant of God.

"The methods of raising funds for charitable and religious purposes which I found in operation when I came to Lexington was as follows: There were six objects for which contributions were systematically asked: Foreign and Domestic Missions, Education for the Ministry, the Publication of Religious Tracts and Books, the Bible Society, and Sabbath-schools. No collections for these objects were ever taken in church. In place of this the congregation was divided into six districts, and a collector appointed for each district. Then the clerk of session was required to furnish each of these collectors with a list of all the members of the church residing in his district. When each member had been seen and his subscription obtained, the lists were returned to the session and the money remitted. This plan had been found to work in this church far better than any other. For sixteen years the average contributions had exceeded three thousand dollars per annum.

"On one occasion Gen. Thomas J. Jackson was appointed one of the collectors for the Bible Society. When he returned his list it was discovered that, at the end, copied by the clerk of session, was a considerable number of names written in pencil, to each of which a very small amount was attached. Moreover, the session, recognizing very few of the names, asked who these were. Jackson's characteristic reply was 'They are the militia; as the Bible Society is not a Presbyterian but a Christian cause, I deemed it best to go beyond the limits of our own church.' They were the names chiefly of *free negros*."

CHAPTER XI.

1848–1861.

PENTECOSTAL SEASONS.—SPECIAL PRAYER FOR THE APPROACHING MEETING OF SYNOD.—ITS FERVOR AN INDICATION OF APPROACHING REVIVAL, WHICH OCCURRED IN HIS ABSENCE.—EFFECTS OF THE REVIVAL ON THE CHURCH.—ANOTHER REVIVAL, EXTENDING FROM NOVEMBER, 1853, TO FEBRUARY, 1854.—FULL ACCOUNT OF ANOTHER IN 1856.—PROPOSITION IN 1857 TO COLONIZE.—THE CHURCH BUILDING ENLARGED.—EFFORTS FOR THE COLORED PEOPLE.—SABBATH-SCHOOL FOUNDED BY GEN. T. J. JACKSON FOR THEIR BENEFIT.—WORK IN BEHALF OF TEMPERANCE.—ANECDOTE ABOUT HIS PREACHING AGAINST A MILITARY BALL.—HOME MISSIONARY WORK.—STEMS A TORRENT OF INDIGNANT OPPOSITION TO A PUBLIC LECTURER.—REV. W. J. BAIRD, D. D.—HIS PULPIT POWER.

> "For, when the power of imparting joy
> Is equal to the will, the human soul
> Requires no other heaven."

THE ministry of Dr. White was blessed with many pentecostal seasons. Wherever he lived revival after revival occurred, to refresh the hearts of the people and add many to their numbers. As we have seen in Scottsville and Charlottesville, so it was in Lexington on a larger scale. With a wider field, a richer experience of personal piety, more wisdom in winning souls, and more pulpit power acquired by study and practice, his harvest seasons were more abundant in the last nineteen years of his ministerial life than in the first nineteen.

He believed in revivals, worked and prayed for them, was not satisfied without them. The Holy Ghost worked in him so mightily that he could not rest when his church was not making perceptible progress, but strove night and day for a revival. And God heard him. He sowed in tears and reaped

His First Revival in Lexington. 145

in joy. His spirits always ran low when the songs of Zion mourned. His countenance, usually so full of light and strength, was an infallible index to his heart. While not giving way to gloominess or despondency, it was easy for those who knew him well to see at such times a settled thoughtfulness on his brow. His correspondence with his friends always brought it out. Whatever might be the occasion of his writing, at the conclusion he would add a line about his discouragement and ask an interest in their prayers. His conversation with the members of the church would turn on the subject and stir up their zeal and enlist their prayers. In his sermons he would note the discouraging signs of the time, and rouse the people of God from their slumbers to prove the Lord of Hosts by prayer and personal effort. Nor would he cease until he saw the people aroused.

In this experience he was not singular. Revivals always come to such men, go where they may, unless the place be a Chorazin or Bethsaida. "He that goeth forth and weepeth, bearing precious seed, shall doubtless come again with rejoicing, bringing his sheaves with him."

His measures to revive his church were drawn from the Scriptures and applied in a wise and wholesome manner. Wildfire was not allowed. His views on this subject, as well as his methods of work, are laid down fully in his book, entitled *The Gospel Ministry*, pp. 173–204. The following accounts of some of these revivals will be suggestive of some of them:

"In October, 1849, when I had been in Lexington a year, the Synod of Virginia met in Petersburg. During this year the congregation slowly but steadily increased. The troubles in which the church had been involved with my predecessor had driven many from the place of worship. These gradually returned. The church had been humbled and taught to realize their dependence on God, and a spirit of prayer began to prevail. Seven made a profession of conversion during the year. On leaving home for Petersburg, I proposed that, at the stated congregational prayer-meeting, always held on Tuesday evening, special prayer should be offered for the blessing of God on the meeting of Synod. The unusual number that attended this meeting, and the fervor of the prayers offered, awakened the hope that God was about to visit them with a season of refreshing. Nor were they disappointed. I was absent for two Sabbaths. The pulpit was occupied on both days by one of the professors in college, and only the stated services were held. No extra efforts whatever had been employed. When I approached the town on my return, I enquired of one of the most irreligious men of the place, whom I met in the road, for the news. His reply both surprised and delighted me. It was in these remarkable words, 'All I know is that there is a great revival of religion in your church.' I had no sooner entered the town than I discovered, in part at least, the truth of what the man had said. As I passed up Main Street, a number of my friends came out to welcome me home and tell me that a number of persons were asking what they must do to be saved. The proposition was made and pressed that I should preach that night. But I declined. It was Tuesday, and that night was the time of our stated prayer meeting. I wished first to see, I told them, how much there seems to be of a spirit of prayer.

"The hour for the meeting came. They had had no public meeting of any kind since the Sabbath. The lecture-room contained double as many people as I had ever seen at a prayer-meeting before. There was deep solemnity and tenderness. They who were called on to pray were evidently and deeply impressed with their message to the mercy-seat. They wasted no words. They indulged in no vain repetitions. Their prayers were brief, pointed and spiritual. An appointment was made for preaching in the lecture-room on Wednesday night. The house was densely filled. I appointed an inquiry meeting, to be held in my study on Thursday evening. Some twelve or fifteen attended. The work progressed steadily and very quietly during November, December and January. Through November we had prayer-meeting or preaching every night and no service in the day. Through the two following months the meetings were less frequent. Yet cases of awakening continued to occur. The church register contains the names of forty-five members added to the church as the fruits of this revival. Besides these a few joined other branches of the church.

"This revival thoroughly harmonized the church and effaced every trace of the wound inflicted by their former troubles. During the four succeeding years there were a few additions at every communion, and a very healthful state of religion prevailed. The liberality of the church greatly improved. They increased my salary and abounded more and more in the grace of giving. The increased size of the congregations made additional pew rents necessary, and these could be provided only by filling up the vacant space around the pulpit.

"In August, 1853, several very interesting cases of conversion occurred. This seemed to give new life to the church, and through September and October following the desire for a revival greatly increased. But no other conversions occurred until the middle of November. Yet all the meetings were well attended. The Sabbath-school was flourishing; much harmony and brotherly love prevailed in the church. Some who had been neglectful, even of public worship, now became constant in their attendance. Washington College and the Virginia Military Institute were well filled and well conducted. The young men belonging to these institutions were punctual and decorous in their attendance. They filled the spacious galleries of our church. One of the twenty-two gentlemen who had joined the church in the last revival was the keeper of the principal hotel in the town.

One of the substantial fruits of this conversion was the closing of his bar. For four years no spirituous liquors had been sold at that tavern, and language cannot describe the full extent of the good thus accomplished.

"Now, I have never been accustomed to hold protracted meetings for the purpose of *getting up a revival*, but have always held such meetings when the interest excited by the ordinary services of the church seemed to make them necessary.

"About the middle of November, 1853, as I sat one afternoon in my study, I was both surprised and delighted by a call from two of our principal merchants. They were gentlemen of intelligence and influence. They were heads of families, pew-holders, whose wives were members of the church, constant attendants on worship, but had hitherto appeared quite careless as to their personal interest in religion. They promptly announced the object of their call. In a way they could not accurately describe they had become sensible of their sinful and undone condition, and desired to know what they must do to be saved. Such had been their early training that they were soon enabled to embrace Jesus Christ freely offered to them in the gospel. This was quickly followed by other cases of the same sort. For about three months we now enjoyed one of the most quiet seasons of refreshing I have ever known. There was but little increase of public services. Once or twice a week I usually held a meeting for inquirers. Rarely more than four or five at a time attended these meetings. From November 12, 1853, to February 12, 1854, the church register exhibits a list of forty-three names added as one of the fruits of this season of refreshing. Of these, twenty-one were males and twenty-two females; as in the previous revival, there were twenty-two males and twenty-three females.

"We were careful not to hurry young converts into the church, seldom or never admitting them under one or two months. About this time we adopted the plan of taking persons recently converted, or supposed to be so, under the care of the session as candidates for church membership. In some cases persons held this position for several months before they were admitted, and some, after trial, were advised to withdraw their application.

"Notwithstanding these precautionary measures, candor compels me to confess that sufficient pains were not taken in many cases to secure a more thorough work of grace before admission to the Lord's table. I am painfully conscious of having too often sought to convince inquirers that they had valid ground to hope they had been accepted of God. They were not sufficiently left to their own exertions and the guidance of the Spirit. They had too much mere human help. The result, I fear, in some cases, was delusion, and in others, where the work might have been real, it was still superficial. Had I my time to live over, I would trust less to my own exertions and more to the work of the Spirit.

"In October, 1855, the Synod of Virginia met in Lexington. The impression made by this meeting was salutary. The business of Synod was transacted with the utmost harmony, and the preaching both instructive and impressive. Still, no awakening occurred among the impenitent. During the succeeding winter, however, the church was in a healthful state, and all promised well. When our stated quarterly communion, on the second Sabbath of March, approached, the pleasing discovery was made that there were six applicants for admission to the church. The social character and position of these applicants were such as to promise good to the church. Nor were we disappointed. Perhaps a larger amount of good never resulted from the reception of the same number of members.

"I should have said also, that in January of that year much mischief was threatened by the passing of our chief hotel, which had for seven years been a thorough temperance house, into the hands of those who avowed their purpose to make it '*a genteel drinking establishment.*'

"Notwithstanding this, the reception, early in March, of the six members referred to, was graciously followed by other cases of religious awakening, which so multiplied that by the middle of April we were blessed with a revival of greater extent and power than either of those already referred to."

From *The Central Presbyterian:*

"THE LEXINGTON REVIVAL.

"We omit some editorial matter to make room for the following deeply interesting letter from Dr. White, of Lexington. Nothing can be more cheering and profitable to Christians than the perusal of such accounts of God's gracious dealings with his people in answer to prayer.

"LEXINGTON, VA., *May* 30, 1856.
"REV. DR. HOGE:

"MY DEAR BROTHER: When we met at Union Seminary a few weeks since, you requested me to furnish for *The Central Presbyterian* a statement respecting the work of grace with which God has recently blessed the Lexington Church. I deemed it premature to do this until the present time. On the last Sabbath, the first communion since the revival commenced was held, and the results on that occasion justify a compliance with your request.

"For twelve months preceding our communion in March last, the church had been in a very cold state. Everything good in our midst seemed to languish. Two communions passed without any additions on examination, and only seven additions were made during the whole year. .

"The meeting of our Synod here in October was highly prized by the church and people generally. For many weeks after the adjournment the remark was frequently made, 'How delightful was the meeting of Synod!' It has since appeared that in a few cases impressions were made on the unregenerate which led them to Christ.

"About the middle of February a verbal communication was made to me *confidentially*, that a few females had united in special prayer for a revival. The fourth Thursday in February came, and was observed, as usual, with much solemnity. About this time the principal hotel of the village, which for seven years had been a temperance house, passed into other hands, and preparations were made to open a spacious and attractive bar. The contiguity of Washington College and the Virginia Military Institute, superadded to many other considerations, rendered this in the highest degree undesirable. The proposed change was resisted by the officers of the two institutions and others with much zeal. Advocates of the new enterprise, neither few nor weak, appeared on the other side. Meetings were held, speeches made, and newspaper articles written, until much bad feeling was engendered.

"This excitement was greatly increased by a serious disturbance in college on the evening of the 22nd of February, occasioned by the unlawful introduction within its walls of intoxicating drinks. All this seemed unfavorable to the revival of pure and undefiled religion. But 'God's ways are not as our ways, nor his thoughts as our thoughts.'

"In the midst of this conflict our first communion for the year came. During the week preceding the second Sabbath in March, the pleasing discovery was made that six unusually interesting cases of conversion to God had recently occurred; and when we met on that Sabbath to commemorate the dying love of the Saviour, the six persons thus hopefully renewed were received into the church. This precious communion was like a gleam of sun-light breaking through the darkness of a stormy night. Many said, 'It was good to be there.' But still the storm raged, and no indication of other awakenings came. The main body of the church appeared to be engrossed with the contest still going on, or sunk in profound slumber. 'The night was dark and dreary.'

"But another sign of the breaking of day was seen. An anonymous letter was brought to me from the postoffice. The writer is entirely unknown to this hour. It was in these words:

"'The writer of this feels it her duty, in the midst of so much that must sadden the heart of our dear paster, to inform him that, although there seems to be no outward manifestations of the presence of God's Spirit among us, she has reason to know that the Spirit is operating on the hearts of many of our young people, and a few professing Christians are endeavoring to arouse themselves from their long slumber. This is written to encourage our pastor, because outward manifestations of interest do not seem to exist.'

"Now, too, a member of the Ann Smith Academy expressed her surprise, on coming home from school, that several of the young ladies of the Academy 'had for several days appeared very serious, that they were often seen separated from the other girls, conversing and reading the Bible together.' The daughter of a pious father, too, sought an interview with him to ask what she must do to be saved.

"Just in this state of things came the terrible calamity which ended in the death of young Booker (young Booker was a student of Washington College who had been accidentally shot by a pistol in the hands of a fellow-student, his room-mate and warm personal friend). This sad story is well known to all your readers. He lived, to the surprise of every one, more than two days, during all which time he reaffirmed his faith in Christ with so much clearness, warned and exhorted his attendants and friends so faithfully, and prayed for them so fervently, that many were at once savingly awakened.

"One week after his funeral, the Rev. John H. Bocock, in compliance with a promise made to me several months before, came to preach for us. He preached five sermons, which many will never forget. A week after he left, the Rev. B. T. Lacy, also in compliance with a promise made some time before, came and helped us. God greatly helped him.

"The number of those attending the meetings for religious inquiry now amounted to sixty. We arranged our meetings so that they should not interfere with the ordinary duties either of the citizen, the student or the cadet. All went on calmly, but very earnestly. The irreligious and the unconcerned expressed astonishment at the absence of all appearance of disorder or excess.

"We were also favored during the time with several sermons from the Rev. J. H. Smith, of Charlottesville, and Rev. Wm. G. Campbell, of Staunton, and one very unexpectedly from my excellent old friend and brother, Rev. Wm. Hamersley, and two from one whom I shall make free to call one of the sons of our own church, the Rev. Chas. M. See. All these brethren were blessed in their own souls, and made blessings to us.

"Considerably more than two months have elapsed since this gracious work commenced, nor has it ceased. The extra preaching has ceased, but still unmistakable tokens of the presence of God's Spirit are seen.

"The town, the College, and the Military Institute shared about equally in this blessed work.

"Last Sabbath the Lord's supper was celebrated in our church, and we deemed it proper to give to those who, two or three weeks before, had put themselves under the care of session as candidates for church membership an opportunity to confess Christ before men. On that occasion fifty-five were received. Of these thirty were males and twenty-five females. Six others still stand as candidates, and several others are still anxiously seeking the way of life.

"Fifteen students of college have united with the Presbyterian and five with the Episcopal Church, while nineteen cadets have joined the Episcopal and two the Presbyterian Church. One student and three or four cadets have also joined either the Baptist or Methodist Church; a third cadet awaits the consent of his father to join our church.

"A most delightful spirit prevails. The young men of the two institutions worship together with the utmost harmony. Asperity has been banished. The angry controversy about the tavern bar has long since ceased, and the very atmosphere of schools and village seems imbued with the Divine Spirit. To all 'who love our Lord Jesus Christ in sincerity and truth' it has been, and still is, a time of calm, yet very high religious enjoyment. Surely nothing but that religion which rises to the highest and stoops to the lowest could produce the change now distinctly seen in individuals and through the community.

"Last Sabbath was a day never to be forgotten by our people. Fifty-five young disciples, rising in the midst of an immense audience and singing as they arose and stood—

> "'Jesus, I my cross have taken,
> All to leave and follow thee,
> Naked, poor, despised, forsaken,
> Thou my all from hence shall be.'

This was a scene not to be described. My faith is scarcely strong enough to warrant the expectation that I shall live to see another like it. But be this as it may, the recollection of this will go with me through life, and cheer me in death.

"Thirteen of those admitted were baptized, among whom, I cannot refrain from stating, was the cherished friend of Booker, who so unintentionally and so sadly to himself had been the occasion of his death. When this esteemed young man presented himself for baptism, almost the whole audience wept. Gratitude to God went up from many a heart, that out of so deep an affliction so rich a blessing had been brought.

"The worship was closed by singing the good old hymn, commencing—

"'How firm a foundation, ye saints of the Lord,
Is laid for your faith in his excellent word.'

The singing of this hymn, associated in the minds and hearts of the children of God with all that had preceded it, called forth feelings which bore them far towards heaven.

"Yours truly and affectionately,

"WM. S. WHITE.

"P. S.—The books and tracts of our Board of Publication have been eminently blessed in the awakening of the careless, the guiding of the anxious, and the confirming of the young convert. There has been such a demand for these publications that we were obliged to order a fresh supply by express.

"The revival seemed to begin and, for a long time, to be confined to a small portion of the church. Let the pastors of large and sleeping churches take courage. 'Where two or three are gathered together *in my name*, there am I in the midst of them. W. S. W."

"Immediately after the communion on the second Sabbath in March, I left home to assist the Rev. B. T. Lacy in a sacramental meeting at Salem, Roanoke county, and to visit my daughter at Christiansburg, Montgomery county. Proposals were then made to me to leave Lexington, of so inviting a kind that I was strongly inclined to do so. I said to those making it: 'If the angry excitement prevailing continues, I shall leave.' But I reached home just as young Booker died, in time to preach his funeral sermon, found the letter of my anonymous correspondent, the revival in progress, and so determined to remain.

"This revival added sixty-eight to the membership of the church, the majority of whom were young men. Many of these were well educated, and most of them were in the way to be so. The church was not only enlarged, but strengthened. The cases of apostasy were fewer than those of either of the preceding revivals. Indeed, we had great reason to be thankful that the number of such was so small in each case.

"From June, 1856, to the present time, October, 1864, the church has enjoyed no general revival. The largest number received in any one year since was nineteen on profession and ten on certificate.

"But the congregation had so increased that it was deemed advisable in 1857 either to colonize and build a new house of worship, having a pastor to each, or else to enlarge their house of worship and remain together.

"I very sincerely expressed my willingness to agree to either plan. If they deemed it best to colonize and build a new church, I would willingly take charge of either if desired, or retire altogether. My proposal met with no favor.

"After many meetings, and after asking the advice of the Presbytery, in 1859 they entered upon the enlargement of the building then in use. They added ten feet to the length of the building, and a wing to the right and left of the pulpit, each twenty feet square, with considerable increase of the galleries, especially for the accommodation of the colored people. The work was a complete success. The church was much enlarged and beautified, at an expense of something over $4,000. The lecture-room also was improved, at an expense of $1,200.

"A congregational meeting was now held, and a proposition unanimously adopted to re-assess all the pews and relet them. This succeeded, and every pew was at once taken at an increased price. The church now enjoyed a large measure of prosperity. The congregation was considerably increased in size, the prayer-meeting well attended, and the two Sabbath-schools, one for the whites and the other for the blacks, were full. The latter of these schools was organized in 1856, by Major (afterwards General) Thomas J. Jackson, and was superintended by him with distinguished energy and success, until he was called to act so conspicuous a part in the defence of our invaded country. The singleness of aim, the purity of motive, the enlightened zeal and practical wisdom of this man, whose fame is now wide as the world, made him a blessing to the church which no language can adequately express. He joined the church with six others, on the 22nd of November, 1851, and soon after was elected a deacon. As his biography has already been written, and as it will hereafter be rewritten until the civilized world will be familiar with the leading traits of his character and the events of his life, no more need be said here. For about ten years it was my privilege to sustain to him the two-fold relation of pastor and personal friend—a privilege I shall prize as one of the richest of my life until my work on earth is ended.

"From the beginning of my professional life, I have felt a deep interest and made special exertions for the spiritual good of the colored people. I have stated before that, when I came to Lexington I found the church edifice, then recently erected, though large, not large enough to accommodate many of this people. To obviate this, my first effort was to preach to them on Sabbath afternoon. For a time many attended and seemed interested; but their practical exclusion from our house of worship had turned them to the Baptist and Methodist churches. Only about a dozen, and these chiefly old and infirm, were communicants in our church. Death and removal soon diminished their number to only two or three, and nothing else was done to supply their places. I record this with no little shame and mortification.

"After some years I proposed to the church that Saturday

afternoon should be allowed to them, on condition that they would attend on a service to be held by me at that time for their benefit. Now, too, they attended well for a time, but soon fell away. The truth is, that they had become so enamored with a boisterous sort of meeting that they could not relish our calm and quiet method of proceeding. As the labor was seen to be too arduous for me, the church employed a younger minister, admirably fitted for the work, to take the oversight of them as his special charge. He labored faithfully for a time, but with no visible sign of success. Thus attempt after attempt has failed.

"But the Sabbath-school, founded by General Jackson for their benefit, was a decided success. This distinguished man threw himself into this work with all of his characteristic energy and wisdom. Whatsoever he did prospered. To the moment he was always punctual at the opening of the school. Although wholly ignorant of the science of music, and having neither ear nor voice for singing, he yet learned so to sing

"'Amazing grace, how sweet the sound
That saved a wretch like me,'

that the school would recognize it and carry it along. Sabbath after Sabbath he would stand before his school of blacks and raise this hymn and tune for them.

"He issued monthly reports to the owners of the slaves. These reports he delivered in person, calling each month at every house where one of his pupils lived. When necessary he conferred with the family about all matters connected with the behavior or misbehavior of the pupils.

"Under his management this school became one of the most interesting and useful institutions in the church. So deep was the interest he felt in it that, during the war, when he was at the front, in the midst of active campaigns, he would find time to write asking about it, and otherwise showing how closely it lay on his brave heart. This school is now (November 17, 1864) prosperous and doing good."

The school continued in operation over thirty years, and was at last brought to a close only when the necessity for its continuance passed away.

These statements about General "Stonewall" Jackson by Dr. White are corroborated by Mrs. Margaret Preston, the General's sister-in-law, in an article published by her in *The Sunday-school Times* of December 3, 1887. She writes as follows: "And when the major had become a general, and was sweeping back and forth through his native Virginia at the head of his army, he rarely wrote a letter home in which something was not said about his well-beloved Sunday-school. Success or defeat, anxiety or suffering, glory or grief, nothing made him forget it, or cease to be interested in its welfare."

If Dr. White had depended solely upon his pulpit and pastoral work, his success as a minister would have been less marked. He did much extra work, which seconded his main work by increasing the area of his usefulness, multiplying the number of his friends, and preparing the way for his pulpit power. He took hold of everything with wisdom and earnestness that could be made subsidiary to preaching, so that his success was the aggregate result of many efforts in many directions. As his work among the negroes led to the development of the working power of General Jackson and others in the same way, so his efforts in the matter of intemperance set others to work in this direction, and drew friends to his side.

WORK IN THE TEMPERANCE CAUSE.

Two days after coming to Lexington with his family, November, 1848, the election of General Z. Taylor to the Presidency of the United States took place. On that day the streets of the town were filled with drinking men, and about twelve o'clock the fighting began. Never before, and never since, have we seen so many personal combats take place in so short a time and in so small a place. Between the courthouse and the upper tavern on Main street we saw many in quick succession. A part of the time two were going on at once, the one of which was between two very old and gray-haired men.

The Scotch-Irish settlements in the Valley of Virginia were noted for three things: churches, academies of learning and distilleries. The latter flourished in spite of the former, and, among a less sturdy, intelligent and godly race of people, would have led to utter demoralization.

Dr. White's great heart was stirred as he beheld the aboundings of this iniquity. We have heard him over and over again, in the family circle, count up the distilleries in the county, and lament the almost universal use of alcoholic stimulants in both county and town. He determined, by the help of God, to abate or destroy the evil. He joined the Sons of Temperance, not because, as we heard him say, he thought it the best thing, but because he believed there was nothing wrong in it, and because, if he "could not get a long, straight hickory to kill a snake in his path, he would take any stick he could find, however crooked." He addressed them on public occasions in Lexington. He went out into the county of Rockbridge in every direction to make speeches. He influenced others to do likewise. He talked with the country people when they came to town on the subject, made appointments through them for public gatherings at different places. Thus he kept up the agitation of the popular mind on the subject. Twice we recollect that he, after speaking at two points in the country, went home with the distillers in those neighborhoods to spend the night, and made himself as agreeable as possible, by conversation on any and every other subject than that on which he had spoken in public. One of these distillers volunteered, as he was leaving the next morning, to say to him: "I do not want to say anything rashly, but I think I will never distil another drop." And he kept his word. This was one of the peculiar talents of Dr. White; he could denounce a sin with the utmost sternness in such a way that the sinner would not take it amiss. In a few years distilling was almost entirely abandoned throughout the county.

Home Missionary Work.

Throughout life he was devoted to Home Missionary work. When he lived in Nottoway his regular work extended over this county, with those of Amelia and Dinwiddie. But his zeal for God and for souls drove him at times into the regions beyond. When he lived in Charlottesville, a large part of each summer was spent in travelling through Madison, Culpeper, Green, Orange, Fauquier, Rappahannock, and other counties, preaching in school-houses and farm-houses, as well as churches. As he was lame, he always took one of his sons along with him through these counties, to open the gates and let down the check-rein for his horse to drink. When he lived in Lexington he did the same sort of work, helping the brethren in the upper end of the Valley of Virginia, and in Southwest Virginia. The Lord sent times of refreshing to Salem, Christiansburg, Blacksburg, Wytheville, Union, in West Virginia, and other places that he visited. Thus his labor was rewarded, and his heart warmed up with fresh zeal for work at home on his return. He preferred spending his vacations in this way to lolling at the watering places, or sight-seeing in Europe.

On these excursions, besides preaching the word, he made many temperance speeches and speeches on education, and did a great deal of wayside, colloquial preaching. These two causes lay next to the gospel in his heart. We have heard him on the road with strangers defending the University of Virginia, at a time when public sentiment was running strongly against it, and advising a liberal education for young men as the best possible money-investment for them. His reasons are distinctly remembered after the lapse of over forty years, although but a child when we heard them.

To make himself agreeable to every one was his constant aim. Not only in his own house, but on the roadside, in the stage-coach, wherever his elbow touched that of a fellow-man, rich or poor, well-dressed or ill, educated or ignorant, he laid himself out to make time pass pleasantly.

As a conversationalist he never argued or made speeches, nor did, as Macaulay says of Samuel Johnson, "fold his legs up to have his talk out," but exchanged sentiments, told stories, dealt in pleasantry. Conversation was with him colloquial, mind acting upon mind and thought playing between,

"*Heart-affluence* in discursive talk,
From household fountains never dry."

On missionary excursions this served him a good turn; for when he had ingratiated himself into the good will of a man by pleasant intercourse, he would, by a versatility often remarked upon, give conversation a serious turn, and by a well-told anecdote or a sentence or two breathing the spirit of the gospel, plant a religious truth in the mind of his friend.

One of the elders of his church once said of him, that he showed this versatility sometimes in the pulpit. When he saw his audience growing drowsy he would tell an anecdote to wake them up, then go ahead. He could turn in a moment from the deepest seriousness to humor, and that too without effort or affectation. We remember hearing him once, on a missionary tour, bolt out an outlandish word in his sermon. Riding away from church we asked him why he did so. "Did you not see," he replied, "that the congregation was becoming listless and some of them sleepy?

I used that word just to wake them up and get their attention." And he did it.

Another instance illustrative of this talent is given by the *Religious Herald*, a Baptist paper published in Richmond, Va., dated September 8th, 1887. "This about *dancing* we clip from the correspondence of the *Western Recorder:* 'About thirty years ago, we heard old Dr. Wm. S. White, Stonewall Jackson's pastor, at Lexington, Va., preach a sermon from the text, "Be not conformed to this world." In the course of his sermon he had a good deal to say about dancing, and we have never forgotten some of his observations on that subject. For instance, "A sister with whom I was remonstrating for sending her daughter to a dancing school said to me, 'Well, she had better dance than talk scandal.' 'Madam,' said I, 'you are paying your daughter a very poor compliment. You are saying that she has not sense enough to carry on a conversation without resorting to scandal, or else you are saying that she is so brimful of scandal that she must needs talk it out at her head or dance it out at her heels.'"

"'Again, "But people are continually asking me if dancing in the abstract is wrong. Well, no; and if you will only *dance in the abstract* you will never hear any objection from me. But unfortunately I've never known any one to dance in the abstract. All the dancing that ever I knew was in the concrete." We really think this is one of the smartest things that we ever heard anybody say on this subject.'"

"Yes," says the *Baptist Herald*, "old Dr. White *was* smart, and, what is better, he was an able and successful minister and pastor."

He never forgot that he was the servant of Christ, and anywhere and everywhere sought out opportunities of usefulness. He would cheerfully leave the most entertaining company to speak a word for God to souls. Stopping at a country tavern, called "Blue Ridge Hotel," in Botetourt county, Va., and learning, after supper, that the Sons of Temperance were to hold a stated meeting not far off, he left his company, went to the lodge, and made a little speech. Years afterwards, stopping at the same tavern, we met one who was present and heard the speech, who gave a long account of it and the good done to the cause.

Thus he did the work of an evangelist and made full proof of his ministry. The thought of hiring himself out to a congregation to do so much work for so much pay could never have taken root in his mind. Yet he did not neglect his special charge, but felt bound in conscience to lay out his strength for those over whom God had made him overseer.

No minister of the gospel could be further removed from what King Charles calls "the ghostly influence of my chaplains" than was he. He was intensely human; he loved all sorts of genteel society. When a visitor at a public place, such as a "health resort," he mixed with the people in the parlors, on the piazzas and lawns; he used his room to sleep in, but for little else. No one would ever take him to be a preacher from his dress or manner.

A pleasant little incident once occurred with him at the Warm Springs, Bath Co., Va., which has been going the rounds of the newspapers for years. Sometimes it is told of one minister and then of another. The last account we saw of it gave the names of the parties as a clergyman of the Church of England and a member of the British Parliament.

After sitting for an hour with a party of gentlemen in the parlor of this "watering place," one of whom was Senator Orr, of South Carolina,—then, if we remember aright, Governor of his State - he arose to leave. As he was walking across the floor, limping, with a limp peculiar to him from childhood, Mr. Orr sprang to his feet and recalled him, saying, "Dr. White, were you not chaplain at the University of Virginia in 1840?"

"Yes," replied the Doctor.

"Well, I thought so; I recognized you by your walk; I was a student there then."

Dr. White answered pleasantly, "Governor, my infirmity seems to have impressed you more deeply than my preaching or conversation—a rather equivocal compliment, is it not?"

"Oh!" replied the governor, with the most excellent wit, "Pardon me, Doctor, but I think there is a compliment in it after all. Is it not better to be recognized by one's *walk* than by his *conversation?*"

Combined with versatility, zeal, sweetness and humor, was, as Dr. R. L. Dabney calls it, his "lion-like courage." He never drove a measure through his session, nor forced his own ideas upon his congregation. But when the time came, he could oppose a host, even of the good and mighty.

In the winter of ——, the Rev. Dr. W. J. Baird was invited by the ——— to deliver a series of lectures in Lexington, on his travels in Europe. When Dr. Baird came, and was in the town, and notice given, some of the gentlemen of the place, lawyers, professors, politicians, and others, learning that his name was on the list of the one thousand clergymen, who had petitioned Congress to prohibit slavery from the territories, made a great clamor about his abolitionism, in order to drive him from the town, or throw cold water upon his lectures.

Dr. White, though a decided pro-slavery man, determined to stand by him, as the invited guest of the community, and introduced him to the audience the first evening with a speech, giving his reason for so doing, which he closed with the well-known words, "Sink or swim, live or die, survive or perish, I give my hand to this brother." He prevailed. The people, as a mass, stood by him, although the agitators stayed away and sulked in their homes.

The pulpit work of Dr. White was characterized principally by spiritual power. He believed in the preparation by the Holy Spirit for public worship of the hearts of both preacher and people, and came from the mercy-seat to the pulpit. He tried to see the face of God before looking into the faces of his audience, and to bring fresh feeling from God to the work. Therefore, the blood mounted to his face and his soul glowed with intense ardor. As Mr. Longfellow poetically said of his favorite preacher, one could always "hear his heart beat."

While not eschewing the graces of rhetoric or the methods of logic, they were always subsidiary to the one design of making the truth plain. They never caught the eye in his preaching more than the frame that holds the light in the darkness.

Yet his study was not only an oratory, it was a workshop also. He was fond of books, and made a good use of them, although perhaps not so patient and plodding a student as some others. His sermons in manuscript show an exactness of method that did not impress us when delivered. It is obvious from these that he studied closely, and carried "beaten oil into the pulpit." Out of the hundreds in our possession, not one can be found whose order is not regular, and that does not abound in thought.

Rev. Dr. Dabney writes: "I have heard from him many able, well-knit, doctrinal sermons, especially while chaplain at the University."

Dr. Plumer writes: "His pulpit was his throne." Perhaps these two heard him more frequently than any of his professional brethren. In sermonizing, we would say, Ezra was his model, who "read in the book, in the law of God distinctly, and gave the sense, and caused them to understand the reading."

CHAPTER XII.

1861-1865.

A "Union Man" at the Secession of South Carolina.—What Changed his Mind and that of his State.—Abolitionism and Secessionism.—List of those in his Church and Congregation who Perished, or were Disabled for Life in the War.—Depreciated Currency.—Peace in the Midst of War.—Extract from a Letter of his Son who Fell in Battle.—False Philanthropy of Abolitionists.—Their Agency in Bringing on the War.—The Nat. Turner Insurrection.—John Brown's Diabolical Scheme.—The Southern People on the Defensive for Thirty Years Prior to the War.—Gen. Hunter's Ruffianism in Lexington.—Shells, Burns and Sacks the Town.—Gen. Averill's Raid; a Thorough Gentleman.—Chaplains in the Northern Army.—The Gayety among the People.--Sir Walter Scott's Review of the French Revolution.—"The Lost Cause."—Grace Triumphs.

> "Where cattle pastured late, now scatter'd lies
> With carcasses and arms th' ensanguin'd field,
> Deserted."

"THE opening of the spring of 1861 found my family and congregation in the enjoyment of a measure of prosperity rarely possessed in this world. We had health and competence. Five little families that had gone out from our family altar now had such altars of their own. One darling boy was prosecuting his studies for the ministry with eminent success. The youngest had just entered Washington College, being in his sixteenth year.

"The church was harmonious. The two Sabbath-schools, the prayer-meetings, the worship of the sanctuary, were well attended, and a communion had rarely occurred for years without gratifying additions to the church. How good and how pleasant it was thus to live under the fostering care and love of the God of peace!

"But fearful omens of great trouble appeared in the North. A sectional President and Vice-president of the United States had been elected, in the autumn of 1860, by a bare plurality of votes, and several of the Southern States had quietly withdrawn from the Union. On the 4th of March, 1861, the President-elect was inaugurated, and it became evident at once that it was his purpose, and that of the party which had placed him in power, to attempt the forcing of the retiring States back into the Union at the point of the bayonet.

"Virginia had not withdrawn from the Union, and an immense majority of her people were strongly opposed to this measure as the wisest and best means of seeking redress for the wrongs the whole South suffered at the hands of the North. With this feeling I sympathized with all my heart. I deprecated what then seemed to me like 'burning the barn to kill the rats.'

"The newly elected President issued a proclamation on the 15th of April, 1861—a little more than a month after his inauguration—calling for seventy-five thousand men to coerce the retiring States back into the Union. Of these, Virginia was required to furnish a specified quota. This was an undisguised declaration of war on the part of the general government against certain States composing a part of that government. Virginia now felt that she no longer had the option of peace or war, nor any option between a war of invasion or a war for defence. It had been decided for her that she must and should fight, and that she should join in an invasion of her sisters of the South.

"Her decision was soon formed. As she must fight, she claimed the poor privilege of deciding whom she should fight. So she promptly withdrew from the Union, and placed herself on the defensive, by the side of her invaded sisters.

"Such a revolution in public sentiment at once occurred as I never witnessed nor read of. Thousands, nay, tens of thousands, of those who, up to this time, were as true friends to the Union as any government ever had, at once became its enemies The flag, for which they would have died on one day, they would have shot the next. Thus the war began.

"I am not now concerned with its history. I wish merely to leave for my children a few notes, referring chiefly to the sad interest my own household has had in it. I have recorded the views which determined my course in the matter."

We insert here several letters, written during the war, not only to show his course in the matter, but because they refer to certain facts of much importance in its history.

"LEXINGTON, VA., *Dec.* 13, 1860.
"TO THE REV. JOHN S. WATT:

"MY DEAR BROTHER: . . . I had seen Dr. Palmer's sermon in the *Witness* before your letter came. Still, I thank you for the copy. Dr. Palmer can hardly be so simple as really to desire the breaking up of this great confederacy. He must have preached thus to scare the Yankees into terms. . . . The fountain of all this evil lies deeper than men of either party are now willing to confess. The addition of territory, the influx of foreigners, the extension of the right of suffrage, have altogether given the centrifugal force such an ascendancy over the centripetal, that I fear it is impossible to keep our Confederacy in its orbit. And then abolition has been so convenient a smut-ball for each party to use in blackening each other, that at last they have all become blackened together. The leading men of the country are thoroughly corrupt, and we are to have another fearful confirmation of the doctrine of human depravity. Man is too great a sinner to govern himself. . . .

"There is to be a great gathering here to-morrow, and I have been warmly urged to speak. Even the Federal judge of this district has pressed me to do so. But no, sir. I will not. I preach now on such texts as these, 'The word of God is not bound'; 'Be not afraid, only believe'; 'He that ruleth his spirit,' etc.; 'Let patience have her perfect work'; 'Your adversary, the devil, goeth about,' etc. I recently studied and sought to unfold the character of his satanic majesty in full. I never did it before. I wished to make the people acquainted with their new ruler. So, you see, I agree with you as to his present preëminence and power.

"But keep cool. The bursting of the boiler of a steamboat would be as nothing to the explosion that would occur, if you or I get in the wrong box. Our brother-in-law, ———, and his son ———, are run-mad secessionists. The secession spirit is rising and spreading in Virginia. Dr. Junkin roars against it like a lion. . . ."

"LEXINGTON, VA., *March* 2, 1865.
"TO THE REV. WM. BROWN, D. D.:

"MY DEAR BROTHER: . . . . You greatly misunderstand me, if you suppose I ever intended to say that my personal sins had not had their share in provoking God to subject us to the horrors of the war. No; most sincerely do I confess that I have sinned enough, in all the relations I sustain, to have merited all I have suffered or may yet suffer. But I meant to say what even now I repeat, that I did everything in my power to prevent it (the war).

"My opposition to secession was so decided and so publicly expressed, as to expose me to no little personal rudeness. A prominent member of my church took such offence at something I said from the pulpit, that he rose from his seat, and, in a very angry tone, loud enough to be heard by all who sat near him, denounced me. And on the next day I was told that another man had said that I must and should be taught to behave better.

"This occurred more than a year before the war began; and yet I never did behave any better; for as late as the 15th of April, 1861, I made a speech to a crowd of Union men, advocating their views. On the following day Lincoln's proclamation came, which I then regarded, and now regard, as a declaration of war.

"Thus forced to fight, I claimed the poor right of choosing whom to fight. Necessity was laid upon me to *rebel* against *him*, or my native State. I chose the former, and became a rebel, but never a secessionist."

"A sort of madness seemed to seize upon this people some thirty years ago, 1*st*, In regard to African slavery; and 2*nd*, In regard to the unlimited extent and populousness of the country.

"As to the first, the abolitionists contended that African slavery was in itself an unmitigated evil; or, as they were fond of expressing it, 'the sum of all abominations,' and should be repented of and abolished at once, regardless of all consequences both to the master and his slaves.

"On the other hand, the secessionists contended not only that this relation was sanctioned by the word of God, but that it was in itself a great social, political and moral good, and as such ought to be perpetuated through all time and disseminated through all space.

"Massachusetts was the mother of the former, and South Carolina the mother of the latter heresy. By these extreme views the whole country was agitated, nay, torn into wrathful factions, and the halls of the national legislature became battle-fields, not always *bloodless*. The two great political parties seized upon this negro question as one well fitted to be employed for mere party purposes; and as such it proved an instrument that bore down all opposition.

"As to the second: The acquisition of territory and the extension of the right of suffrage to every male citizen twenty-one years of age, weakened the centripetal and strengthened the centrifugal forces in the political system. This evil was fearfully aggravated by the influx of vast hordes of ignorant foreigners clothed with the full powers of American citizens as soon as they set foot on our shores. At the rate of three hundred thousand per annum they poured into this country for some years prior to 1860. Ten thousand had been known to land in New York in two days. Of these every male became a qualified voter at twenty-one years of age. Chiefly because of the negro population at the South this tide emptied itself wholly into the North and West. With such an ascendancy in numbers, all of whom were fired with jealous hatred of the educated and high-toned white population of the South, nothing but a miracle could have prevented the ruin that has come.

"When the time came to strike, the people of the North found the constitution in their way. That constitution sanctioned African slavery in the South, gave the negro power at the ballot-box, secured autonomy to the States as sovereign over their own affairs. But all this was at once ignored. The negroes were emancipated and enlisted as soldiers by the thousand, and State sovereignty set aside as useless political trumpery. Virginia, that had given several States to the Union, was cut in half, in cold blood, as though she had been so much public domain. She who had stood as a breakwater between the two sections, using every legitimate means to avert the civil war up to the last, who sent a peace commission to Washington, with an ex-president at its head, after the secession of some of the States, and who took up the gage of battle only because she could not bathe her sword in the blood of her natural allies, was drawn and quartered as though she had been the chief offender.

"But I have wandered from my chief design. The war

began in April, 1861. The community in which I live, and especially the church and congregation to which I minister, were strongly averse to war, and did all we could to prevent it. But when it was forced upon us, with a unanimity that could hardly be exceeded they resolved to meet the issue. Whatever may be said of other parts of the country, it is not true of this, that the people were drawn blindfolded into this sad work by the politicians.

"It so happened that the great body of our leading politicians, I mean our most noisy and meddlesome politicians, sympathized with South Carolina, and had, all through the winter of 1860 and '61, striven to attach the people to her cause, but failed, utterly failed. Indeed, the civil war was very near beginning in the streets of Lexington on the 13th of April, 1861, between a handful of secessionists, urged on by some of the sort of politicians described above, and the mass of our private citizens. *But for the intervention of Gen. Thomas J. Jackson, blood would then have been shed,* a fact but little known, yet worthy of lasting remembrance.

"But what the politicians could not do, despotism could do, and did. We were not willing to join South Carolina, but we were still more unwilling to assist in violating the constitution by joining in a war of invasion waged upon a sovereign and independent State. It is well and personally known to me, that the entire mass of the men most active *for the Union*, in the commotion raised in our streets on the 13th, gave themselves to its overthrow on the 16th of April. Not an effort had been made, by speech or otherwise, to bring about this change. President Lincoln's message came, and this alone wrought the mighty change.

"My own congregation and my own family became at once deeply involved in this mighty struggle. The invading forces were already on the march upon our northern border. Thirty-five communicants of my church and thirty members of my congregation, not communicants, were soon in the ranks and on the weary march to meet the foe. Of the first were two of my own sons, the oldest commanding and his younger brother a private in a volunteer company composed almost exclusively of the students of Washington College.[1]

"These sons were soon followed by our youngest, who entered the ranks of his brother's company when only sixteen and a half years old. This boy was soon followed by a fourth. The eldest of the four, after some hard fighting, was compelled by ill-health to resign his commission and retire from the service. The younger, who entered with him, became the captain of the company, and fell, instantly killed, August 30, 1862. The sketches of his life, referred to above, contain all that need be said of his career.

"During the three years and seven months now spent in this war my church and congregation have furnished one hundred and six privates and officers. Of these, seventy-three were communicants, and thirty-three were not. Of the members of the church twelve have been killed, two have died of disease, and five disabled by wounds. Of the congregation six have been killed and three have died of disease. Total casualties, twenty-eight.

"Members of the church killed are—

Joshua Parks,	William Page,
J. B. McCorkle,	William C. Preston,
Henry Payne,	William F. Cocke,
D. G. Houston,	Charles Nelson,
Alphonzo Smith,	Joseph Chester,
Capt. H. A. White,	Gen. T. J. Jackson.

"Members of this church disabled by wounds are—
Col. J. K. Edmondson (arm lost), Capt. Frank C. Wilson,
Capt. Frank Preston (arm lost), Thomas D. Houston,
R. K. Estill.

---

[1] See *Sketches of the Life of Captain Hugh A. White*, by his father, pp. 46–48.

"Members of the church who died of disease are—
 Dr. Joseph McClung,   Samuel M. Lightner.

"Members of the congregation killed are—
 F. Davidson,   Capt. M. X. White,
 George Chapin,   Capt. Greenlee Davidson,
 William Patton,   Gen. E. F. Paxton.

"All these, with scarcely one exception, were men of irreproachable character, and the large majority were men of the highest social position and moral worth. Their names are worthy of perpetual remembrance. Their vacant places in the house of God are sad remembrancers of our irreparable loss.

"The state of religion in the church since the war began has not been in all respects encouraging, and yet there has existed, and still exists, much to gratify its friends. During the first three months a daily prayer-meeting was well attended. This was afterwards held once a week. The subject of prayer in all of these meetings was the deliverance of our country from her invaders and the return of peace. The places in our church made vacant by the absence of those in the army were more than supplied by the presence of refugees, which prevented any perceptible diminution in the size of our congregations on the Sabbath. Many very gratifying cases of conversion occurred among our young men in the army. These, from time to time, came home and were admitted to communion.

"For a year or two after the opening of the war, a spirit of worldliness seemed to seize not a few of the members of the church. The fear of poverty, blending with both hatred and fear of the enemy, threatened seriously to lower the moral and religious tone of the church. Speculation ran high. Some who had been leaders in church work became languid and remiss. This is still too much the case. Yet our sufferings have not been without the sanctification of the Spirit. The currency has depreciated to such an extent, and the tenure by which all property is held has become so precarious, as to restrain some not under the influence of higher and purer motives. It seems to be the purpose of God to lessen the love of men for money by rendering it almost valueless.

"Gold is now worth thirty-fold as much as the government currency. And as everything offered for sale—even the most common necessaries of life—is held at specie value, prices are fabulous. I paid a year ago $690 for two hogs; more recently I paid $2,000 for a very ordinary horse, and $10 per bushel for oats; and am now asked $400 per ton for hay to feed him on. As two tons of hay and fifty bushels of oats would be a moderate supply for a horse for the winter and early spring, this will call for the sum of $1,300 to feed my $2,000 horse. Butter brings $6 per pound, and eggs $3 per dozen. Boarders at our village hotel pay $400 per month, or $4,800 per annum. Common English broadcloth brings $250 per yard, and an ordinary felt hat for a gentleman $150. I have just hired for the ensuing year a very ordinary woman for my kitchen, fifty-five years of age, for $600, and must have one for the house at the same price. Firewood is $60 per cord. And yet every one, except those who live on fixed salaries, is living as well and cheaply as before the war. Producers purchase what they need of merchants and others by paying in the produce of their farms at these enormous prices. One congregation in this vicinity pays its pastor one hundred and eighty barrels of flour, worth $45,000. This enormous sum is equivalent to his salary before the war of $1,000, or rather, the one hundred and eighty barrels of flour would have been worth before the war $1,000.

"I have passed through various stages of feeling since this war commenced. The anxiety and gloom were at first almost intolerable. The vastly superior numbers and resources of the North, our own want of every element of strength, except intelligence and courage, our isolated condition from all the rest of the world, caused by the blockade of all our ports, made me very doubtful of success. When the Secretary of State, Mr. Wm. H. Seward, assured the governments of Europe that they would easily 'crush the rebellion in ninety days,' I partly believed him. Through many a dark night I lay sleepless on my bed thinking of the mighty hosts they could pour into Virginia from North and Northwest. In this conviction I would think of my sons in the army, whose presence had always contributed to make my home so pleasant, of the hardships to which they were exposed, and the probability of their death. By such thoughts my peace of mind would be so utterly destroyed that relief could be found only in prayer.

"But time, experience and a deepening conviction of the justice of our self-defence, and above all, the help and blessing of God, quieted anxiety and fear, gave me tranquillity and peace of mind, so that, for three years, I have habitually slept soundly, and attended to my duties, both social and professional, with a high degree of satisfaction and comfort. God has been a present help to me in trouble. Even in the death of my son, slain in battle, who was all that a son could be to his father and mother, I have had a very sweet experience of God's great goodness in giving him to us, in making him what he was, and in taking him to himself just *when* and *as* he did. I firmly believe that he had filled the allotted measure of his days, that he had accomplished his mission, and answered the end of his being. He ardently desired to preach the gospel, but his will was to do and suffer the will of God. Of all the beautiful and truthful remarks recorded in his published life, none are more so than what he says to his mother on the forty-fourth page, viz.:

"'God in his providence has permitted these afflictions to

befall us; and, my mother, if he rides upon the storm, if he guides it to please himself and accomplish his own purposes, shall we murmur or repine?—shall we so magnify our wishes and plans as to shut him from our view? What if our desires and purposes are thwarted and our happiness blasted, does this make him any the less wise or just or good? What if darkness, that may be felt, gathers over us, is it not all light with him? Could we catch a glimpse of God, and of the blessed purposes which he is carrying out, how soon we should wipe away our tears, blush to think of our murmurings, and run with glad hearts into his arms. You know how your children used to do. They might fret and cry when their plans were crossed, but when they found they had been wrong and you right, how gladly did they run to you, and love you all the more tenderly because you had interposed your better wisdom to control them. Thus should we all now do with our Heavenly Father. The issue of all this commotion is with him. He will certainly bring light out of this darkness and joy out of this sorrow. Weeping may endure for a night, but joy cometh in the morning.'

"The remnant of my pilgrimage on earth is rendered far more lonely by his early death. But this remnant is brief, and its termination will bring me into joyful and never-ending communion with him and many others who have gone before."

On the death of this son he wrote several letters, which we insert here, in whole or in part, to show the state of his mind at this time:

To the Rev. Dr. Wm. Brown:

"LEXINGTON, VA., *Sept.* 6, 1862.

"MY DEAR BROTHER: My son Hugh is in heaven. His body perished on the plains of Manassas, on the 30th of

August—the scene of his heroic bravery more than a year ago. I can learn nothing of the particulars, except that he was killed instantly. General Jackson's adjutant-general writes merely this: 'Hugh was killed in the battle of Satturday. He fell gallantly leading his men. I sincerely sympathize with you in the loss of a son so faultless as a Christian and a soldier.'

"This is all, but it is enough. I am thankful to God that I had so costly an offering, when called for, to lay on so sacred an altar. I am now more anxious than ever that the object for which he has sacrificed his precious life should be attained. . . . But his redeemed soul is safe, and I look up through my tears, and in that rejoice.

"One of my kind friends, a lady of my church, wrote me a consolatory letter, in which she says, 'I sorrow with you in the loss of as noble a son as a parent could mourn for; so modest and respectful, so kind and earnest and honorable was he always, that the crowning gift of piety seemed only to add lustre to a character already so good that I could see nothing in it that needed to be corrected or reformed. With everything to render him dear to you, a comfort as well as a pride, how sad, *almost hard*, it seems that he should be the one taken away. And yet, while you sorrow, you may rejoice that God has thus taken to himself the best you had to give. Oh! how little of bitterness there is in giving back the good and pious to their Father and our Father in heaven!'

"In Hugh's last letter he says: 'I feel more and more deeply that I must live altogether for God and in God.' My heart is so filled with sadness, and my eyes with tears, that I cannot write much. I accept what you say of living habitually in the service of God. This I have been endeavoring, though imperfectly, to do for forty-three years."

To the same:

"LEXINGTON, VA., *Nov.* 19, 1862.

"MY DEAR BROTHER: I feel very sensibly the need of some communion with you, that my spirit may be refreshed. The times press heavily upon me, and my faith is feeble. I strive to look through the cloud, that I may find light above, which I cannot find below.

"It seems to me I miss my dear boy more and more. I miss him whenever I put on my overcoat, for at such times he always helped me. I miss him when I mount my horse, for even then he helped me. I miss him when I pray, for now I dare not pray for him. I shall miss him till I die, when I hope to meet him.

"This hope makes the expectation of death pleasant, especially when faith is vigorous. But alas! my faith is often so feeble that even this hope affords me little comfort. This is all selfish, however, and I ought be ashamed of it. Help me, my brother, that I fall not."

"The people of the North profess to seek the good of the negro in thus invading our soil. They seek the good of the black at the expense of the white race. They demand that they shall be emancipated and placed in a condition of equality with us—that the two races shall live socially and politically as one. To their emancipation I have no objection, so far as the whites are concerned. Since I possessed sufficient intelligence to form a judgment in the case, I have been convinced that it would be a real good to the white man. The question is, what shall we do with him? Can two races so different from each other possess the same country on terms of entire equality? Must not the one or the other perish? The warmest philanthropy must pause before such a problem.

"But in truth they have no special fondness for the negro. One of the most distinguished men in the State of

Ohio said to a friend of mine, 'Only consent to wipe the blot of African slavery from our national escutcheon, and we shall have peace.' My friend replied, 'I have no objection to the emancipation of this people, but tell me how we can better their condition. What shall we do with them?' 'Do with them?' replied the kind-hearted philanthropist. 'Do with them? Why, hang them, shoot them, drown them. I care nothing for them; *only wipe out this blot.*'

"The mayor of Rochester, N. Y., told me, in 1860: 'About fifteen years ago we adopted measures designed to drive the negroes then here from our corporate limits, and to prevent others from coming. And they succeeded well. When those measures were first adopted every barber in the city was a black man. Now there is not one. Three-fourths of our cartmen and dray-drivers were negroes. Now the number is very small. The truth is, sir, we do not like the negro. His presence is every way distasteful to us. We have three reasons for preferring white laborers to black, namely:

"'1. The white man will do double the work in the same time.

"'2. He will do it twice as well.

"'3. He can live on one-half as much as the negro.

"'You know and like him; you have room for him, and work suited to him, and I wish you to keep him.'

"This man had sense, was candid, liberal, just and generous; so I replied, 'Only prevail on your politicians to adopt your sentiments, and all danger of disunion and war is over. We are perfectly willing to bear the responsibility in the sight of God of holding them in their present condition until we can prepare them for a better.'

"But I have no heart to enlarge upon a theme so hackneyed, so misunderstood, and so misrepresented. I thank God that their conduct and condition in my congregation have steadily and rapidly improved since the commencement of the war. During this time there has been less vagrancy and insubordination than ever before. They seem to appreciate their dependence and their obligation to their owners as they never did.

"I have not yet abandoned the hope that God has something better in store for these people than their abandonment to the tender mercies of false philanthropists. Still, we have greatly sinned in our neglect of their instruction.

"This neglect is not because of any want of humanity, or even of true affection for the race. There are monsters in human form everywhere. In all lands there are husbands and fathers who maltreat their wives and children. So there are masters among us who maltreat their slaves. But the prevailing spirit is one of great kindness, showing itself in innumerable ways. Their mutual dependence begets mutual attachment. I could fill volumes with incidents, occurring under my own eyes, illustrating this statement; but I write for my own people, especially my own children, and not for the abolitionists.

"The truth is, there has been no true peace in this country for about thirty-five years. About the year 1830 the purpose was fully formed at the North either to abolish slavery in the South or to exterminate the white race. To this end they formed extensive combinations; raised large sums of money; sent out emissaries; issued books, pamphlets, newspapers, false and bitter. They spared neither pains nor money to rouse the blacks to insurrection and bloodshed.

In the summer of 1830 they succeeded in a small section of Southampton county, Va. Urged on by one of their emissaries, inflamed by their incendiary publications, a few were induced to attempt the extermination of the whites. In one small section they succeeded in slaughtering some seventy persons, chiefly old men, women and children. The dastardly *Yankee preacher* who had been chiefly instrumental in exciting this insurrection made his escape under the cover of night, and the insurgents were soon vanquished."

[Mr. White was living and preaching the gospel in that part of Virginia at that time, and writes from observation. We have often heard him relate orally some of the most thrilling events of that insurrection.]

"The South was thus and then thrown on the defensive. Stringent laws were enacted, which would never have been thought of but for the purpose of a necessary self-defence, and for which we of the South incurred the reprobation of the North. The negro was restricted in his privileges, and the vagrant Yankees who prowled through every part of our country, impelled by avarice, ambition or malice, were subjected to no little severity, which was richly deserved. For almost thirty years this sort of war raged with a constantly increasing violence. The halls of Congress were the scene of many angry and shameful collisions. Civil courts and church courts were at times thrown into a state of confusion by the introduction of this question. Much blood was shed by the opposing parties in the newly settled portions of our country—the one disputing and the other contending for his right to hold slaves in the territories.

"At length, in 1859, a diabolical scheme to murder the whites and liberate the blacks was put in execution by one John Brown on the border line between Virginia and Maryland, at Harper's Ferry. He had been preparing for this outbreak by importing arms in large quantities into a desolate valley on the Maryland side, beyond the river, and opposite the Ferry, where he had been living secretly for many months. Besides army rifles of the most approved pattern, he had many boxes of pikes—a blood-curdling weapon to look at—consisting of a wooden shaft, from ten to fourteen feet long, with a flat, pointed, steel head, long enough to impale a human body of ordinary size, and a guard to prevent its penetrating the bed on which the sleeper lay, so as to be difficult of extraction. At the dead hour of the night the negroes were to be armed with these instruments, set to work murdering their masters and mistresses, marching southward, and receiving recruits as they advanced into the country. A more cold-blooded and atrocious plot of the greatest magnitude never entered the brain of man or demon.

"Of course it failed. The emissaries whom Brown had sent before into Virginia, ostensibly engaged in different lawful callings, yet really paid to excite the negroes to insurrection and prepare them for his coming, failed in their mission. The negroes suspected their intentions, and refused to enlist. When Brown entered the Ferry, and began his work of burning and blood-shedding, the whites rose in arms, surrounded and forced him and his band into a small brick house, and kept him at bay until a *posse* of men from the regular army of the United States, commanded by Captain—afterwards the renowned General—Robert E. Lee, arrived on the ground, arrested and turned him over to the authorities of the State of Virginia, by whom he and several of his associates, after due trial before the law, were hanged.

"From even this very brief outline of the warfare waged upon us for about thirty years, it is not difficult to see why our rulers deemed it indispensable to impose restrictions, both on masters and servants, which seriously interfered with the duties of the former and the privileges of the latter.

"Previous to the inauguration of this state of things, servants were taught to read, colored men were licensed to preach the gospel, and became pastors of congregations of their own race; the marriage and parental relations were respected; they lived in families, had family worship, were not only permitted, but urged to train their children and govern their households according to the word of God. When a boy I often attended family worship held in the houses of my father's servants and of other servants in our neighborhood. Then the white and colored races were friends; they respected, confided in and loved each other.

"But in an evil hour the tempter came, and the scene was changed. If we had been let alone the condition of the negro would have steadily improved; public sentiment would have turned decisively in favor of a gradual emancipation under the influence of the most sagacious minds in the State, who, in public speeches and pamphlets, were already advocating it.

"During this war, which is now near the close of its fourth year, the negroes have remained faithful to their owners, except in portions of the country overrun by the enemy. As a race they are very credulous. Where the master has been forced to flee for his life before the foe, leaving his home in flames and his family impoverished, the negro, believing his pretended friends, has gone off with them. In this way some sections of our State have been almost depopulated of both the white and the black man.

"In June, 1864, the enemy, twenty thousand strong, entered the quiet village of Lexington. General David Hunter was in command, a man whose notoriety among our people made him terrible to the timid and detestable to all. He seemed to riot in the alarm excited by his presence among women and children. In two cases, when respectfully applied to in person by ladies of the highest refinement and greatest prudence, for some protection against his ruffian troops, who were tramping through their houses, destroying or bearing off their food and furniture, not leaving the apparel and bedding of their infant children, he replied to one of these ladies with a brutality that would have disgraced a savage: 'These are the natural consequences of war, and you must bear them as best you can.' To the other he said: 'I know your father and brothers; look to them to protect you.'

"Thus encouraged, the work of ruin went on, especially in the houses of these two ladies, until scarcely a morsel, and, in one, not a morsel of food was left, and scarcely an article of apparel or bed-covering was left. Several other families in the part of the town more immediately under his command suffered nearly as much.

"By the special order of this commanding officer the Sabbath day was spent in first robbing and then burning the residence of Governor Letcher, the beautiful residences of two of the professors of the Virginia Military Institute, the spacious and tasteful barracks of the Institute, a large flour mill belonging to a peaceful citizen, besides the large warehouse owned by the State of Virginia.

"The Institute was robbed of its library, containing many rare and costly volumes, of its splendid paintings, and last, of a bronze statue of General Washington, a copy of that in the Capitol at Richmond, the pride of the State.

"The splendid residence of the Superintendent of the Institute escaped destruction, in consequence of the extreme illness of his married daughter; and this residence is now all that remains of that once beautiful establishment—barracks, professors' houses, mess hall, hospital, and offices, are all in ashes.

"Washington College, endowed by 'the father of his country,' was sacked, its library and paintings carried off, the rich and costly furniture of its public rooms either given to the negroes or carried as trophies to the North; nearly every pane of glass in it was broken, and all needful preparation made for its burning, which was prevented only by the expostulations of a gray-haired trustee.

"I omitted to state that they shelled the town before entering it. Twenty houses were struck, some of which were seriously damaged, and two were ignited, but the fire was extinguished. Six shells passed over the parsonage, one exploded in the garden, and one in the stable-yard. But not a person was struck. Many very narrowly escaped.

"They robbed me of corn and hay worth $500. They cut

the curtains from my carriage, and carried off a portion of the harness. A well-dressed and well-mounted captain and lieutenant attempted to rob me of my carriage and harness, but were prevented by the sergeant appointed by General Averill to guard my premises. Last of all, they robbed me of my favorite horse, 'Charley,' one I had used under the saddle for nine years—a horse almost as well known through the county of Rockbridge as his owner. A faithful servant plead with the robbers not to take 'old Charley' from 'master,' urging that both were old and lame, and that Charley could not be of much use to them. But the pleadings were all in vain. It is not wonderful that my good servant, John, should close his account of his efforts to save Charley by saying, 'Master, these Yankees are the beat of all the rogues I ever saw, black or white.'

"General Averill, commanding the Federal cavalry, acted like a gentleman. He made every practicable effort to check the robbers of private property. He stationed a guard at every house where it was asked in his district, and punished severely in my presence several men brought before him on a charge of spoiling private houses. It is very rare that I attempt to prophecy either on high or low themes, but I did say repeatedly during the three days of army rule in Lexington, 'Averill is altogether too much of a gentleman to be permitted to hold a command very long under such a superior as the brutal Hunter.' And so it came to pass. In about two months from the time of their visit to us he was relieved of his command. Notwithstanding, the opinion was very general, both in their army and our's, that he was the best cavalry commander they had.

"I moved freely among their officers and privates. In no instance did I meet with personal insult. On the whole, they were respectful and polite. In my first interview with General Averill I told him politely, but firmly, that my principles and sympathies were all with my native South; to which he promptly replied, 'I am not surprised to hear you say that.'

"I scrupulously avoided all general conversation, especially on the war, or anything connected with it. My intercourse had respect wholly to securing guards for defenceless families.

"It was very obvious that there were several distinct parties in their army, differing widely in their principles, and much embittered towards each other in spirit. Some comprehended and appreciated in some degree our position. Many gave unmistakable proof, not only of a want of true sympathy with the negro, but of strong hostility towards him. The general and his staff were well supplied with these people as body servants, and the exactions they made upon them, both in the way of personal attention and actual labor, far exceeded anything to which we Virginians had been accustomed. The remark was often made by officers in my yard, 'I am not fighting for the negro. I would as soon shoot a negro as a rebel.' Such men dissuaded the negroes from going with them.

"On the other hand, many had no other idea of the war than that it was fomented and prosecuted exclusively to free the negroes, put them in possession of the homes and property, and make them in all respects the equals of the whites.

"And yet again there were many, especially foreigners, who were fighting only for present compensation and the prospective possession of our farms.

"There was every grade of intellect and character among them, from the gentleman and scholar down. Perhaps, as a whole, they are shrewder than the mass of our army. But, on the score of amiability and kindly conduct, good taste and good manners, as far as my observation has gone, their common soldiers are immeasurably below ours. This is true also of some holding office. The most unmitigated ruffian I ever encountered in human shape was a man named Berry, captain of the provost guard, who at the beginning of the war, as I learned from a member of Averill's staff, was a common Irish hackman in Baltimore. A recital of his brutalities would be too offensive to good taste, and too painful to the better feelings of our nature for record here. Sooner or later he will receive his reward.

"I was several times compelled to move through large and densely crowded portions of their encampment, even on the Sabbath day; and I record with astonishment and pain the fact that I never saw or heard of a chaplain, nor could I discover that a hymn was sung, a prayer offered, or any form of worship observed through all that holy day. All, too, were idle, except the very small number deemed necessary to rob and burn the public buildings—all of which was done on the Sabbath.

"I asked one of their majors if they had no chaplains. He replied, 'O yes, we have a great many; almost one to every regiment.' I answered, 'I am astonished then that you have no worship to-day.' He replied, 'Our chaplains are not of much account. They seldom or never preach. I have not heard a sermon, or even a prayer, for many months.'

"After they left, I heard of three or four chaplains who inquired of some of the ladies of my congregation for me; said they knew me, had met me at the North, etc. One of these seemed to be *enjoying* himself at 9 o'clock on Sabbath morning, standing near and looking at the flames as they consumed the private residence of Governor Letcher, while Mrs. Letcher and her children were sitting on some trunks which, with their own hands and with great difficulty, they had rescued from the flames. This man said to a daughter of Governor Letcher, 'I know Dr. White pretty well, and have thought of calling at his house to see him; but, as I learn he is a very warm Southern man, I have concluded not to do so.' All of them seemed afraid to encounter 'a warm

Southern man,' as none of them sought my acquaintance or paid me a respectful call.

"I omitted to state in the proper place, that General Averill made his headquarters in my yard, within forty feet of my study door, and his signal corps encamped in my garden. This was a great protection to my dwelling and other houses in the yard, but this protection did not extend, as I have already stated, to my carriage-house, stable and granery.

"On the whole, with the exception of the buildings burned and the robberies inflicted on the store-rooms and wardrobes of many families, the damage was as slight as could have been expected from a hostile army of twenty thousand men encamped for three days in and immediately around a village of twenty-five hundred inhabitants. May it please God soon to terminate this cruel and unnatural war.

"Such are my views of the folly, weakness and depravity of men, that my expectation of good from any form of government are faint. I am not, nor ever have been, a secessionist. Yet, when a party was formed at the North, which became large enough to get the government into its hands, which did not scruple to sanction the nullification of laws of the national Congress, and which forbade to the South rights of property in the territories guaranteed by the constitution, whose executive called for Virginia bayonets to impale the bodies of our nearest neighbors and dearest friends, the time for rebellion with a view to revolution seemed to me to have come. I wish, therefore, my children to know that their father was not a secessionist, but *a rebel, an honest, earnest rebel.* As such he has suffered much and may suffer more. Of this he does not complain. If it should please God to frown upon the effort to resist such injustice, and to subject us to still greater sufferings, nay, even to subjugation and death, he may do no more than he may justly claim. Thus has he dealt in other lands and ages, with nations nearer and dearer to him than we can claim to be. Though my portion should be poverty, imprisonment and death, I hope to be able to say with a tranquil spirit, 'Not my will, but thine, be done.'

"For myself, by the help of God, I can live happily and die peacefully under any form of civil government. Paul and Silas in the jail at Philippi, with their feet and hands in the stocks, under the iron despotism of Nero, were prayerful and joyous. Our blessed Lord himself had his birth, grew to maturity, and laid the foundation of his church, in equally troublous times. Why cannot we, the citizens of 'a kingdom which cannot be moved,' carry forward the work they began with equal joyousness and alacrity?

"The whole country seems to be sinking into a state of demoralization. At no time during a ministry of thirty-eight years have I known so much sensual gaiety among professedly pious people, so much drinking of intoxicating liquors, and so free a participation in promiscuous dancing. The present winter of 1864–'5 has been equally characterized by suffering and sin. Scarcely a family can be found in which death has not recently made inroad. Many families are very scarcely supplied with the commonest comforts. An aged widow told me recently that all the corn she had on which to sustain a family of eight members amounted to ten bushels, for which she had paid five hundred dollars. And yet at no period since the settlement of this Valley have there been, in the same length of time, as many gay assemblies. Crowds of young people pass from house to house, with little to eat and less to wear, and spend the entire night in dancing and revelry. Sorrow and suffering in themselves uniformly make bad people worse. 'The sorrow of the world worketh death.' This is divinely true. The state of things is far worse in other sections.

"Meantime the dangers and suffering of our people, the probability of our subjugation by our enemies, increase daily. Five or six of our most important cities and towns have been evacuated by us and occupied by the enemy within the last few weeks. Just now a force is approaching us which we have not the means of resisting, even for an hour, and the strong probability is, not to say certainty, that our lovely valley will be wholly in their possession in a very short time. And yet the people revel with almost frenzied excess. We are told that the people ate, drank, married wives, and were given in marriage until Noah entered the ark, and the flood came and took them all away. I have always thought this was a modest and delicate way of stating that they continued their social revelry, their feasting and dancing, until the flood actually came, and have sometimes felt a childish curiosity to know whether they discontinued their sport on the hills when the valleys had been submerged.

"A redeeming feature in the case is the readiness with which the people contribute to the support of chaplains in the army. With a few months past more than twenty thousand dollars has been paid into my hands for this purpose by the churches of Lexington Presbytery—an average of eight hundred and seventy dollars to a church.

"The gaiety of our people in the midst of suffering reminds me of a paragraph in Walter Scott's *Review of the French Revolution*. After the execution of Robespierre and the overthrow of the Jacobin party, Scott says: 'Society began to resume its ordinary course, and business and pleasure succeeded each other as usual. But even social pleasures brought with them strange and gloomy associations with that valley of the shadow of death through which the late pilgrimage of France appeared to have been lain. An assembly for dancing, very much frequented by the young of both sexes and highly fashionable, was called 'the Ball of the Victims.' The qualification for attendance was the having lost some near and valued relation or friend in the late Reign of Terror. The hair and head-dress were so arranged as to resemble the preparations made for the guillotine, and the motto adopted was "We dance amidst tombs." In no country but France could the incidents have taken place which gave rise to this association, and certainly in no country but France would they have been used for such a purpose.'

"This occurred soon after the massacre in which ten thousand of the best citizens of Paris perished from the pikes, sabres and clubs of assassins within a space of three days, in addition to the thousands who perished on the guillotine. Scott wrote long before our time, or he might have coupled us with France.

"The capital of Virginia and the Confederacy has been evacuated, and the enemy has taken possession of it. The officials, both of the State and Confederate governments, have fled, and the reasonable presumption is that our army, now some fifty miles from Richmond, will either capitulate or evacuate the State. Anarchy begins to prevail, and danger and suffering increase with almost every passing hour The brief view I take, by which my mind is kept calm and tranquil, may be thus stated:

"1. God can deliver us from our enemies if he will.

"2. If he does not, it will be best that he should not.

"3. And if he does not, then the people of God have greatly the advantage of those who are not his people. God only knows what is really and permanently best for us, and both his justice and mercy concur in assuring us that he will order or permit only what is best.

"My greatest concern by far is for my two sons now in our army, especially the younger of the two, who is the youngest of my children, and of whose spiritual safety I have no assurance, not even a well-grounded hope. I can only say, God of the covenant, fulfil thy promise to be a God to thy people and their seed. Hearer of prayer, hear me.

This dear boy was brought home late in last November badly wounded. He had gone ahead of his regiment with only one companion, when they were fired upon by the enemy at the distance of one hundred yards. His companion was instantly killed and he wounded. His clothes were pierced by seven balls. One passed through the calf of his left leg. This was at Rood's Hill, Shenandoah county, Va.

"The fondest hopes of his parents and friends were that so signal an escape from death would result in a change of heart. But he recovered and returned to the army without giving any evidence of conversion. All I know now is that he has been in some very hard fighting within the last few days. Whether he has escaped, been wounded, captured or slain, is yet to be learned. The anguish of such suspense no language can express. And yet I hope that my faith in the covenant is firm. I am not without comfort. God will undoubtedly do what is wisest and best, and to know and believe this ought to be enough. And, then, this dear boy has been the object of concerted prayer by parents, brothers, sisters and friends for many years. Shall not some of these prayers be answered? I think they will.

"The tendency of human nature to extremes in their opinions and feelings was never so apparent to me as at present. The large majority tend strongly to presumption or despair. The former seem to have no doubt, the latter no hope of success. Reverses do not dispirit the former, nor do successes cheer the latter. Neither can explain very satisfactorily the grounds of their hopes or fears, and it is difficult to decide which is the more unhappy of the two.

"They who were original and active secessionists belong chiefly to the former class. They made so many prophecies that have not been fulfilled, one would think some suspicion of their fallibility would be forced upon them. But it seems not. Although gold is now worth sixty-five dollars for one in Confederate money, flour twelve hundred dollars a barrel, bacon ten dollars a pound; although a poor preacher had to pay four thousand seven hundred dollars for a very ordinary horse and cow, still they have no doubt but that our currency will soon be as good as gold, and the said horse and cow sell for a hundred and fifty dollars. In many cases it taxes charity very heavily to give such people credit for sincerity. But many, I have no doubt, are thoroughly sincere. 'The wish is father to the thought.' They belong to that class who are described by the poet in the familiar lines—

> 'Hope springs eternal in the human breast;
> Man never is, but always to be blest.'

The latter class see ruin in every bush and hear it in every sound. They were never well-informed as to the origin of the war, and could never see sufficient cause for it. When once commenced, and especially when our enemies became our invaders, they warmly espoused resistance for self-defence. Nor did they so much oppose the enemy for what they did, as for doing it without constitutional warrant. They would have favored the adoption of a constitution authorizing all that had been done, but were offended because the enemy first adopted unconstitutional measures, and then altered the constitution so as to bring their measures into harmony with it. These persons felt themselves forced by the Washington cabinet to rebel either against State or national authority, and they chose the latter.

"Virginia, as a border State, having the District of Columbia and the national capital on its boundary, at once became the battle-ground of the war; and although victory often perched upon our banner, although the invaders were often driven from our borders in the wildest confusion and with appalling loss of life, yet, by reason of their superior numbers, after four years of desperate fighting, they have succeeded in getting possession of much the larger part of our territory, including many of our principal cities and towns. Large portions of our richest and most highly-cultivated lands have been swept as with the besom of destruction. Our finest dwellings, with their out-buildings, our mills and churches, have been reduced to ashes. One may travel for miles through what was once our most populous and prosperous sections without seeing a human habitation or a living thing Such ravages have filled the minds and hearts of those just described with thoughts and feelings too sad to be borne without some animosity. And when to all this is added the fact that few, very few, homes can be found in which there was one or more of suitable age to enter the army out of which one or more has not perished in the conflict, then it is not surprising if many despond and some despair. Several of my own acquaintance have become hopelessly insane, and some have unquestionably died of a broken heart.

"Pressing demands have been made upon every pastor, as well as upon other Christian friends, for consolation for such. In some places, especially in the larger cities, the preaching has been too much of a war-like nature Ministers of the gospel, in some cases, have erred in thinking they were called to rouse the people to a sterner and fiercer spirit of resistance. But the great majority have abstained from such a course. 'Comfort ye, comfort ye my people,' has been the voice chiefly heard from the pulpit, and to the great mass of God's own people this has been a welcome message.

"An intelligent lady said to me yesterday, in deep distress, 'It seems to me I have no faith at all. I certainly have not enough to determine whether the Lord is on our side in this war or on that of the enemy.' I replied that we had no warrant to decide such a question by faith. The Scriptures tell us that 'faith cometh by hearing, and hearing by the word of God.' Now, the word of God gives us no information on this question. We can have no scriptural faith on the subject. But this word is full of instruction that appeals directly to our faith. For example, 'The Lord

God omnipotent reigneth;' 'The very hairs of your head are all numbered;' 'A sparrow shall not fall to the ground without your Father;' and 'All things work together for good to them that love God.' If you have no faith in these words your condition is deplorable indeed. If you have, then you may be comforted, come what may. This simple view seemed to quiet her mind.

"One has said, 'If the thing prayed for is not in the promise, it is a sin to ask for it, and if it is, then it is a sin not to expect it.' Faith accepts as true, really, unalterably, eternally true, what God has said, and this not because it seems reasonable to us, but simply and solely because God has said it.

"April 10, 1865. Tidings have just come that in a battle on the 2nd instant our youngest son was captured. We know nothing more. How taken, or where he is confined, we know not. From him we have not a note or message. Nor is it likely that we shall for many a weary day. 'Be anxious for nothing.' And yet anxious I am. The whole of my brief remnant of this mortal life must be full of earthly sorrow. But comfort in God may abound. For this I fervently pray.

"Of our elder son no tidings whatever have been received. For his safety I am anxious. God of the covenant, help and deliver thy servant.

"April 15. Both of our sons have reached home in safety. The younger escaped as by a miracle. Surely God's goodness calls for our warmest gratitude and praise.

"Our brave and honored army, overborne by vastly superior numbers and utterly exhausted by continued marching and fighting without food or rest, has been compelled to surrender. Our capital and commonwealth are now under the heel of our enemy. Scarcely a doubt exists that we are to be a subjugated people, ruined as to all political power, and sorely straitened for a time for the necessaries of life. But these things are not paramount. We have other relations than political. I am a husband, father, minister of the gospel, as well as citizen of the State. If our social and religious privileges are not denied us we can endure all else. One may be good, useful and happy under any form of government, provided the mind and conscience be free. True religion has prospered under all forms of civil government. Our blessed Lord can surely do more to make his people permanently happy than men and devils can to make them miserable. Though persecuted, we will not be forsaken; though cast down, we will not be destroyed.

"God's purposes are hidden from mortal sight, but I rest calmly in the belief that these purposes will move steadily on to wise and beneficent results.

"The fearful struggle of four years has ended. The work of carnage and death is over. Forced back into a position from which we sought to escape, the mortified victims of a power we have hated, I bow reverently to God. Acknowledging the obligation wisely imposed by his word, I submit to 'the powers that be,' because they 'are ordained of God.' I make no further record of these sad times, except to express my deep and painful apprehensions for the future destiny of the negro and of my own descendants. The former will probably waste away before the superior power of the whites. The latter will be, I fear, by a slow process, amalgamated with their conquerors, until they cease to be recognized and applauded for the noble traits that have hitherto distinguished them.

"For myself, now at the age of sixty-five years, with many physical infirmities, there remains but little, very little, of earthly ill to fear or of earthly good to expect. The time of my discharge is near, and through the grace of God abounding in the Lord Jesus Christ, I have a very comfortable hope that, when the time of my departure shall come, I will be enabled to say, with the apostle, 'I have fought a good fight, I have finished my course, I have kept the faith; henceforth there is laid up for me a crown of righteousness, which the Lord, the righteous Judge, shall give me at that day; and not to me only, but unto all them also that love his appearing.'"

CHAPTER XIII.

1861-1865.

THE STRIFE BEFORE THE WAR.

WHEN Dr. White says, "The truth is, there has been no true peace in this country for about thirty-five years," he is supported by facts well known in the South in his time, and brought to light in every reliable history of the abolition movement in this country. *The sentiment of abolition did not originate in the North*, as the ill-informed suppose, but in the South.

The first newspaper published in this country, whose one avowed object was opposition to slavery, was edited by Elihu Embree, in Jonesborough, Tennessee, under the style of *The Manumission Intelligencer*. True, Mr. Embree was a New Jerseyman, but the supporters of his paper were Southern people. Its issue began in March, 1819. From the same source, in 1820, an octavo monthly began its career, under the title of *The Emancipator*.

The doctrine of these papers was gradual emancipation by the States. Not until September 2, 1829, did William Lloyd Garrison issue *The Genius of Universal Emancipation*, in which, for the first time, the policy of immediate and forcible abolition by the general government was advocated, and which in time became *The Liberator*.[1]

The first societies in this country organized to spread this sentiment took their rise in Tennessee and North Carolina. As early as 1825 these two States were covered over

---

[1] See the *Life of W. Lloyd Garrison*, Vol. I., p. 141. The Century Co. 1885.

with them, and gradual emancipation was the sentiment of the great majority.

The legislation in the border Southern States was moving strongly in this direction at a very early day. In 1821-'2, Mr. Faulkner introduced a bill into the House of Delegates of Virginia, favoring a scheme of gradual emancipation. In the discussion of this bill, Mr. Moore characterized slavery as a "curse"—"the heaviest calamity which has ever befallen any portion of the human race;" he spoke of its irresistible tendency to undermine and destroy everything like virtue and morality in the community; of its disastrous effects on the general prosperity by making agriculture degrading for the whites; of its check upon population, and its danger in case of invasion.

This speech was endorsed by the Richmond *Enquirer;* and the *Whig,* commenting on it, asked, "What is the question of who shall be president—of banks, of roads, and canals, of tariffs—to this?"[1]

In this same debate Mr. Broadnax boldly asked, "Is there one man in Virginia who does not lament that there ever was a slave in the State?"

In their fifteenth annual report (1832) the American Colonization Society speak of the "great movement" then going on in Maryland and Virginia.[2]

Probably the most noted political pamphlet ever published in Virginia was the *Ruffner Pamphlet,* which advocated gradual emancipation from an economic view of the subject. This pamphlet was signed by some of the most distinguished men of the State, and reflected a sentiment that had been growing from colonial times.[3]

Thus we see that the movement was going forward with great force when the counter movement of forcible and im-

---

[1] See *Niles' Register,* January 21, 1832, p. 378, quoted in the *Life of W. Lloyd Garrison,* Vol. I., pp. 251-'2. The Century Co. 1885.
[2] *Ibid.*   [3] *Ibid.*

mediate abolition by the general government was initiated. On this doctrine the abolition party was formed. It spread with great rapidity. Their organization was extended "at the rate of nearly one new society a day."[1]

State societies were formed; newspapers published; books and tracts, stigmatizing slaveholders with the most opprobrious epithets, scattered broadcast over the land; wood-cuts of the most horrible kind were secretly put into the hands of the blacks, as Senator Benton said in 1835, "to inflame the passions of the slaves."[2]

So wide-spread was the circulation of these incendiary publications, and so dangerous their tendency to incite insurrection among the slaves, that President Andrew Jackson, in his Message to Congress, December 7, 1835, introduced the subject, suggesting "the propriety of passing such a law as will prohibit, under severe penalties, the circulation in the Southern States, through the mail, of incendiary publications intended to instigate the slaves to insurrection." In this same year Mr. John C. Calhoun introduced in Congress a bill making it a penal offence for postmasters "knowingly to deliver to any person whatever any pamphlet, newspaper, handbill, or other printed paper or *pictorial representation*, touching the subject of slavery, where, by the laws of said State, district, or territory, their circulation was prohibited."[3]

The abolitionists, moreover, invaded the South with schoolmasters and school-mistresses, who secretly fanned the flame of insurrection among the negroes, and with travelling venders of different articles of merchandise, who did likewise.

In these and numerous other ways insurrections were actually excited in the South, in one of which, in Southampton county, Virginia, August, 1831, fifty-five whites were murdered outright. As Dr. White says, this was the work

---

[1] *Life of W. Lloyd Garrison*, Vol. II., p. 79.
[2] *Thirty Years' View*, i., 577.
[3] *Ibid.*, i., 586; *Life of W. Lloyd Garrison*, Vol. I., p. 232.

chiefly of a Yankee school-master; and John Brown's right-hand man, John E. Cook, was also a school-master in Virginia while preparing for that insurrection.

Not content with all this mischief-making at home, the abolitionists strove to excite the animosity of Europeans against the South, and succeeded in rendering slaveholders a by-word and a hissing in many countries. They even attempted to prevail on the Free Church of Scotland to declare slaveholding a ground of exclusion from the sacraments of the church, which Dr. Chalmers characterized as a "new and factious principle of administration, for which she can see no authority in Scripture, and of which she can gather no traces in the history or practice of the churches in apostolic times."[1]

Of course the Southern people resented all this. The work of gradual emancipation by the States, which was popular throughout the South, and was landing emigrants in Liberia by the hundreds, was suddenly arrested; the newspapers took the matter in hand; books and pamphlets were written mass-meetings were held to denounce abolitionism; platform speeches were made; vigilance committees organized to keep a lookout for dangerous emissaries; bills passed by legislatures to prevent the circulation of seditious writings; the help of Congress invoked, as we have seen, and the supreme court appealed to.

And so a war of words raged throughout North and South on the lines of public travel, in public houses, in churches, by the family fireside; the halls of legislation, national and State, became avenues in which rencounters took place, not always bloodless; negro riots occurred; the mails were rifled and contents burned publicly in the streets; scaffolds were erected on which to hang the disturbers of the public peace; prominent men were mobbed in different cities; and school-books were changed to suit the prevalent ideas of the sections.

---

[1] See *Life of Dr. Chalmers*, Vol. IV., p. 571. Harper & Bros. 1852.

Thus the strife went on, waxing more and more fierce, until actual hostilities with arms began in 1861. The language of Dr. White—"there has been no peace in this country for about thirty-five years"—is in strict accordance with fact.

While acting as General Agent for the American Tract Society in Virginia he was sent, in the spring of 1835, to New York and Boston to attend a convention of those interested in the tract work. In a diary kept at the time by him we find some notes bearing on this subject. After the lapse of fifty-five years, in which time the greatest event in the history of the United States has taken place, "the war between the States," and the emancipation of the slaves, these notes will interest the thoughtful reader, the more so because, on a fly-leaf of this diary, we find the following postscript, written near the close of the war, October 6, 1864: "The views herein expressed of slavery and abolitionism have undergone no material change when now the terrible civil war predicted in this paper is actually upon us."

The notes in the diary read as follows: "Of all the new and extravagant things at the North, nothing can equal the furious and fiery spirit of the abolitionists. . . . Avowing the purest benevolence for the colored race, they exhibit a spirit towards those of their own color both violent and reckless. One of them, and he a minister of the gospel, told me he was ready at any time to shoulder his musket and march against his white brethren of the South. . . . This man was city missionary in Boston. Another told me that no man was under any obligation to pay debts which had been contracted under the slavery system; that no citizen of Virginia was under the slightest obligation to obey those laws which were designed to regulate slavery, and that the constitution of the United States was an iniquitous, a bloody compact.

"This man I convicted in a public company of having once

sold slaves to a considerable amount, and of travelling at that moment to make fiery abolition speeches on the proceeds of those very sales. This man is the notorious James G. Birney, of Kentucky, once a respectable lawyer, a highly reputable citizen, a kind-hearted, benevolent and charitable neighbor and friend. At an unhappy hour he had imbibed the sentiments and spirit of this cut-throat crew, and in a moment all rational and consistent benevolence and charity forsook his breast, and now nothing is left but an undefined and undefinable sort of compassion for the blacks, with a hatred for those of his own color which nothing can satisfy short of their blood.

"Indeed, the whole party seem literally to riot in the anticipation of soon witnessing the utter extermination of the whole slave-holding population, and of the establishment in their place of the blacks. It really seems to me that a black skin, covering any sort of a heart, is the only sure passport to their confidence and kind feelings.

"This party, however, constitutes a small portion of the population. Public sentiment is violently enlisted against them. No religious society in Boston will allow them the use of their house of worship, nor will the civil authority grant them the use of any of their public buildings. . . . . . Upon the whole, I love my Northern brethren all the better since seeing them in their own houses. And the more I love them the more I hate abolitionism as such, which, in my eyes, is as a black wart standing out upon a comely and attractive face.

"The Bostonians are not satisfied with treating me kindly. They have given me six hundred and twenty-five dollars for the Society in whose service I am travelling, and that, too, without my asking for it.

"The Yankees are a noble race. But I am not writing a book. I am merely recording a few memoranda for the amusement of my children when I am taken away."

As a specimen of Dr. White's graphic style of narration, we copy from the diary the following incident: "On my return from this delightful meeting one of those incidents occurred which serve to remind us forcibly of our utter dependence on God and of our constant exposure to death. I had taken my seat with the stage-driver, that I might have an opportunity to converse with him about his peculiar duties as a professing Christian, he being a member of our church. We reached the Rivanna, which we were to cross in a ferry-boat. A gentleman and lady were all who were in the stage.

"Before entering the boat the gentleman left the stage, deeming it unsafe to pass the river in so confined a situation. The lady and myself retained our seats, she in the stage and I with the driver. The horses entered the boat rather too precipitately, so that, as the foremost wheels of the stage struck the boat, its moorings gave way, and off went the boat down stream, the horses being on board and the stage in the water. I kept my seat until the hind feet of the wheel horses losing their hold, the poor animals slided slowly into the water, holding to the end of the boat with their fore feet.

"The water now began to pour through the boot of the driver's box, and the stage was so completely filled with water that there was barely room above its surface for the lady's head. I saw that, in an instant more, we must lose all hold upon the boat, and that the stage, horses, passengers and all must be precipitated into the stream together. For my own part I decidedly preferred taking the water [Dr. White was a lame man], so I sprang into the river and easily swam to the shore we had just left.

"I had scarcely left my seat when what I had anticipated occurred, horses, stage, driver and lady all came with a tremendous splash immediately behind me. The horses fell with so much regularity, and so untrammeled by the harness, that they instantly recovered and swam with amazing spirit towards the opposite shore

"Several times the top of the stage could scarcely be seen above the water. The driver kept his seat and the lady her's. We utterly abandoned all hope of their escaping a watery grave. Several boats were sent out to meet the stage, but no regard was paid to this proffered help. In truth there was no time to try experiments.

"It was a scene truly sublime and almost overpowering to the spectators. I had swam until I reached the muddy bottom, when I immediately turned to see what had become of my companions in danger. I stood all the time up to my waist in water, too much concerned about the result to go ashore.

"The driver had the precaution to give the horses the reins entirely, and, sitting, whip in hand, he gave them the lash freely as they arose above the water, until at length, to the amazement and joy of all, they reached the opposite shore in perfect safety. Surely the Lord compasseth our path at all times."

CHAPTER XIV.

1866–1871.

HEALTH FAILS.—OFFERS HIS RESIGNATION TO THE SESSION; DECLINED, AND AN OFFER OF SUPPORT FOR AN ASSISTANT MADE, PROVIDED HIS HEALTH NOT RESTORED BY REST.—CORRESPONDS FOR ASSISTANT.—HEALTH NOT BEING RESTORED, INSISTS ON RESIGNING.—ACTION OF THE CONGREGATION.—BECOMES PRINCIPAL OF THE ANN SMITH ACADEMY.—LETTER TO REV. JOHN S. WATT.—A TOUCHING SIGHT.—THE SCHOOL SUCCEEDS.—RESIGNS.—LETTER OF THE TRUSTEES ACCEPTING.

> " Howe'er it be, it seems to me
> 'Tis only noble to be good ;
> Kind hearts are more than coronets,
> And simple faith than Norman blood."

"NOVEMBER 2, 1866. Maladies which have disturbed me for more than two years have at last resulted in a total suspension of my ministry. Enfeebled in body and mind, wholly incapacitated for labor, I have been compelled to retire from the pulpit. The chief source of my sufferings is my throat. For more than thirty-nine years I have preached in-doors and out, at every season and in all states of the weather. I have often preached twice a day for two weeks, and have never, until now, suffered in the least degree from my voice or lungs. But suddenly the evil has come upon me. For more than a year I have had a troublesome cough, attended by great debility. I preached regularly twice on the Sabbath, and lectured one evening in the week, with no other inconvenience than great prostration after each service.

"Still, as I did not improve while at work, I tendered my resignation to the session. It was promptly and unanimously declined, and a resolution adopted with equal promptitude and unanimity exempting me from all professional duties, both public and private, until January 1, 1867, meantime continuing my salary, and pledging themselves to provide a substitute for the pulpit, and to supply my place themselves in visiting, and otherwise superintending the congregation. They moreover avowed, without a dissenting voice, that if, when the first of January came, I was still unable to resume my duties, an adequate salary should be continued, while no duty would be required but such as I could perform in my study; and that they would proceed to call a collegiate pastor, for whose support they would provide, in addition to my own. This was more than just; it was eminently generous. My heart filled, and I could not restrain tears of gratitude. The abuse of the wicked can be endured with calmness, but such kindness from God's people almost breaks my heart.

"I am, therefore, now wholly laid aside. For almost forty years God called me to speak, and now, with equal distinctness, he calls me to be silent. Surely I should yield to the one as promptly and cheerfully as the other. In great mercy he has given me two sons who occupy important positions as heralds of the same blessed gospel which I have so long proclaimed. This is a great comfort to me, and helps me to 'be still and know that he is God.'

"All my symptoms, however, are better. My general health has improved very much. The soreness of the throat has ceased. My voice is clearer and stronger, and the cough has lessened.

"I desire to wait patiently upon God, and to have my 'expectation from him.' 'The Lord is my light and my salvation; whom shall I fear? The Lord is the strength of my life; of whom shall I be afraid? For in the time of trouble he shall hide me in his pavilion.'"

Dr. White laid down his pen at this point; nor did he ever take it up again to write another line of "notes" on his life, although he lived six years longer, and wrote on other matters. He seems to have considered his life as virtually ended by his retirement from regular, professional work. The course pursued by the church was not what he expected, and he doubtless decided in his own mind that the interests of all concerned required little, if anything, to be said about it at the time.

We have gathered from his correspondence and from the minutes of the session of the Lexington Church all the facts necessary to complete the record of his life.

We have seen from his "notes" that the session declined his resignation when it was first offered, and gave him a vacation of several months. In a letter to his son George, dated October 29, 1866, he makes a minute statement of this action of the session, viz.:

"The session had a full meeting a week ago, and resolved to discharge me from every professional duty, in public and in private, until the first of January next, meantime continuing to me my full salary. . . . The session also agreed that 'if my health was not restored on the first of January, then to continue to me a salary of $1,000, requiring of me no duty but such as I could render in my study, and that they would then proceed to call a collegiate pastor, whom they would support by voluntary contribution. This was extremely generous. They met in my study, and insisted that I should remain with them during the pending of these matters. My heart filled and my tears flowed. I can quietly endure the abuse of the wicked, but such kindness from God's people almost breaks my heart.'"

In a note on the margin of the page he adds:

"I should have stated that this action was taken by the session on my tendering to them, and through them to the church, the resignation of my pastoral charge."

From this letter two facts are perfectly clear: the first is, that Dr. White did not offer his resignation under a promise of the session to provide for him a maintenance as pastor emeritus. He could not have known what was at that time in their minds; and if he had, he could not have known whether the congregation would approve their act. "The action was taken," he says, "on my tendering to them, and through them to the church, the resignation of my pastoral charge."

His resignation was evidently the discharge of a duty, in which he walked by simple faith in God, who would overrule all things for good; it was going forward in the dark.

The second fact made evident by this letter is, that he could not have been misinformed or mistaken in what he wrote. It is rarely the case that so many details of any transaction are given in a friendly letter without any design for publication. The meeting was "a full one"; it was held only "a week" before he wrote; "in my study"; after their insisting on his remaining "with them during the pending of these matters"; they agreed to continue "a salary of $1,000"; .. "to call a collegiate pastor," and to provide for his support "by voluntary contributions." He then states the effect of their action upon his feelings in language identical with that on the last page of his "notes."

By this act of the session, Dr. White was led to open correspondence with a young minister, one who had grown up in the church, and for whom he felt a love so deep and strong that he was sure they could coöperate with cordiality. This young minister agreed to act as his colleague, and wrote to him accordingly.

For reasons which we have not been able to ascertain, the session changed their mind. The collegiate pastor was not employed. The first of January passed without such an improvement in his health as justified his resuming the full duty of the ministry in so large a church. Accordingly, on the 9th of March, 1867, he again tendered the formal resignation of his office, and asked the session and congregation to concur with him in an application to Presbytery to grant it. The session, in meeting March 12, 1867, acceded to his request, and at a congregational meeting, held April 13, 1867, his resignation was accepted. An effort was made to defeat this action by the offer of a substitute, declining to accept his resignation, and offering Dr. White an assistant. But the substitute was lost.

This action, though taken in congregational meeting, was not agreeable to the majority, and trouble began to arise. The division of the church was threatened. Dr. White, with characteristic self-forgetfulness, promptly prevented any such catastrophe. In a letter to his son George, dated May 27, 1867, after the words, "The strong aversion of many, nay, a large majority of the church, to unite in my request to Presbytery," he adds, "The desire was to procure an assistant. But this was opposed by a part of the session, and finally by all except Mr. ——. But I was firmly resolved, by the help of God, that there should be no division, no wrangling, and had a brief letter read from the pulpit by Dr. Kirkpatrick, which fully quieted the matter, and so the dissolution was effected with the utmost harmony."

When General Washington resigned his place at the head of the army with which he had won the nation's liberty, it was by general consent. When Cincinnatus resigned the dictatorship of Rome, and retired to his farm, he sought his personal ease. When Samuel, the last and noblest of the judges of Israel, stood aside from power and influence, 'twas because he was growing old, and the people were clamoring for a king. But Dr. White resigned at *sixty-six* years of age "from a firm conviction that your" (the church's) "best interests made it necessary," and by his personal influence prevailed on "the large majority" to submit to a party in the session.

The minister of the gospel who is called of God to the work never wants to "retire from business." The labor of his vocation is its own reward. The joy of that communion with the Lord which he finds in his work has a peculiar fascination for his mind. He has meat to eat that others know not of. And this is the reason why, of all men, he is the most reluctant to retire from work. Even when failing health, or the infirmities of old age, lay the necessity upon him, the heart pines to be at it again. It has been playfully said that "the grace of resignation is the last grace God gives a minister of the gospel."

When Dr. White was called to Lexington, in 1848, the living promised him by the church was $1,000, and the use of the manse. This was soon raised to $1,200, and was promptly paid throughout his ministry. Although the town of Lexington did not grow appreciably, yet such was the growth of the church in the time of his work among them, that immediately upon his retirement they called Dr. Moses Hoge, of Richmond, on a salary of $2,500 and manse. The church had become one of the strongest in the Synod in every way. Its size, compared with that of the town of twenty-five hundred inhabitants, was phenomenal. It would be difficult, if not impossible, to find a parallel case. The town was full of men and women who regarded him as their spiritual father. By his personal presence and sympathy, as a "son of consolation" during the war, he had carried the comfort of religion to almost every house.

To stand aside from such a pastorate, and see another take his place in the affections of the people; to have an effort to retain him on a living salary, as pastor emeritus, rejected, and see another called to do his work with a promise of twice the salary he had ever received, was calculated to stir up jealousy and a factious spirit. But just the opposite was conspicuously displayed. He interested himself in helping the people to get a minister; and when at last one came, he welcomed him with open arms, waited upon his ministry with docility, and upheld his hands in every way.

In a letter to his son George, dated July 25, 1868, he

writes: "I have made several excursions into the country to preach, and enjoyed it very much. I expect to preach here (Lexington) to-morrow for the first time in two years. . . . The last minister called to the pastorate of this church was the Rev. Mr. Lowry, of Selma, Alabama. But he too declines their call, and they meet again on the 3rd of August to make another effort. They are becoming terribly disheartened, and appearances at present portend a split. Some ill-feeling and some wrangling begin to appear. I was told recently from a high source, that if I would permit my name to be used I would be elected by acclamation. Of course I declined. I told him my work as pastor of this church was fully finished in July, 1866. But I do feel great anxiety about them."

Having resigned from a sense of duty, in the face of poverty and a homeless old age, he was not the man to return to office again. His step had been taken dispassionately, in the fear of God, and was therefore without repentance.

Not very long after this the Presbytery of Lexington met in Lexington. He attended its sittings awhile daily, and occupied a chair in front of the pulpit. "His appearance was very venerable and impressive," says the Rev. R. H. Fleming, who was a member of the court. "The moderator called on him to address the body, which he did with marked effect on all present." Among other things, showing the decision of his mind about the step he had taken, he said, with that warmth and forcefulness which was characteristic of him, "Brethren, forty years ago I heard the voice of God speaking to me and saying, 'Preach my gospel,' and now, with equal distinctness, I hear him saying, 'Stop preaching.'" The Rev. John A. Scott, of Duffield, W. Va., recollects, among other remarks, this, "I thank God he has permitted me to preach the gospel for forty years." Thus was he permitted, like the great apostle, to finish his course with joy

To have resigned at sixty-six years of age because his throat was sore, was surely a mistake. Events proved it so. Rest entirely restored him. To begin at that time of life a struggle for existence, under all the circumstances, seemed a desperate venture. But he saw no escape from it, after leaving his pulpit and manse.

He had laid by a small patrimony years before, and added something to it while teaching in Charlottesville. This was swept away by the war. His noble spirit would not allow him to accept a living from any while he had power to earn it for himself. The same greatness of heart that could not bear the thought of holding on by "sentimental sufferance" to a place in the church which he could not completely fill would not allow him to be a pensioner upon another's bounty. He could lay down his salary, vacate his home, and hazard all the ills of a penniless old age for the church which, by God's blessing, he had carried up to the front rank in the Synod of Virginia, but he could not eat the bread of idleness under any circumstances.

The Ann Smith Academy, a school of high-grade for young ladies, being vacant, and being "pressed upon" him, he accepted the position of principal, and entered upon its duties in September, 1868. An experience of twelve years in conducting a school of this sort in Charlottesville prepared his mind for the task before him. He knew all about its cares and toils. Yet he took hold, at the age of sixty-eight years, with characteristic courage, determined to throw into the enterprise all his enthusiasm and strength, and make it a success.

In a letter to one of his sons, dated July 25, 1868, he writes thus: "I am about to buckle on the harness as a teacher again. It would be impossible to find a more comfortable home than we have here. But I am idle, and this is enough to render any home distasteful. The trustees and many others press the Ann Smith Academy upon me. I hope to get Mr. Wm. Jordan and his wife to keep the house and accommodate the boarders, including your mother and me in the number. We shall accordingly vacate our delightful rooms here and take far inferior ones there. Your mother will take the little girls. May it please God to enable me to do something more in this line before I die. Now that he has given me a measure of health I never expected to enjoy again, I must use it in his service, or greatly sin."

His strength of purpose is seen in a letter to his brother-in-law, the Rev. John S. Watt:

"*November* 26, 1866.

"My Dear Brother: They talk of calling an assistant. But . . . . and others are opposed to this for the reason, as they express it, that it is less cruel to starve one man than two. If I resign, then, at over sixty-six years of age, I begin life afresh a great deal poorer than I was forty years ago. But I may have voice enough to teach, if not to preach, and if not, then use enough of this right hand to keep some merchant's books. God helping, neither you nor I need despair."

His wife entered with him into this work with her whole heart. She too, though nearly seventy years of age, became a teacher of girls, having her room and classes to which she gave her time every day.

There is something very touching and inspiring in this sight: two old people, who had spent their whole life in the service of God in the church, broken in fortune, enfeebled by age, of their own accord stepping down from prominence and competency, declining to live with their children because, as they often said, "if they could not help, they would not hinder" them, and going into the school-room to earn their bread "by the sweat of their face."

And they did it so meekly, so sweetly. Not a word of complaint fell from their lips, even in the hearing of those who knew them as children know loving and confiding parents. Like God-fearing saints they accepted the hard lot of a struggle for bread in old age as a dispensation of mercy from a loving heavenly Father. They went to their task without a murmuring word, nay, counting it a joy to "please God" by doing "something more in this line" before they died.

The boarding department of the school was entrusted to a friend of long standing, Mr. Wm. Jordan, who filled the place completely. The teaching was done by himself and wife, with the following faculty, viz.: Miss Francis Mary Exall, from Reading, England, who had entire charge of the music department; Miss Jane Reid Venable, of Farmville, Va., had charge of the preparatory department; Miss Mary Francis Witherspoon, of York, S. C., managed the department of higher English; Prof. D. Rodes Massie, the department of languages; Mr. Edwin C. Moorman, of Powhatan county, Va., taught mathematics. From the size and accomplishment of his staff, it is obvious that Dr. White's ideas had not diminished with age. Miss Witherspoon, having married Dr. Lewis Duncan Mason, of Brooklyn, N. Y., resides there, and is an authoress of increasing fame. Her husband is a distinguished physician and a lineal descendant of the very celebrated Rev. Dr. John M. Mason. Miss Exall married Mr Wm. Chaplin, member of Parliament from Torquay, and is now a widow.

Dr. White won the hearts of his assistant teachers as of his scholars. We have in hand a letter from Mrs. Dr. Mason, abundantly showing the truth of this statement, which on many accounts we would like to insert.

The school proved a success. It paid all expenses from the start, and yielded a surplus. But it soon became evident that the strain was too heavy for him, enfeebled, as he was, by old age, and his superabundant work and anxiety during the war. His strength gave out sooner than he expected. A succession of attacks, attended by sinking spells that exhausted his strength, after three years of work, convinced him and his children of his inability successfully to carry on the enterprise. His spirit was willing, but his flesh was weak. So, at the end of the third session, with the earnest advice of his sons, he volunteered his resignation to the Board of Trustees.

It was a common saying with him that he would not hold a place that felt itself independent of him, and which another could be gotten to fill better than he could. To hang on to a place for the loaves and fishes, his noble spirit could not brook. The place must hang on to him as indispensable to its interests. "Woe to a preacher," he used to say, "when he ceased to be indispensable to his church!"

The same motive led him to resign the principalship of the Academy that led to his resignation of his pulpit. He entered both as the servant of God, and, finding his work beyond his strength, turned it over to another. On two former occasions he had it seriously in mind to resign his pulpit, because he thought he might be more useful elsewhere. Thus, December 13, 1860, he writes to a friend: "I cannot help feeling that the time has come for me to seek a smaller and more obscure position. A few months ago I thought I should leave and embark in teaching a female school, but the Lord hedged up the way, or, rather, he seemed to do it." This refers probably to the effort of Dr. Joseph M. Atkinson to get him to take charge of the Institute for young ladies at Raleigh, N. C.

Again he sought the office of evangelist. February 19, 1858, he writes: "There has been a steadily deepening conviction on my mind for more than twelve months that a man may be found better fitted to fill my place than I now can. . . . Could I not resign my present charge for the office of evangelist, to be appointed and sustained, say, by West and East Hanover Presbyteries, with a special view to visit all the churches in their bounds, directing my labors mainly to the awakening of the ruling eldership and the increase of candidates for the ministry, extending my work into frontier and destitute portions of the land? . . . It does seem to me that, with the small modicum of *uncommon* sense, and the more respectable modicum of *common* sense, that God has given me, I could thus do more for the seminary, the colleges, the common schools, and the press of our church, in the little time now remaining to me, than in any other way."

Dr. Plumer says, as we have already seen, that no man *better understood his own powers* than Dr. White. He succeeded at everything he undertook throughout life. The merit of success always showed itself, whether teacher, or agent, or preacher, or presbyter. Even in the last effort of his life, as principal of Ann Smith Academy, he succeeded, as may be seen from the following letter:

"LEXINGTON, VA., *August* 3, 1871.
"REV. W. S. WHITE, D. D.:

"DEAR SIR: The Trustees of the Ann Smith Academy have instructed me to acknowledge the receipt of your letter of resignation. They accept the same, and in doing so, tender to you their hearty acknowledgments for the able manner in which, for three years, you have presided over the institution, and their sincere regrets that your health will not admit of your longer continuance at this post of usefulness. They express the sentiments of the whole community when they assure you that your resignation creates a vacancy which they cannot hope adequately to fill.

"Commending you to the care of the Father of mercies, they pray that your honored and useful life may be long spared in the midst of this community, where the marks of your abundant labors are everywhere visible.

"Very truly and respectfully, your friend and brother,
"JNO. W. PRATT, *Pres. of Board of Trustees.*"

CHAPTER XV.

1871–1873.

RETREATS TO THE HOME OF HIS DAUGHTER, MRS. HARRIET MCCRUM.—SERENE AND CHEERFUL OLD AGE.—HOW HE APPEARED TO HIS BRETHREN; *e. g.*, REV. G. W. LEYBURN AND REV. DR. WM. S. PLUMER.—HIS CHIEF DESIRE IN PROSPECT OF DEATH.—LEADS HIS PHYSICIAN TO CHRIST.—IMPRESSIVE INTERVIEW WITH JUDGE J. W. BROCKENBROUGH.—ANECDOTE OF HIS PATRIOTISM.

> "What if I sleep and then awake
>   On the future's distant shore;
> Where the rose of love and the lily of peace
>   Shall bloom forever more?
>
> "Then let the earth go round and round,
>   And the sun sink into the sea;
> For whether I'm on or under the ground,
>   Oh! what will it matter to me?"

THIS was in August, 1871. Old, infirm, homeless, he is at that sad time in life when our burdens are the heaviest and our power to bear or throw them off the least. He has made a last, despairing effort to serve his God, his church and his generation. He has sunk beneath the effort. Full proof has been made of his ministry. The judgment of his sons concurs with his own. He *must* give up to the inevitable. He hears the voice of God calling him out of the struggle to unbuckle his harness and be still. Bowing meekly and solemnly, yet with a sorrowing heart to think that he can do no more for that cause which he loves so dearly, he quits the field.

Unable to speak in public or teach a school, he yet has some ability with his pen, for the proper use of which he feels accountable. Under this conviction the "Notes" which compose the staple of this volume, and occasional articles for the religious press, were written. He was never idle, but used up the last shred of his time in the service of God.

This ardor and intensity were not confined to the church. He served his country as well. His love of country and her institutions, especially his native State, Virginia, would rouse him even from a sick bed. Long after he had left the walks of men, and confined himself to his sick room, learning that his friend, General Kemper, was before the people as a candidate for the governorship of the State, he was taken by his physician in a carriage, and on the arms of friends, to the polls, to cast his vote. As he was brought out of the courthouse, some one in the crowd exclaimed, "Game to the last;" and the *Lexington Gazette*, in its columns the next week, compared him to "Gideon at the fords of the Jordan, faint yet pursuing."

He was a Virginian to the marrow of his bones. In a letter to Dr. Wm. Brown, about their contemplated journey to the General Assembly in Rochester, New York, in 1860, he writes:

"I don't mean to dress up. I was buying a hat the other day, and the seller said, 'You'll not see one man in twenty with that sort of a hat on at the North.' Then, said I, it's the hat for me, because it's old Virginia."

Throughout life he felt a strong aversion to leaving his native State for any other, which was revived with power whenever he had to consider seriously a call to work in another.

Unable to serve his church or State in any other way than by the occasional use of his pen, he finds a delightful retreat in the home of his daughter, Mrs. Harriet McCrum. Reading, writing, playing with her children, and receiving his numerous friends, he spends a serene old age, "abounding in hope by the power of the Holy Ghost." Visitors often found it good and profitable to their souls to look into his cheerful countenance, and listen to his words of wholesome entertainment. His delight in conversation never failed him.

At times he sat alone and kept silence, while meditating on his inability to serve God in the ministry. At other times he was grieved because he had no home of his own, where his children and grandchildren might gather for social reunions. But his faith in God, and his "good hope of glory through grace," manifested themselves in so much peace and joy, that his conversation proved a fountain of pleasure to those who sought it.

That it may be seen how he appeared to others in his last days, as well as to his children, we give below several letters from men known throughout the church, whose ministry was cotemporaneous with his; *i. e.*, Rev. G. L. Leyburn, Sr., Rev. Dr. W. S. Plumer, Dr. Bissell, and Dr. J. L. Kirkpatrick.

[*For the Central Presbyterian.*]
"Testimony of a Departing Veteran.

"I was in Lexington, Va., between two and three weeks ago, and called to see our venerable friend, Dr. Wm. S. White. I had heard, previous to making the call, that he was so unwell as to be "laid up," but thought it might be a temporary indisposition, such as, at times, of late years, he had passed through. When I saw him, however, and heard him express himself, I began to think that he was probably soon to receive the Master's call. I thought I saw something of the seal of death upon his features. But his face never so impressed me, as a venerable and striking one, in the degree that it then did.

"He called me, almost as soon as I got in, to his bed-side; in his usual friendly way (which any one acquainted with him will remember), expressed his pleasure at seeing me; told me how much comfort he had had in the calls and the prayers with him of my brother, who resides in the vicinity, and repeated what he had at other times said of the friendship between them of so many years. . . . . . These words of his, spoken at such a juncture, have renewed in my mind the thought, how precious, how heaven-like, how immortal are Christian friendships!

"'The fellowship of kindred minds,
Is like to that above.'

"Then, asking me to lead in prayer by his bed-side, he said, 'Brother L——, I am getting near; but I am peaceful— I am peaceful.' And then he added, seeming to me particularly to wish to utter this testimony: 'I have spent forty-two years in the gospel ministry; I have no regrets for that; I am thankful that I have spent so much of my life in that work.'

"Making the prayer as he had requested, when I rose from it I saw that he seemed still for a few moments engaged in silent devotion, with his arms resting on the elbows upon his breast, and his hands stretching upwards Then turning to me, he repeated his testimony, I think as to his peace of mind in the prospect of the great change (and he needed not to tell me on what that rested), as well as in respect to his ministry.

"I expected and wished to see him again, for the chamber where such a servant of God meets his end is a privileged place; it is a vestibule of heaven; we may obtain more than we confer in the visit to the departing one. But it so happened that I did not get there again; it was therefore my last earthly interview with him. . . .

"WINCHESTER, VA., *December*, 1873.   G. W. L."

[*From the New York Observer.*]

"LETTER FROM DR. PLUMER TO LEVI A. WARD, ESQ., OF ROCHESTER, N. Y.

"MY DEAR, KIND FRIEND: You will remember that blessed meeting of the General Assembly of the Presbyterian Church in your city in 1860. I can never forget it. At its opening Dr. Spring offered one of the most copious and edifying prayers I have ever heard. Although it was twice as long as the prayers we commonly hear before sermon, yet all were sorry when he ceased to plead at the mercy-seat.

"The prayer was followed by a very practical and powerful discourse from Rev. Dr. Wm. A. Scott, of California. The preacher had just crossed the Rocky Mountains by the 'pony express.' For eleven days and nights he had travelled continuously, not knowing, for a considerable part of the way, what moment the Indians, then hostile and excited, might make a murderous attack on the party. But God spared his useful life, and he preached to us with simplicity and power.

'The Assembly thus opened was remarkable for many things. It was large. It did much important business. The hospitality shown by you and your neighbors was boundless. An excellent temper governed the Assembly. There was an abundance of good preaching. It was the last Assembly that invited any Southern man to fill any high post in the North. It was the last Assembly in which the South was represented. . . . But a chief object in writing to you is to say something of the last days of the Rev. Dr. Wm. S. White, who recently died at Lexington, Va., honored and beloved in all the land.

"You will remember him as somewhat lame. Your considerate Committee of Arrangements kindly placed him at a fine hotel hard by the church. Here he was handsomely entertained. Out of the Assembly and in waking hours he was almost constantly surrounded by a pleasant group of gentlemen, most of whom had never seen him before. They were attracted by his manly and noble countenance, by his easy, courteous and affable manners, by his marked humility, and by his ardent love to Christ and his people. Often have they spoken of the love and admiration he drew forth by his winning ways.

"At his death Dr. White was seventy-three years old. He had been a preacher forty-eight years. In his life he had done a great work for the Tract Society. He had, at different times, controlled two very important female schools. He had been chaplain at the University of Virginia. He had had charge of four different churches. He delighted in pastoral work. His pulpit was his throne. His people were his joy and crown. I think you would like to hear something of the last days of this great and good man.

"About eight years ago Dr. White's throat or lungs became somewhat affected. He suffered more or less till near the close of his life, when a bad cold aggravated all his symptoms. He lived a few weeks and then was no longer on earth. To him death had no terrors. It was the highway to the joy of his Lord. For some months before his decease Dr. White had confidently anticipated a very early departure out of time into eternity. Yet he was always happy to see his friends, particularly his brethren in the ministry. Thinking and talking of death did not distress him. He spoke of leaving the world with as much composure as if he were going on a visit to one of his children. He said he had lived his allotted time on earth. Except for the sundering of ties very tender and strong, the prospect of dying did not cost him a pang. He would have greatly rejoiced to be allowed to preach the blessed gospel, but he never murmured at the silence enforced upon him by disease. He said, 'I have been greatly honored in being allowed, in my poor way, to preach the glorious gospel, and now my Master, who called me first to preach, wills me to sit still and be silent; and I will try and obey him in a proper and becoming manner, as a Christian ought, with patience and resignation to his holy will. If I know my own heart, I desire to glorify God in sickness and in health.'

"The old adversary, the lion of the evening, would not let this old hero of the cross pass away without annoyance. He sometimes disturbed him with fears that he would yet be left to fall into some sin that would greatly dishonor

God. Again he suggested that his sins were too great for God to forgive. But these conflicts were short. The truths, 'My grace is sufficient for thee,' and 'He is able to save to the uttermost,' were blessed to drive away the arch enemy.

"Dr. White's interest in the church of Christ grew stronger and stronger to the end. He delighted in hearing of any progress the gospel was making in any part of the world. He took great interest in the proceedings of the Evangelical Alliance. As his vision was good (he had second sight), he read with great pleasure everything he could get on the subject. He said he thought it augured well for the church of Christ. He loved God's people of every name. The hymns beginning—

"'I lay my sins on Jesus,
The spotless Lamb of God,'

and—

"'Jesus, lover of my soul,
Let me to thy bosom fly,'

were as soothing cordials to him.

"With the exceptions already stated, Dr. White's peace was like a river. It was the peace of God that passeth all understanding. Lying very still for a while, one heard him say, 'I want to go home.' Supposing his mind might be wandering, one said, 'You are at home.' He replied, 'Oh! yes, I am at my earthly home, but I want to go to my heavenly home, to be with Jesus. Here I have a good, sweet home, with my dear wife and children, and it will be a great trial to part with you all. But I want to go to my heavenly home. I have two precious sons gone before. Will not they rejoice to welcome their old father to glory? And will it not be joyful to see my blessed Saviour and Redeemer in his glory and dwell with him for ever?'

"To the wife of his youth he said, 'Look up to God, my

dear one. Jehovah will be your Husband, your Father and your Friend. It will not be long before you follow me.'

"He knew his Saviour as long as he knew anything. His full and final release was apparently without pain. He fell asleep in Jesus.

"Thus there has left us as true, as generous, as candid, as faithful, and as loving a man as you will find in a lifetime.

"My love to all around you.

"Faithfully yours, WM. S. PLUMER."

[*From the New York Observer.*]
"THE LATE WILLIAM S. WHITE, D. D.

"MESSRS. EDITORS: The recent tribute of Dr. Plumer to his old friend, Dr. White, in the *Observer* touches the heart of another friend in the North.

"Nearly forty years ago it was the privilege of the writer to be Dr. White's assistant, and then his successor, in the general agency of the Virginia Tract Society, just entering upon the 'volume enterprise' of the American Tract Society, inaugurated after a noble speech made by Dr. Plumer before them at their anniversary, May, 1834. His fellow-worker begs leave to bear his attestation to what the distinguished professor has so well and so justly said of one of the most true, devout, and earnest servants of Christ in Virginia during the last forty years, and to drop this simple immortelle on the grave of the honored and beloved pastor and friend of his youthful ministry. S. B. S. B."

The Rev. Dr. J. L. Kirkpatrick, Professor of Philosophy in Washington and Lee University, wrote of him to *The Central Presbyterian*, viz.:

---

[1] This is Dr. Bissell, now of New York city, who assisted Dr. White in his early manhood in the American Tract Agency in Virginia.

"His life—whole life—is such a testimony that nothing could have been added to its value by the experiences of the dying hour. It was a life of unremitted, self-denying labor in the service of the Redeemer as long as strength was given him to stand in the pulpit, or a voice to proclaim the offers of salvation to a perishing world, and afterward to its close a life of suffering, but of suffering that no less decisively evinced his love to the Saviour than his most devoted labors in preaching the gospel; it was borne in such a sweet spirit of Christ-like resignation; through it all he, the patient, was so bright and hopeful. Never has it been my happiness to witness a more 'beautiful old age,' or so cheerful, nay, so cheering, a sick room.

"Who of the ministers of our church, belonging to the generation in which we live, is more worthy of as high a tribute of commendation and honor as it is lawful for man to bestow on man? I am sure that no member of our Synod possessed in a larger measure the confidence and love of all his brethren and of the Christian people of the State. If he was more loved and esteemed in Lexington than elsewhere, it was only because we saw more of him than others did and knew him better."

The governing motive of his life was strong to the last—to honor God. He used to quote with approbation a remark of Dr. Doddridge: "I am more afraid of dishonoring God than of dying;" and frequently said he was much afraid he would yet, in some way, bring reproach on the gospel of Christ.

In a letter to his son George, dated October 26, 1867, after he had resigned his pastoral charge, and when confined to the house with sickness, he thus wrote: "Your reflections as to God's dealings with me are just and seasonable, and I cannot express the comfort I feel at being thus written to by a dear son. I need instruction and counsel from every quarter, for I am passing through the deep waters. My condition is novel, and, in some respects, so trying, that unless I receive large supplies of grace, I shall not end my mortal life in accordance with my long-cherished and oft-repeated principles. *I greatly desire that the closing scenes of life may not be marred by any deformity or blot.* May God, in whom I have ever lived, be my guide unto death." In his last days he often, very often, quoted Psalm lxxi. 18: "Now also, when I am old and gray-headed, O God, forsake me not, until I have shewed thy strength unto this generation, and thy power to every one that is to come."

His physician, Dr. J. W. McClung, had a large practice, was about sixty years of age, the head of a family, and was accounted one of the best men by nature in the community. But he was not a Christian; had never given himself to the Lord Jesus, nor publicly confessed him. Dr. White's heart was moved for him so deeply that he strove to show him the error of his ways and bring him to God. Nor did he abandon his purpose until it was consummated. On his dying bed he had the joy of leading to Christ him who ministered to his body.

LETTER FROM REV. T. P. EPES.

"WOODSTOCK, VA., *May* 23, 1889.

"DEAR BROTHER WHITE: Some time ago, while we were resting in our room at Dr. Hopkins', on our return from Presbytery at Shepherdstown, I promised to put in writing for you some account of some incidents in your father's sick chamber a few weeks or months before he 'fell on sleep.'

"You must pardon the delay in executing the promise then made in Charlestown. You know, the pages of memory are like palimpsest manuscripts, written over many a time. Nothing is ever lost, but often the process of restoration is tedious, and, for accuracy, requires a leisure hour to bring out clearly the underwriting. Even now I cannot relate to you the details of these occasions in such vividness and tenderness as will account for the fixed impression upon me, as permanent as life. I was a susceptible boy then, and from childhood had been taught to hold your father in veneration, though I had never known him till I entered Washington and Lee University as a student, in September, 1870.

"A few evenings before the first visit of which we were speaking, the families of Mr. McCrum and Professor White had been called to his bedside, at bedtime I think. He had sunken through weakness into a state of inability to communicate with those about him, and had lost knowledge of his outward surroundings; yet the continuity of consciousness in the soul was not suspended, and rational thought was not interrupted.

"Locked in in this state, he comprehended the cause, that it was from physical exhaustion. This he took to be death. This conviction first forced itself upon him on discovering his loss of power to communicate with those around him, while as yet he was still cognizant of their presence. His spirit yearned to say some tender word of farewell to each one in the room, especially to speak once again to your brother Tom. 'There' (waving his hand) 'sat my boy Tom, and I did want to plead with him once more to come to Jesus, and could not.' For a time his heart was bitterly pained and distressed at leaving him still out of Christ. 'But,' said he, 'it was only for a little while, for I felt sure that a covenant-keeping God would bring him to me after I was gone.' And as he spoke this confidence to us, his face lighted up with the assurance of hope, emanating from a faith which is the substance of the things we hope for. 'And,' he added, 'he will do it.'

"Presently his senses became so feeble that they failed even to bring in a knowledge of his surroundings, though the mind was still active and clear. Now, as he thought he was passing away, eager expectancy of the imminent meeting with the Lord filled him with glad emotion, which beamed in his eye then while he spoke.

"Later in the night his physical powers revived, his senses were re-opened, and he discovered, with bitter disappointment, that he had not passed from earth, but was returned to life in the flesh.

"Thus, in substance, he related this strange experience. I wish I could give it to you in his own words, of which a number inhere in the above account in its descriptive terms.

"As he was talking, a shadow of compunction suddenly came over his face. His lips quivered, and his countenance told unmistakably that the tears which were streaming from his eyes were tears of repentance. This he explained immediately by saying, 'And it was wrong; if God wants me to stay, he has something for me to do, and I ought not to want to go; but I cannot see what it is.'

"I have seen men in pangs of remorse for sin; I have seen them in the agony of conviction of sin; I have seen them in sweet contrition under a sense of sin pardoned; but nothing has ever produced such an impression of the sinfulness of sin as the sight of this aged servant of the Lord, ripe like a shock of corn, weeping in godly sorrow for that which before we had always esteemed a grace and a triumph of faith; and nothing has ever revealed to me more clearly the essence of sin as 'lack of resignation to God's will' as he defined it.

"One of us said to him, 'Doctor, you have much to live for; *you have taught us what sin is.*' My companion during this visit was young John McCoy, my room-mate, who is now a useful elder in the church of his native town, Franklin, Pendleton county, West Virginia. The exhibition of the fact that faith may be of such a character as to bring quiet and calmness even to a dying father when leaving a yet unsaved son, and without ability to speak once more to him, impressed him, he tells me, more than anything else in this deep spiritual experience of your father. It was indeed marvellous. It reminded him of the faith of Abraham, when preparing to offer Isaac. This faith in the covenanted mercy of God, you tell me, has been justified by the conversion of your brother since; and we have an exemplification of the fact, that to take such comfort from faith is reasonable.

"A week later, perhaps, I was again with your father. This time alone, if I remember aright. During the visit Judge Brockenbrough came into the room. Hearing of his restoration from this collapse prompted him to stop on his way home from his afternoon law lecture, as it had occasioned my call.

"You remember Judge Brockenbrough's august, portly presence, his massive head, his strong shaggy brow, his judicial face. He, too, was growing infirm and clumsy and unwieldy to himself from age. He drew his chair to your father's bedside, close by his pillow, and expressed his gratification at finding him restored in such measure to strength and comfort. Dr. White thanked him, and related somewhat of his recent experience, emphasizing that to depart and be with Christ would be far better. Judge Brockenbrough spoke feelingly of the priceless comfort of such a Christian state, and expressed with genuine pain his regret that such comfort and peace were not his in view of his own approaching end.

"Your father then took his hands in one of his, and placing the other upon his shoulder, or head, as the Judge bent forward over his bed, assured him that such a peaceful state might be his; told him that often he had thought of and prayed for him in preaching, commended our Lord as a Saviour to him, and persuasively said to him, that to see him a Christian was one desire of his heart which he longed to have granted before his departure.

"During the conversation, Judge Brockenbrough's frame shook and trembled, and tears trickled down his cheeks. In answer to these appeals he several times ejaculated, 'I will try,' 'I hope so,' and finally, asking his prayers, he rose from his chair, their hands still clasped in gentle pressure. For a moment in silence they looked into each other's faces, and then the Judge turned and moved, in deep thought, from the room, without another word on the part of either.

"I too, scarcely daring to speak 'good bye,' followed quietly down stairs, feeling indeed that God did have something for him to do. I know nothing of Judge Brockenbrough's religious history afterwards. My impression is that he died in the communion of the Episcopal Church.

"I have never witnessed a tenderer scene between men, nor one which more strongly illustrated the supremacy of 'things unseen and eternal.' As these two old men talked about these things, their frankness, their simplicity, their earnestness was sublime, and comported with nothing but realities. The world was behind them. They were on the confines of eternity; they knew where they were standing, and did not hide the serious verity of the position from each other. I saw it, and watched them in awe. . . .

"One incident of the first visit to your father's room I forgot to mention. Your mother was sitting in her usual quiet way by the window towards which his bed faced. As he was expressing his longing for heaven, he waved his hand towards her and said, 'Not because I want to leave you, but because I want to be with him (pointing upwards), and you will come soon.'

"Affectionately yours,
"T. P. Epes."

Dr. White completely recovered from his throat complaint that forced him to suspend his ministry. His appetite became strong and his lungs perfectly sound. His mind was as clear and vigorous as ever. Yet he fell sick in an unaccountable manner. Sinking spells, like the one seen by Mr. Epes, with unconsciousness, lasting for several days, followed one another at intervals of different length.

In one of these intervals, his physician, seeing the end approaching, cautiously and sorrowfully communicated his fears to him, saying: ' Doctor, I am very sorry to have to inform you that, in my judgment, you have not long to live, and to suggest that if you have any preparation to make you had better do so at once."

The dying man looked up, and asked: "Doctor, how long do you think I may live?"

"Only a few days, at most," said the physician.

"Well," rejoined the patient, "you need not be sorry to tell me that;" and, with a brightening countenance, added, "*That's the best news I've heard for twenty years.*"

During these attacks his friends would generally lose hope. Yet the flame would shoot up in the socket again; he would rally, and seem as well as usual. At last the appointed hour came. This time the attack lasted several days, and, on November 29, 1873, about twelve o'clock M., he sank so gently that they who were looking upon him could with difficulty say when he fell asleep.

CHAPTER XVI.

MEMORIAL NOTICES OF DR. AND MRS. WHITE.

BY THE SESSION OF THE CHURCH.—LINES BY MRS. M. J. PRESTON.— BY THE SYNOD OF VIRGINIA.—THE FACULTY OF WASHINGTON AND LEE UNIVERSITY.—THE "CENTRAL PRESBYTERIAN."—REV. JOHN S. GRASTY, D. D.—REV. DR. BALCH.—LINES BY REV. DR. J. A. WADDELL.—MEMORIALS OF MRS. WHITE.—BY THE SESSION OF THE CHURCH AND MRS. PRESTON.

> "His life was bright—bright without spot it *was*,
> And cannot cease to be. No ominous hour
> Knocks at his door with tidings of mishap.
> Far off is he, above desire and fear;
> No more submitted to the change and chance
> Of the unsteady planets. Oh! 'tis well
> With *him!*"

BY THE SESSION OF THE CHURCH.

THE following minute was adopted and ordered to be spread upon the records of session:

"In tender remembrance of our former pastor, who served this church in the gospel ministry for nearly twenty years, with devout gratitude to God for the blessings conferred through his instrumentality, that we may stimulate ourselves to renewed diligence in our calling, and that we may present to those who may succeed in bearing rule over the church an example worthy of all imitation, we place upon our records the following brief memorial of the Rev. Wm. S. White, D.D., who departed this life at the residence of his son-in-law, Mr. J. T. McCrum, November 29, 1873, in the seventy-fourth year of his age:

"He was born in Hanover county, Va., in the year 1800. He received his collegiate education at Hampden-Sidney College, pursued his theological studies at Union Seminary, and began to preach June, 1827. His degree of "D. D." he received from Princeton College, 1851. He labored first as a domestic missionary in the counties of Nottoway, Amelia, Dinwiddie and Lunenburg. From Nottoway he went to Scottsville, Albemarle county, where he remained two years. About this time his energy and practical skill in dealing with men pointed him out as an agent for the American Tract Society, which post he filled with eminent zeal and efficiency. In the year 1836 he went to Charlottesville, where he was at the same time pastor of the church and the founder of a female school, which took its place among the most popular institutions of learning at that time in Virginia. He was also, during his residence at Charlottesville, chaplain for two terms at the University of Virginia, and in 1848 he received and accepted a unanimous call from this church to become its pastor. This connection, commenced at a critical period in the history of this congregation, was continued, with unchanging fidelity on his part and with undiminished love on the part of his people, and without a day's disturbance by offence or misunderstanding on either side, until it was solemnly terminated by the providence of God, which disabled him for active duty any longer. How much grace, wisdom, prudence, integrity, self-control, watchfulness and labor was demanded to accomplish this result can be fully comprehended only by those who were connected with the affairs of this church immediately preceding his pastorate, and who mourned over the existing strife, bitterness and heart-burning, and who trembled at the imminent danger of schism that would be irreconcilable. How thankful were we to a gracious Master who rescued us from this danger, and how we admired our pastor, who with firm but gentle hand gathered us into harmony again!

"Nor was pacification the only or the chief blessing of which he was the instrument. It pleased God greatly to enlarge the membership of our church. During his first year forty-two were added by examination, in 1854 forty-two more, in 1857 sixty-one; and even in the last year of his enfeebled labor there were nineteen additions, while each intervening year, though less notable, bore steady fruit. Few of God's ministers in modern times excelled Dr. White in pastoral work. His varied acquaintance with men, and his Christian sympathy, made him trusted as a counsellor and sought for as a comforter. Every one felt at ease in the presence of so genial a representative of Christianity, while at the same time he never was tempted into levity unbecoming his sacred profession. All his varied excellences were conspicuous and charming in him as moderator of session. Surrounded by his brethren and advisers he seemed to feel the confidence in them which he inspired for himself. Always well acquainted with the business in hand, but never dogmatic, he skillfully guided the deliberations of the body to a harmonious conclusion. Never while he presided over this session was there a single instance of unkindliness manifested among the members, and very generally the decisions were unanimous. As a member of the higher courts of the church he was influential in his wisdom, his familiarity with the business before the body, his unselfishness, and his attractive manner of speaking. His standing with his brethren and his position in the church at large were all that he could wish, and the more honorable that, being unsought, they were unembittered by jealousy. Nor was he more remarkable for the ability and steadfastness with which he supported his own branch of the church than for his charity to all sister churches. Nor did he take his distinguished place because he was thrown only among men of mediocrity. He was the cotemporary, with more or less difference of age, of such ministers in the Synod of Virginia as Dr. Benjamin Rice, Dr. Baxter, Dr. Speece, Dr. Ruffner, Dr. McFarland, Dr. Jesse Armistead, Dr. McGuffey, Dr. Plumer, and others. Likewise, by his residence at the University and at Lexington, he was subjected to the test of comparison with men noted for more than usual culture. Also in his day some great questions were agitated. He met with Jeffersonian infidelity about Charlottesville; he acted in the controversy which divided the Presbyterian Church in the United States; he was in the midst of the great revival period, with its power and errors; the temperance movement, with its true philanthropy and hurtful fanaticism, called for his consideration; and in his latter days the relations of church and state were presented to view in our late struggle. He watched by the cradle of Union Seminary, and labored all his life for its success.

"It is not meant to claim for Dr. White any exaggerated importance in connection with any of these great questions, but it is simple truth and justice to affirm that never in regard to any of them did he commit a serious error.

"Thus did it please God in his providence to test his servant by the vicissitudes of a life unusually varied, and thus, in the judgment of those who knew him best (must we not believe, by the judgment of his Master?) he proved himself true in every relation of life—as husband, father, citizen, preacher, pastor, Christian. And one test yet remained—the last. He had come to us when we were torn by distraction, and we saw how, by the grace of God, he could show the power of religion in calming the stormy waves of passion. Infirmity came upon him, and he exhibited that rare grace of humility in counting himself unable for the work that was before him, and so he gave up the church he loved, and that loved him, into the hands of another. And yet another lesson he was to learn, and teach us while he was learning it: the work that he loved was just on the one hand, and the crown was just on the other; but he was not permitted either to do the work or to take the crown; but, between the two, he was called on to lie upon a couch of languishing, and wait for the words, 'Well done, enter thou.' He waited and taught us to wait, and he has entered into the joy of his Lord.

"We did not drape in black the church for his funeral. Why should we? There was nothing mournful there. Elisha did not mourn when he saw the chariot that bore Elijah from mortal vision; he cried, 'My father! my father! The chariot of Israel, and the horsemen thereof!'—anxious only not to lose the ascending prophet's mantle. And so we, if we may but share our pastor's spirit, needed not to weep when we saw a full life brought to a full end, and stood as a congregation with bended heads to receive his benediction at the close of the noblest sermon he ever preached—the sermon of a perfect life."

The following lines, adopted by the session, were composed by Mrs. Margaret J. Preston, and had the following caption:

"HARVESTED.

"WILLIAM S. WHITE, D. D., DIED IN LEXINGTON, VA., NOVEMBER 29, 1873, AGED SEVENTY-THREE.

"It was late in a life's calm autumn;
　The green on the blades grew sere;
And ripened, and rich, and mellow,
　The corn was filling the ear.

"In the flush of the budding springtime,
　Had the living seed been sown;
And under the dews of heaven,
　In shade and in shine had grown.

"The heat of the noon would wither,
　At times, its marrowy leaves;
It bent to the brunt of the tempests
　That darkened the summer eves.

"He knew how to temper and portion
　The sunlight, the cloud, the air;
He knew what its root most needed,
　He saw what its blades could bear

"And once and again he lopped it,
  For sake of the fruit, he said;
And bravely it bore the wounding,
  Tho' under the hurt—it bled.

"And so, when the dim November
  Came with its mists at morn,
And the autumn frost into whiteness
  Was bleaching the tassel'd corn;

'When the golden ears were fruitened,
  And the grain was sweet to the core,
Then the Master, who saw it needed
  To stand in the field no more—

"For the cold and the mould of winter
  To shrivel and shrink its leaf—
Said, *Put in thy sickle, Reaper,
  And garner my full-ripe sheaf!*"

At a meeting of the session of the Lexington Presbyterian Church it was—

"*Resolved*, That Dr. Pratt be requested to deliver a discourse memorial of the life and character of Dr. White."

BY THE SYNOD OF VIRGINIA, IN WINCHESTER, OCTOBER, 1874.

"The Rev. William Spottswood White departed this life in Lexington, Va.

"He was born in the county of Hanover, Va., July 30, 1800. His parents were connected with the congregation gathered in that part of the colony by the Rev. Samuel Davies. His collegiate education was at Hampden-Sidney, and while a student of that institution the ministry of its venerable president, Dr. Moses Hoge, was blessed in awakening such convictions of sin as led to his conversion.

"His theological studies were pursued under the instruction of the Rev. John H. Rice, D. D., and he was one among the first students under that eminent professor of theology in Union Seminary. He was licensed to preach the gospel by Hanover Presbytery in 1827. His first field of labor was in the counties of Nottoway, Amelia, Lunenburg and Dinwiddie, but after one year it was mainly in Nottoway. Sometime during his service in this county he was ordained to the full work of the ministry.

"In June, 1832, he removed to Scottsville, Va., and was installed as pastor of the church in that place. After two years of service here, during which his labors were greatly prospered and the church greatly increased, he accepted an appointment as General Agent of the Virginia (a branch of the American) Tract Society, with a special reference to the 'volume enterprise,' which was resigned after two years of arduous and very useful work.

"In May, 1836, he was settled as pastor of the church in Charlottesville, giving for a time a portion of his labors to the neighboring churches of Bethel and South Plains. During his residence here he conducted a large and prosperous female school, and was twice elected as chaplain to the University of Virginia.

"In September, 1848, Dr. White, having accepted a call to become the pastor of the Presbyterian Church in Lexington, Va., removed to that place, which was his home till called to rest from his labors.

"Such is a mere outline of the principal events of this long and useful ministry. If filled up with the details which might be supplied, it would present before us the portrait of a beloved, devoted servant of Christ, worthy of the admiration of all and to be held in everlasting remembrance. Our departed brother was a man of uncommon endowments. With no relish for metaphysical subtleties, or abstruse speculations of any sort, he had a solid, vigorous understanding, a thoroughly good common sense, a wide knowledge of men and the springs of human action, together with a remarkable tact in finding access to them. He was an able, earnest, impressive and most successful preacher, with a rare gift for illustrating the subject in hand, both by similitudes and by incidents of general history, or those which had come under his own observation. In every field in which he was called to labor his ministry had an ample seal of the divine blessing. His fine social qualities, together with his tender sympathy, amiable, pacific disposition, and fervent piety, endeared him to all as a friend and pastor. He was an eminently wise, good and loving husband and father, and his household was a scene of affection and peace. In every relation of life he was an example worthy of imitation. His end was full of Christian peace; his memory is precious among us, and his name remains among the good and the great which so profusely adorn and enrich the history of the Synod of Virginia. We thankfully adore that grace by which Christ has been magnified, both in his life and in his death."

The following account of the memorial services of the Synod of Virginia, at which the foregoing paper was adopted, is taken from *The Young Virginian*, a monthly periodical edited by the Rev. William T. Price:

"SYNODICAL MEMORIAL SERVICES.

"The services referred to occurred on Saturday morning, October 24, 1874, at Winchester, Va. The first hours of the session had been chiefly occupied in hearing reports from committees.

"Dr. William Brown's paper was an affectionate tribute to the memory of Rev. W. S. White, D. D., whose useful labors in Nottoway, Scottsville, Charlottesville and Lexington, along with abundant services in other departments and places, and exemplary Christian life, have rendered his name very precious to the whole church.

"Profound silence reigned over the assembly, and every sentence was heeded that told how good and faithful brethren had toiled, triumphed and died. After a momentary pause, upon the conclusion of the memorial, Rev. Dr. Preston, of the First Church, Richmond. one of Dr. White's spiritual sons, felt constrained by his emotions to arise, and, with words tremulous with filial admiration, bore touching witness to the usefulness of that pastor, in his opinion the grandest and best of his race. He hoped that other brethren would be encouraged to labor on in hope, so that, when they passed away, some spiritual son would rise up and call their memory blessed.

"Dr. Pryor, the friend of Dr. White's youth, who had known him intimately all his ministerial life, referred sweetly to the lovely and pleasant relations that had ever existed between them.

"He called attention to the fact, that while Dr. White was received into the church by Dr. Hoge, and had been greatly influenced by his ministry, yet the first permanent and saving impressions were made by the fidelity of the Rev. E. Pollard, an humble and obscure licentiate. This person, a licensed minister, never received a call, and was never ordained. He visited the outposts of Hanover Presbytery, trying to do good wherever he could induce any to hear him.

"Mr. Pollard became much interested in young White's spiritual welfare, and having met him one Sabbath afternoon near Hampden-Sidney, he conversed with him on the subject of religion, and the student was savingly impressed.

"This fact was mentioned, Dr. Pryor said, to encourage brethren in humble spheres of service to work for Jesus, and he may use their works in bringing about grand results.

"Dr. B. M. Smith felt that, as mention had been made of Dr. Moses Hoge's influence, it was also due to the memory of the Rev. Mr. Pollard to say, that his instructions had been rendered very influential by the divine blessing in moulding the character of the useful pastor, Dr. White, whose life the Synod now commemorated.

"The frequency with which God blesses humble men in working out great results should be an encouragement to us all to *labor in season and out of season*. The speaker agreed to what had been said of Dr. White, that, while great and noble, he succeeded because he looked for and received power from above, and so consecrated his time, talents and opportunities. Like greatness and usefulness might be attained by us all, were each to make the life-long effort to use faithfully the gifts bestowed upon him, and to seek continually the indwelling of the Holy Spirit.

"The last to speak was the Rev. Dr. Kirkpatrick, whose privilege it was to enjoy precious seasons of prayer and conversation with Dr. White in his last days. On the speaker's return from the previous meeting of Synod, he heard of his alarming illness, and hastened at once to his bedside. What he said in that interview amounted to this: 'My work on earth is done, and I wish to be where I can begin anew my Saviour's service.'

"On the evening preceding his death, he was heard to say, 'I want home.' It was supposed that delirium had returned, and one said to him, 'You are at home.' 'O yes,' he said, 'I know I am at home, and a better home none need ever want; but I want the home where my Saviour is.'

"He soon after went home. A place had been prepared for him, and Jesus had come, as he promised. Truly it is a great blessing to be able to look upon heaven as our home.

"At this point it happily occurred that a ministerial brother, the Rev. J. M. Clymer, proposed that Synod would unite in singing these stanzas of the 635th hymn:

> "'I would not live alway, I ask not to stay,
> Where storm after storm rises dark o'er the way;
> The few lurid mornings that dawn on us here,
> Are enough for life's woes, full enough for its cheer.

"'I would not live alway, thus fettered by sin,
Temptation without, corruption within.
E'en the rapture of pardon is mingled with fears,
And the cup of thanksgiving with penitent tears.

"'Who, who would live alway, away from his God,
Away from yon heaven, that blissful abode,
Where the rivers of pleasure flow o'er the bright plains,
And the noontide of glory eternally reigns—

"'Where the saints of all ages in harmony meet,
Their Saviour and brethren transported to greet;
While the anthems of rapture unceasingly roll,
And the smile of the Lord is the feast of the soul?'

"These appropriate words were sung with much emotion, and then all bowed in prayer, while the minister who had prayed at the bedside of the dying pastor, 'who wanted home,' led the Synod. It was asked of God that the memorials just read might be the means of encouraging the brethren to gird anew for the conflicts before them, and that all may be so admonished to number their days as to apply their hearts unto wisdom. Upon rising from prayer, the motion was put, in a tender and subdued tone, and carried, that unanimously adopted the memorials, and ordered them to be recorded.

"Not a member present will soon forget that memorable hour, and all hearts seemed fused in one by the hallowed influences that reigned over the vast assembly. It was a solemn and tender prelude to the services of another memorial scene, to which many were looking forward on the following Sabbath afternoon. It is well to make solemn and special mention of the holy dead:

"'For the bright memories of the holy dead,
The blessed ones departed, shine on us,
Like the pure splendors of some clear, large star,
Which pilgrims, travelling onward, at their back
Leave, and at every moment see not now;
Yet whensoe'er they list, may pause and turn,
And with its glories gild their faces still.'"

BY THE FACULTY OF WASHINGTON AND LEE UNIVERSITY.

"WASHINGTON AND LEE UNIVERSITY, *Dec.* 1, 1873.

"At a meeting of the Faculty held this day, the following minute touching the death of Rev. William S. White, D. D., was adopted:

"The Faculty of Washington and Lee University have received with profound sorrow the intelligence of the death, on the 29th ult., of the venerable Dr. Wm. S. White, for many years pastor of the Presbyterian Church in this place, and during a part of that time member of the Board of Trustees of this institution. He was also the father of an esteemed colleague, Professor J. J. White. Throughout the term of his residence in our community, Dr. White was the active, untiring friend of this institution, and, in every way possible to him, sought to promote its interests. His influence over its students, both from the pulpit and in private intercourse, was great and ever salutary. For these services we must long hold his name in grateful and honorable remembrance.

"Apart from the claims on our regards above mentioned, Dr. White was worthy of the highest respect for his eminent usefulness as a minister of the gospel, and for the almost unequalled confidence and affection bestowed on him, not by the members of his own communion only, but also by those of other branches of the Christian church, and by the public at large. He was a man of an enlarged catholic spirit, of wide benevolence and most attractive piety, an able advocate of truth and righteousness, a true type of the Christian gentleman.

"The Faculty further express their gratification with the order of the President suspending for this day all academic exercises, that the members of the University may attend the obsequies of one so well entitled to all the respect they could pay to his memory."

"From the minutes of the Faculty.   WM. DOLD, *Clerk.*"

An editorial in *The Central Presbyterian*, by the Rev. Dr. Wm. Brown:

"DEATH OF REV. WM. S. WHITE, D. D.

"This venerable minister of the gospel 'entered into rest' on Saturday, the 29th ult. His age was seventy-three years. While the intelligence of his departure cannot surprise any who knew that his health had been for years quite infirm, yet there are very many who will think with sorrow that they can see his face no more, never again hear a voice which so earnestly and powerfully proclaimed to them the precious message of salvation. . . .

"About the close of the late eventful war, there were manifest tokens that his health was giving way, and as soon as the line of duty was made plain, he resigned his responsible trust, laboring on, however, in another sphere (in charge of the Ann Smith Academy), till the forces of life were too far spent for longer service. From that time he knew that his active work was done. With three of his children immediately around him, in the midst of a people whom he had so long loved and served, and by whom he was cherished with a warm affection, he felt that he had little to do but to 'wait all his appointed days till his change should come.' It was our privilege to see him last September, and to find during an interview of two hours how completely cheerful and happy were his last days. We talked of the past, of the present, and of the future, and concerning it all he seemed about as thankful and hopeful as a man could be. . .

"His decline was gradual; and while unable to engage in active duty, he was at times able to make visits to his children distant from him, and when at home to be occasionally present at the worship of the sanctuary—all of which were greatly enjoyed. While never losing his interest in matters affecting the good of society or of the State, and especially of the church, yet he frequently spoke of dying, and would say that, as he could do nothing more here, he prayed for death, remarking that he did not think it wrong to pray for death any more than to pray for life, but all in submission to the divine will. Since the failure of his health, he would often lament that he was so useless, and would say that, as his work on earth was done, he wished it to begin in heaven. He frequently remarked that he had outlived most of his cotemporaries, and had more friends in heaven than he had on earth, and he took the greatest pleasure in naming them, and in anticipating an early meeting with them above.

"For more than two weeks before his decease he had been confined to his bed with a severe cold. On Saturday, the 22nd ult., he grew decidedly worse, and gradually sank down into the arms of death without any acute suffering. On that day he said to Mrs. White, 'I want to go home.' Thinking that his mind was perhaps wandering, she replied, 'You are at home.' 'O yes,' he answered, 'this is my earthly home, but I want to go to my heavenly home.'

"On Sunday, the 23rd, when he was thought to be dying, a number of his old friends came in to take a last farewell. Observing that there was something unusual taking place, and seeming to understand what was apprehended, he said, 'This is a small matter, a very small matter.'

"During his last hours, when he seemed to know nothing else, if asked, 'Do you know Jesus Christ?'—'O yes,' he would reply, 'he is my Saviour.'

"About midnight he fell into a sleep, from which he did not again awake in this life. But about midday on the 24th he breathed his last, without the least struggle or appearance of pain, and 'entered into rest.'

"Thus was the dear old pastor safely 'harvested,' according to the sentiment so beautifully expressed on another page by one who knew and loved him well: 'Thou shalt come to thy grave in a full age, like as a shock of corn cometh in his season.'

"There is only One who 'knoweth our frame perfectly, but even we can discern to some extent the imperfections of one another, even of the best. But those who had the most thorough knowledge of this good man will say most confidently that such was his character and such his life, that his presence in any community was an unspeakable blessing to it. In his family, no wife could mourn a more devoted husband, no children a more devoted father—'they rise up and call him blessed.'

"As a man, he was eminently amiable and friendly; as a citizen, upright and patriotic He was 'an able minister of the New Testament.' While not given to the profounder studies usefully explored by some, he was endowed with a vigorous mind, which enabled him to hold his subject under the grasp of a strong common sense. This was aided by a remarkable power of illustration, drawn both from facts and similitudes. He had a benevolent countenance, a brilliant, expressive eye, and a voice of great compass and power. All these, animated by a heart full of devout affections, rendered his preaching often highly impressive.

"His social talent was admirable. Full of anecdote and reminiscences of the times through which he had passed, cheerful even to hilarity, yet ever ready, and without any affectation, to turn his mind to the most serious things, his company was sought and welcomed not less by the youngest than by the oldest. He was exceedingly beloved as a pastor, and there are thousands of good people in Virginia who, as they receive the tidings of his death, will think of years gone by, when, in some season of affliction, or other occasion in the family circle, or going to the house of God in company, they 'took sweet counsel together.'

"These remarks could be much extended, as memory brings up its stores of the past; but let this suffice, as indicating our estimate of a beloved brother so widely known, so greatly revered, and who is now everywhere so sincerely lamented. Blessed be his memory! Thanks be to him by whose ascension to heaven such pastors are given to the church 'for the work of the ministry, and for the edifying of the body of Christ,' and under whose intercession they are translated to the church triumphant above."

"*[For the Christian Observer.*
"Sketch of the Rev. Wm. S. White, D. D.
"By the Rev. J. S. Grasty, D. D.

"During the last two years the Synod of Virginia has lost three of its most distinguished members. Dr. Ramsey went first, then Dr. Bocock, and now Dr. White follows Dr. Ramsey was a laborious, patient, accurate expounder of the word, and, under the system which he adopted in connection with such preaching, his congregation grew steadily, and the flock were noted for their attainments in scriptural knowledge. Dr. Bocock was scholarly, impetuous, bold, eloquent, and though irregular and somewhat eccentric, rose at times to the very highest pitch of pulpit eloquence. Dr. White was a man between these two, and possessed a combination of qualities that are rarely found to unite in any single individual.

"The impression that young White made in college and at the Seminary, upon professors, students and the community generally, was favorable and pleasant. Unlike many, he had no blunders committed at this period of preparation to mourn over in the future. His manner was so consistent, his piety so symmetrical, his procedure throughout so proper, that comrades and all others pointed to him as a model. The memory of his exemplary life remained fresh down to the period when the writer himself became a student in Prince Edward.

"After completing his course of theological study, under Drs. Hoge and Rice, he entered upon the work of the ministry in a missionary field embracing Nottoway and the adjoining counties. The sphere chosen was unambitious, but it afforded material adapted exactly to develop those qualities in the young minister which, in the ripeness of manhood, were to make him so useful. Had this preacher, as others have done, waited for a call to a large place, and with a salary to correspond, the whole current of his work and character would have been mournfully marred. But, after consultation with wise men and good, he selected a region of country that seemed to need, more than any other, the ministrations of the word. And yet young White, impeded as he was by certain infirmities of the flesh, might, with a fair show of reason, have excused himself from a field whose duties demanded physical endurance. But this bodily hindrance did not move him, neither was he driven from his purpose by the fear of meagre compensation.

"Souls were to be saved, there was a likelihood of usefulness, the people wanted him, and the youthful minister stood ready to make the experiment. And in this case, as in every other, the bed is easy just in proportion as the hand of providence helps to make it for us. Trouble that often follows the preacher through life can be traced, for the most part, to a wrong step in the beginning. The laborer, either through unhallowed motives or else from failure to enquire prayerfully and submissively about duty, rushes into a section of the vineyard unadapted to his talent. Mischief and sorrow ensue, and then the rumor of these complications becomes the source of further trials. Happy indeed is the young minister who can go without complaint to any position in the church where the Master calls.

"Those missionary days in Nottoway were a period to which Dr. White ever looked back with satisfaction and delight. It was then that he gathered those stores of information in regard to persons of every rank that fitted him afterwards to discharge those responsible and delicate tasks entrusted to his prudence. And here, as elsewhere, one whom God designed for prominence is passed through a school of discipline and preparation adapted to this end. Nottoway, in those days, offered to the preacher opportunities to observe mankind in every grade of society, from the highest to the lowest, and Dr. White was the very man to avail himself of the opening. Hence at one time he was found in the cabin of 'Uncle Jack,' and then again seated a welcome guest in the mansion of the refined, cultured and gifted Dr. Jones. Nor did this contact with the opposites of society ever compromise the minister. But the very contrary of this was the invariable result. The missionary went from house to house, and from familiar intercourse with the people learned to know their wants, and then, when Sabbath came, the discourse was so framed as to suit the needs of every one, from the wealthiest down to the very poorest. Dr. White was deeply pious, loved the gospel sincerely, and preached it in simplicity. He possessed the power of adaptation so remarkably that each class in the community claimed him for its preacher. And yet no one ever charged the minister with selfishness and insincerity. He strove after plainness of speech, so that the ignorant and 'wayfaring' might get their portion in due season.

"Among his hearers was a large element of the colored race. In his sermons he ever remembered the necessities of these untutored ones. He even held special services for their benefit. As a warning to young preachers against high-sounding and far-fetched words, the Doctor frequently related the following: 'One afternoon, an appointment for the negroes, I called upon a visiting brother to occupy my place. He consented, and began the sermon with these words, 'My friends, it is in morals as in physics, like causes produce like results.' When the services were over I ventured to enquire of a colored man what he thought of the preaching. He responded with feeling, 'Master, I did not like that sermon; it had too much *physic* in it for me.'

"Dr. White's bearing was so manly and unexceptionable, and withal so uniformly courteous and gentle, that every family and individual over his wide district hailed him as a friend; for in his open, noble countenance it could be read instinctively that the heart of this servant of Christ beat kindly toward all. Hence, during every year of his sojourn in Nottoway, he gained ground with the entire population, and the friends he made there remained steadfast to the end. So deeply did he grow into the confidence and affection of the people that the prospect of losing him awakened anxiety and universal regret; for he had slowly, but surely, worked his way to a position whence he could be heartily welcomed to a thousand Virginia homes. His coming, without an exception, was anticipated with pleasure, and the announcement that he would preach at any place drew forth large congregations.

"What Dr. White was in efficiency in this field of labor he continued to be as the agent of the American Tract Society, and as pastor, teacher and chaplain in Charlottesville and at the University of Virginia. Indeed, these last positions offered still broader opportunities for the natural bent of his mind, whilst it widened, almost without limit, the circle of his acquaintance; for at this time he was thrown into contact with learned professors; and as the instructor of young ladies and chaplain for young men, he possessed advantages for the study of the disposition of the two sexes rarely ever surpassed. And these facilities were eagerly improved. Youth from every section of the land took home pleasant recollections of the teacher and the preacher, and in after years Dr. White never visited a neighborhood where he did not find some friend of his earlier days waiting to receive him. . . .

"This man has gone to his rest full of years and full of honors, and the Virginia Synod scarcely ever lost a member whose name is as familiar in so many households, and whose labors while living were acceptable to a greater range of culture or to a greater variety in social standing. Considered, therefore, from the standpoint of natural gifts, and the positions that he filled, and the way in which he filled them, the ministerial career of Dr. White was a splendid success, and deserves, as much as that of any other pastor or preacher of the present time, to be held up for imitation before the minds of the young ministers of to-day.

"THE BALANCE OF CHARACTER.

"Before this sketch is closed it will be well to inquire into the precise qualities that entered into the mind and heart of a man who accomplished so much, and this without painful friction. Especially among young men it is a fashion to judge of intellectual excellence by the presence of some one endowment that overtops all the rest. The speaker who startles with scintillations of fancy, the logician who puzzles with his logic, a public caterer of any kind who makes a specific branch of study, this individual attracts the youthful imagination, and is denominated a *genius*. Measured by such a standard as this, Dr. White came manifestly short. There was scarcely a single thing in the whole compass of action or of thought in which Dr. White excelled that was dependent upon the exercise of one faculty by itself. There was altogether too much breadth about his mental powers for this. It would be healthful for our youth to comprehend the fact that eccentricities of every kind are not a sign of strength, but of weakness. Intellect of the highest type is capacious at all points. It was difficult for Goethe's friends to determine whether this most gifted son of Germany ought to be poet, philosopher, statesman, orator, or the commander of an army. And the same was true of Napoleon, Julius Cæsar, Mahomet and others. The more exalted and varied the gifts in the mind-world, the fewer the irregularities.

"The secret of Dr. White's success was in the nice *balance* of forces. In his finely-developed intellect every faculty had a place, and it was these in combination that produced results so opportune. When sitting with him in the Board of Visitors at Union Theological Seminary, or watching his processes upon the floor of Synod, in both of which bodies he stood among the foremost, I observed that while other debaters pressed a single point with skill, Dr. White usually went over the case in all its parts. It was not that he was equal to Dr. Ramsey in his exhaustive methods of research, or to Dr. Bocock in the ardent, scholarly, eloquent outburst of thought, but his power consisted in this, that while certain men of rare, particular gifts occasionally succeeded grandly, this man almost invariably drove the nail directly into the right place.

"He seldom mistook his man or the temper of an assembly before which he stood. With a temperament that corresponded in its make-up with his mental gifts, he warily watched the main chance, and was ready when the moment came. As a pastor, for instance, he was ever *en rapport* with elders, and this not because he lacked force of will, for no man destitute of vigor could have filled such positions, but because he collected the particulars of disposition and character, and then, with the certainty of deduction, calculated the opinions, prejudices and weight of each. And having these at command beforehand, he knew precisely how to act. And I will here venture to surmise that he never, in his entire ministry, *forced* a measure through the session. And yet no pastor's purposes were ever more fully carried out. Dr. White was a diplomat, but with conscience always uppermost. He usually accomplished his plans, but did this in such a way as to leave no room for gall. He watched and often waited for the fruit to ripen, that with a gentle touch he might bring it to his hand.

"He was careful not to lose, if possible, a friend already

gained, whilst he would turn aside, through heat or cold, to add another to the list; for he considered that, to a minister more particularly, there was power in the multiplication of sterling friendships. Yea, it was even best, if principle allowed, to have the good wishes of the humblest, since in the mutations of life the enmity of the feeble may be turned into an annoyance or else a serious hurt.

"Most earnestly did Dr. White seek to make friends among his younger brethren. And the wisdom of this course was justified fully by the sequel; for in every Prestery of the Old Dominion and all over the South there are scores and hundreds of ministers who cherish gratitude in their hearts for the cheering words of counsel spoken to them in days of inexperience by this faithful father in Israel. And there is not a man of this number who did not rejoice in every good thing which befell the Lexington pastor; and the poorest of them all, had necessity arisen, would have divided to him of the weal which fell to his lot. Disregarding such wisdom as this, there have been 'fathers' whose bearing towards their juniors savored of exaction and severity; and while these were tolerated for their ability, yet they elicited no affection, and upon the conscience and recollection abided no sense of obligation. Such men were feared rather than loved, and when missed in the courts, the absence of these *censores morum* was rather a relief than a sorrow.

"Moreover, there was so much of soundness in the moral, intellectual and physical constitution of Dr. White, that he never ceased to be interested in everything which concerned the individual, the family, society, and the church of God. And while a gentleman of the truest dignity, never indulging in a doubtful expression or act, yet he was wide awake to refined humor, and enjoyed a laugh with the heartiness of a boy. It made one think better of his species to witness the freedom of this man's soul from the envious, morose, complaining and uncharitable; for in the sunshine and hopefulness of his sympathizing spirit, it was impossible for anything foreboding and spiteful long to exist. He was a husband of whom the noble wife of his bosom might be proud; a father, upon whose children, if his mantle fall, happy will it be for them, as it shall be a happiness again to those who are to follow. Dr. White, like God's servant of old, ruled his own house; but he ruled it rather through example than by oft-repeated words. The even tenor of his days, the joy that beamed in his open and ingenuous face, that harvest which came to him so richly as the result of his own timely sowing—these visible evidences of how much better it is to be kind and true and good, went further than a thousand sermons to impress upon the family the policy of high manhood.

"Judged by the criterion of the schools, Dr. White was not a great preacher; and yet, tested by the verdict of the multitude (with whom the preacher, as such, has mainly to deal), few ministers in our denomination could secure a larger suffrage. He was ever certain of consideration from the cultivated, while the common people, on the other hand, always heard him gladly. He possessed a rare store of anecdotes, and with these he illustrated the truth so aptly that they who came to hear him once were sure to come again. With a tall figure, broad shoulders, and a head of unusual dimensions crowning all, his appearance in the pulpit was specially engaging. The forehead was not only high, but broad withal, the eye brilliant, the countenance defaced with no imperfect feature. These outward advantages, added to a voice of the deepest and widest compass, and all again crowned with the graces of God's Spirit, fitted him to be, as he ever was, a favorite with the masses. In addition, there fell from his lips now and then in the sermon such revelations of practical knowledge, such masterly thrusts at the inner workings of the heart, that these searching utterances alone left no room for complaint to the most exacting. And upon all, of every degree, either as to literary attainments or social position, there was that in the *tout ensemble* of the man which enforced everywhere, in the pulpit and out of it, the profoundest respect. . . .

"Dr. White in Prayer.

"Three men in the Presbyterian Church of this country towered above all their fellows in the ability which God gave them to lead the soul of the suppliant up to the very altar 'where the cherubim stretched forth their wings over the mercy-seat.' These godly men were Drs. McFarland, Rice and White.

"Dr. McFarland was, so to speak, more simple and childlike in his modes. He drew near to the Father with confidence, and stood at his feet, pleading in gentle, earnest, urgent words, as though there abided in the bosom a certainty of final success. Again and again did he return to the mark, each time with an inspiration that shone around his head and trilled in his voice. . . .

"Dr. Ben. Rice and Dr. Wm. S. White very much resembled each other in prayer. These two and Dr. McFarland were notably dissimilar. On the other hand, Drs. Rice and White were so alike that, with closed eyes, the worshippers could almost mistake the one for the other. The main difference was, if I may express it so, that Dr. Rice possessed a condensed energy, and now and then there gushed forth a sublimity of utterance which did not belong, in the same degree, to the other. But about each there existed a propriety, decorum and genuine majesty that I never knew surpassed. In the outset there was not the quickened pulse, the ardor, the childlike hopefulness and scope (as in Dr. McFarland), but these led off more with the air and mien of the king's officers, who entered the sovereign's council chamber through the accustomed and time-honored forms. . . . .

"A Criterion of Greatness.

"In a word, if greatness is to be decided according to what a person does, then the name of William Spottswood White must be enrolled among the great. For he was tried in four different fields, and one of these the most delicate and difficult possible to be conceived; and yet wherever he went, there followed the plaudit, 'Well done, good and faithful servant.' Can greatness encompass more? Nay, have not the great, defined by certain standards, conspicuously failed where Dr. White confessedly succeeded? Let it be granted that he was not dazzling in his rhetoric, scholastic and formal in his logic, classic in his tastes, and profound and varied in his learning. What boots it to the proprietor of all these, if there be in any man such a rare combination of gifts and graces that the latter can accomplish noble ends for which the former are insufficient? Which of these two classes does the church most need this hour? If there be large attainments, so much the better; but as between insufficiency with this and efficiency without it, no man of sense need hesitate for an answer.

"Not that Dr. White was destitute of culture. Very far from it. He sat a portion of each day in a well-assorted library, and no pastor in Lexington Presbytery knew better how to use it. Yet it was not upon literature, science, or the outcome of genius, that this ambassador of Christ mainly relied. But he held within himself, strengthened and guided by God's grace, that diversity of gifts which is unequalled by all learning, and that roundness and symmetry of character in conjunction with deep piety, and such literary stores as reasonable industry can attain. This is the type of Christian minister which it is healthful and refreshing to set before our young ministers of to-day. True, we want the men of science, the proficient in 'tongues' and philosophy. A few of these the church must have, as watchmen, here and there, upon her walls; but Zion needs most of all a host of the

Lord's servants, upon whom has fallen the mantle of the prudent, self-denying, laborious, cheerful, judicious, wise, and now sainted White.   JOHN S. GRASTY."

[*By the Rev. Thomas B. Balch, Greenwich, Va.*]
REMINISCENCES OF PRESBYTERIAN MINISTERS
BY AN OCTOGENARIAN.—No. 39.

WILLIAM S. WHITE.

"In June, 1839, the Octogenarian was riding in the direction of Charlottesville, in the county of Albemarle. I called at a wayside inn, for the rest of an hour, and my hostess appeared anxious to find out a few particulars touching the traveller. There was nothing obtrusive or officious in her manner. At length she remarked, 'Dr. White to-morrow has sacrament at Charlottesville, and in the evening you will probably meet an elder of his kirk coming home from the preparatory sermon.' 'Thank you,' I replied, 'for that piece of information, and I'll keep an eye on that elder.' 'So do,' she remarked, 'for your black velvet stock gave me an inkling that you were a minister.'

"We rode on at an easy gait, and, rather late in the afternoon, we spied a gentleman, who met up with us in a few minutes. 'Are you from Charlottesville?' I asked. 'Yes,' he answered. 'Are you acquainted with Dr. White?' 'Know him like a book,' he answered. 'Are you a minister? if so, ride up to my house, spend the night, and in the morning I will introduce you to the Doctor, as worthy a man as you could wish to see.' So the head of my steed was turned, and the writer spent a most agreeable night with a Christian family.

"The next morning was cool for a Virginia summer—a crudeness in the atmosphere; and the writer put on a reddish-looking coat, which gave him rather a grotesque appearance. We reached the Albemarle town, and met Dr. White in one of the streets. He was on his way to see a sick member of his flock. 'Go on to the church,' he remarked, 'and take your place in the pulpit.' A large part of the congregation had assembled. In ascending the pulpit, the people gazed at the stranger as if he had been a pope wearing his triple mitre. 'Gaze on, good people,' thought the stranger; 'I am not the pope, nor Michael Angelo, who became, in 1542, the architect of St. Peter's, nor Raffaelle, whose pencil frescoed the apartments of that sumptuous mass of idolatry. This plain edifice suits me better than the cathedral of Canterbury, or St. Paul's in London.' Dr. White entered the pulpit; but just as he took his seat, a man came up the steps and whispered the question, 'Do you need help in putting that man out?' 'What man? Wouldn't you wish to hear him preach?' So the janitor made a hasty retreat. The *eclaircissement* of this queer affair was that, on the Sabbath before, some half-witted man, who resembled the writer, had crept into the pulpit. I should have been amused, had it happened anywhere but in a church.

"My text was, 'Add to your faith virtue, charity,' etc. When the services were closed, a lady approached me, who proved to be a niece of ex-President Jefferson. She had resided at Monticello, the famous seat of her uncle, and I immediately saw that she was a lady of uncommon talents. 'Are you a Virginian?' she enquired. 'A native,' I replied, 'of Columbia District; but Virginia has adopted me, and has become my *alma mater*.' 'It is pleasant,' she remarked, 'to hear a sermon in these days of strife on the subject of charity.' Faith, hope, charity; the greatest of these is charity. 'Then,' I replied, 'my text ought to have read, "*To your charity add*," etc., but it read, "To your faith add charity" as a product of faith, and then the product becomes greater in the deeds we perform for our race; but "without faith we cannot please God."' 'But,' she rejoined, 'have we not disowned our New School brethren?' 'True,' I answered, 'but two cannot walk together except they be agreed. The church is not the place for discussion of litigated points.' 'Then come,' she said, 'and take tea with us to-morrow evening.' My acceptance of the invitation terminated the interview. Dr. White told me that she was the only New School member of his church, and honest in all her convictions.

"The next morning the writer walked out to Monticello. Its owner had died in 1826, and the place had been purchased by a Jewish family. The pastor at Charlottesville had given me a note of introduction to the sister of the proprietor, and in walking along we thought about Sir Walter Scott's Rebecca in *Ivanhoe*. She held Dr. White in great veneration, and occasionally attended his ministry. I paused awhile at the grave of Jefferson, and then advancing, was met by a young man accompanied by a couple of dogs. I do not hate dogs, but the sight of them; for they are nothing more than half-civilized wolves. My note was handed to the young Jew. 'This note of Dr. White,' he remarked, 'will entitle you to all the attentions we can bestow. He is beloved by Jews and Gentiles, and, like Ezra, he delves into the Old Testament, and then couples it with the New.' 'You cannot hold him,' I replied, 'in profounder reverence than your visitor.' He then conducted me through the garden, pointed out the distant views, and led me to the homestead of the statesman, showing its porches, rooms, mosaics, its foreign curiosities and domestic inventions. But of these things I have given an account in one of my twenty-four 'Picturesque Narratives,' published in Stockton's *Christian World*.

"I walked back to the town, and was introduced to Professor Harrison, a fine scholar and polished gentleman. Called on the consort of Professor Tucker, an old acquaintance. Went to hear her husband lecture on moral philosophy. . . . Took tea with the New School lady. She presented me with *a pair of ebonies*, and fifty dollars to help bear their expenses to Liberia. They were sent accordingly with Governor Buchanan. Saw the Rev. Mr. Paxton, just returned from Palestine. Told me that the rose of Sharon was yellow, and that its hue was golden. Many believe that it was red.

"I have seldom met with a minister that made a deeper impression on my memory than Dr. White. He removed to Lexington, in the Valley, where his labors in the ministry were very successful. He was dignified enough to command respect, and yet lowly enough to look for the dew of heaven on all that he attempted to advance in the cause of Christianity, either by oral instruction or by his pen; and now he sleeps in the fern of Shenandoah Valley, not far from the graves of Lee and Jackson, which are frequented by pilgrims from our own and distant lands."

The Rev. Dr. J. A. Waddell, of Roxbury, Virginia, is the author of the following lines:

LINES
SUGGESTED BY THE HAPPY DEATH OF THE REV. DR. WHITE.

"In the first hour of day's decline,
When noon-day's shadows cross the line,
We stood around him as he lay,
And watched him till he passed away.

"The tortured face, the anguished eye,
That mark the time when others die,
Seemed not death's purpose to betray;
We knew not *when* he passed away.

"No mortal tumult heaved his breast;
No mortal pain impaired his rest;
But, like the noon's receding ray,
His sainted spirit passed away.

"As summer clouds at eventide
With unseen motion gently glide;
As stars grow dim at break of day,
Then cease to shine,—he passed away.

"The waves of time so slowly bore
Their precious burden from the shore,
Asleep in their embrace he lay,
And, sweetly slumbering, passed away.

"Thus, on its noiseless wheels of flame,
The chariot for the prophet came;
Affrighted death forsook its sway,
And the immortal passed away.

"'Twas victory for him to die,
And mourners weep, they know not why;
Who would the conqueror's march delay,
When saints to glory pass away?"

MEMORIALS OF MRS. DR. WHITE.

BY THE SESSION OF THE CHURCH.

"IN MEMORIAM.

"The following minute was adopted October 10, 1878, by the session of the Lexington Presbyterian Church, and ordered to be spread upon the record:

"Died, October 3, 1878, aged seventy-five, at the residence of her son, Mr. Thomas S. White, Mrs. Jane I. White, widow of Wm. S. White, D. D., late pastor of this church.

"Mrs. White's membership in the Lexington Presbyterian Church was historic, inasmuch as it was so intimately connected with the pastorate, long continued and specially blessed, of her husband, our pastor.

"We remember with tender affection how faithfully she discharged her appropriate part of the direct duties of her position, and we are well persuaded that her indirect influence was even more potential for good in lightening the labors of her husband, and in encouraging and cheering his heart, and thus strengthening his hands for the arduous work entrusted to him.

"She has ceased from her labors, and entered upon her

everlasting reward, to be enjoyed with him to whom on earth she gave the love and the labor of her life. When his crown is bright with the shining of many stars, some of its lustre will be reflected upon the less conspicuous crown of her who was his true fellow-laborer in winning souls to Christ.

"This simple memorial of her departure from among us appropriately finds a place upon the record-book, in which has been inscribed so often the name of her husband as moderator of this session.

"J. FULLER, *Clerk of Session.*

"[*For the Central Presbyterian.*]
"BY MRS. MARGARET J. PRESTON.

"On Saturday, October 5th, was laid to rest in the Lexington cemetery all that was mortal of Jane Isabella, the venerated widow of the Rev. Dr. Wm. S. White.

"Few deaths occur in this sorrowful world of ours that have not more or less of sadness mingled with them. Yet here we saw our friend, our neighbor, one with whom we had held the most gentle and pleasant intercourse through years of mingled joy and grief, one whose unobtrusive ministrations had never been withheld in prosperity or adversity—such an one we saw laid under the sod almost without tears. There seemed, as we thought of what she had been and what she had done, no room for sorrow, no reasonableness in grief. Faithfully, conscientiously, unremittingly, as daughter and wife and mother, as neighbor and friend and mistress, as a comforter of the poor and a soother of the afflicted, as a pastor's best and truest helper, she had done her duty, with sweet quietness of mind, with calm serenity of manner, and with unselfish endurance. She had ordered, rarely well, all the ways of her household; she had made her husband's home a very home of the heart; she had gladdened and solaced and made smooth for him the entire pathway of his married life, taking upon herself its manifold domestic cares and burdens, that he might be free to give himself without hindrance or stint to the sacred work which he so long and so admirably performed, proving herself thereby a model minister's wife. She had had a life of singular happiness with him, through youth and middle age, and together had they bowed over their one bitter experience of anguish, the death on the field of battle of their noble young son, Capt. Hugh A. White, a loss, nevertheless, that could be borne, seeing that she had such a comforter. She had watched with long and silent submission over the slow decline of this beloved husband, until her ministrations and her care were no longer needed. She had reared, with untiring Christian fidelity, a large family of children, five sons and two daughters; she had seen them all honorably and happily settled in homes of their own; her maternal solicitude had culminated in the fulfilment for them of her highest wishes. She had lived beyond the promised three-score-and-ten, and these five years of borrowed time, spent in patient but saddened widowhood, more than satisfied her. She had no care to linger, if it was God's will that she should go. '*For I have nothing to do now,*' she would sometimes say, half piteously, to the writer of this brief memorial; '*nothing to do; my work is over;*' as if life were not life without the working and the doing.

"From the day she lost her husband the brightness seemed to fade out of life for her. The placid, cheerful, sympathetic face which always heretofore had a smile ready for us who knew her, lost henceforth that sunny tranquillity which had been so pleasant to look upon, convincing all who saw it that there could be in this troublesome world absolute quietness of spirit and content of heart that asked and wished for nothing beyond what was in possession. But when the light of her eyes was taken away, the valley of the shadow began to grow dim about her. When the strong prop was removed the steady heart began to falter. Thenceforth the sweet serenity deepened into something like settled sadness. She never became used to missing the stay of her life-time.

"A second blow followed at no long distance. Her youngest daughter, with whom she had her home, was suddenly snatched away in the hey-day of her young womanhood; and while there was no arraignment of the kindness or wisdom of her heavenly Father, there was a certain bewilderment of sorrow, from which the stricken heart could not react.

"It was but reasonable and natural, then, that the tired hands that had never idled over their work should at last be folded over each other, and that she should softly and quietly receive the summons to the 'rest that remaineth.' It would have been unreasonable and unnatural if on that golden autumn morning her friends and neighbors had felt other than a solemn thanksgiving that the 'shock of corn, fully ripe,' had been gathered into the garner of the Lord.

"To few, with more truth, can the commendation of our Saviour bestowed upon Mary be applied than to Mrs. White. In all the relations of life, and in all its perplexing circumstances, '*she hath done what she could.*' No brilliant work that the world will praise, it may be; but such unselfish service and such fully-performed duty as the eye of God will regard with approval as he pronounces his verdict upon it— 'Well done, good and faithful.' M. J. P."

CHAPTER XVII.

LETTERS OF CONDOLENCE.

FROM REV. DR. WM. BROWN ; REV. DR. WM. S. PLUMER ; REV. DR. B. M. SMITH ; REV. DR. R. L. DABNEY ; MRS. MARGARET J. PRESTON.

THE following letters of condolence are so admirably written, and were so highly valued by our mother, that we think they will be read with comfort by all similarly bereaved, and insert them for the benefit of all such into whose hands this volume may fall.

[*From* REV. DR. WM. BROWN.]

"RICHMOND, VA., *Dec.* 2, 1873.

"DEAR MRS. WHITE: A telegram in the Richmond *Whig* of yesterday (Monday) morning brought the first information that the mournful event had come to separate you from one who had so long and so truly been as part of your own life. In some respects there is nothing which can ever prepare us for this supreme moment, for we must always suffer under the stroke which cuts asunder ties as tender as our own heart-strings.

"But in the midst of all this, I feel assured that you are enabled fully and constantly to recognize the great—I may say the uncommonly great—mercies connected with this dispensation. Your husband had filled up the full measure of years allotted by the Psalmist for manly life; he had filled it well—nobly, indeed—and in the noblest office and work known upon earth. He had been spared with you to see all your children educated and settled in life, and had given you great comfort in them. He had during most of his life been favored with comfortable health. A happy natural constitution, as well as divine grace and a kind providence, led his life peacefully along through enjoyments allotted to few, even among the best of his brethren. I know of no one who had more reason to say, as I am sure he often did, 'He maketh me to lie down in green pastures; he leadeth me beside the still waters.'

"The life of your husband was every way regarded as one of great usefulness, and I do not think I have ever known a man more respected and loved, and deservedly so. To have had your own chosen place by his side through so long a period, and to have been universally recognized as filling it in a manner worthy of such a husband, such a minister of Christ, is a precious heritage to any wife in the day which clothes her in the garments of mourning.

"I need not assure you how sincerely my own feelings are mingled with yours, both in your sorrow and in your comfort under it. I have never known any one outside of my own father's house for whom I had a warmer affection than for my beloved brother now gone; and it will be cherished as one of the choicest memories of my life, that I had in return such unmistakable evidence of a good place in his heart.

"I feel persuaded that a review of the past, so full of 'goodness and mercy,' will constantly strengthen your faith that the Lord will cause them to 'follow you all the days of your life,' and that when they are ended you shall 'dwell in the house of the Lord forever.' The scenes of the present are fast vanishing away; 'the things that are seen are temporal.' 'The places that know us will soon know us no more.' To 'stand complete in all the will of God,'—to know it and do it, and be resigned to it; that, my dear friend, concerns us more than all besides. If that is made sure, everything else is safely anchored by it; no tempest can ever trouble it.

"But perhaps I have written too much. My desire is to

express my heartfelt sympathy with you and with all your children and household. May the covenant blessing of our God rest upon them to the latest generations; and that you may have abiding with you daily the comfort of his love and the fellowship of his Spirit, is the prayer of

"Yours, most sincerely, WILLIAM BROWN."

[*From* REV. DR. PLUMER.]

"COLUMBIA, S. C., *Dec.* 8, 1873.

"MY DEAR SISTER WHITE: I have within an hour heard of the death of dear Dr. White. If you have lost a dear, good husband, I have lost a true and loving friend and brother— a brother made for the day of adversity, as well as for the day of prosperity. I do not think there ever lived a more genial, frank, friendly or sincere man than Dr. White. His wonderful common sense made him one of the most effective men in every station. His candor kept him free from all those detestable littlenesses which mar so many characters otherwise good. I have loved him and communed sweetly with him since 1829, as I had opportunity. My last visit to him was very edifying and refreshing. He is now at rest. Glory be to God for all his mercies given to Dr. White and to others through him. I have often wept with him and often rejoiced with him. But he is at rest now, and you and I are left to fight a little longer. Oh, let us be strong. Let us honor God all the time. Let us remember that Jehovah is our strength. How can we sink with such a prop as our eternal God? If you have the poem, *Yesterday, To-day and Forever*, I ask you to read the first and second books of it. Get also Dr. Alexander's *Letters to the Aged*.

"Give my love to all your children and grandchildren. Do all you can for the glory of God. Be cheerful. The Lord be with you.

"Faithfully yours, WM. S. PLUMER."

[*From* Dr. B. M. Smith]
"Hampden-Sidney, Va., *Dec.* 7, 1873.
"My Dear Mrs. White: You have come to know by experience that sad lot which falls to so many. You are a widow! The joys and hopes and pleasing cares of your past life are at an end. It is no sufficient alleviation of your present distress to remember that it was long before you as a dark cloud. No anticipation can accustom us so to contemplate such a sorrow as yours as to deprive it of its sting when it may have come. My tenderest sympathies are with you. Somehow I have ever felt a peculiar tenderness to the widow. My precious mother was a widow during all that part of her life of which I was an observer; and her widowhood was one of prolonged and painful suffering. It is not surprising, then, that I feel for widows; and yet I remember that of all the classes of persons for which the Bible presents most special promises they are prominent. God is the 'God of the widow and the Father of the fatherless.' He has said, 'Let thy widows trust in me.' And he has made it an element of Christian character of the most prominent place to 'visit the widow and the fatherless.' Do not think, then, for a moment, that God is dealing with you in judgment, or that the deprivations to which your new relations in life subject you have taken from you all relations to sources of comfort and blessing. God has changed your circumstances, but he has not changed himself. He is still a God 'who is near, and not far off.' He is still pitiful and tender. 'Like as a father pitieth his children, so the Lord pitieth them that fear him.' This is one of the most precious of all the comforting promises which the Spirit has written for the afflicted. God is not only a Father who 'chastens,' but a Father who 'pities' while he 'chastens.'

"And then, while he has given you a bitter cup, he has not made it all bitter. What unspeakably precious blessings has he left you! The memory of such a husband is itself a legacy of ineffable value. I doubt not, you have already received, and will continue to receive, from all parts of the country, and from far abler pens than mine, tributes to the eminent worth of your beloved husband. I have known him for nearly fifty years. As boy and man, I have marked his career, and with profit. Few men, living or dead, ever laid me under greater obligations, as contributors to the formation of my own character. I owe him more than I can express. His mode of life, domestic and professional, was one of the examples which, though at a long distance behind, and with very unequal steps, I followed. While in Nottoway, in Scottsville, Charlottesville and Lexington, I was ever taught by him; and much of what little I have done, as I had opportunity, I owe to his example and his encouragement. And then what a blessing in your dear children has God left you. I know they have, in some cases, been sources of affliction in their affliction; but God has rewarded all Dr. White's care and yours in giving you children in whom you may well rejoice. . . . . . And you have, to cherish and comfort you in age, your youngest daughter. So let your heart trust. In sure confidence in your Saviour, faithfulness to your new duties and new relations, you will find new comforts offsetting the sorrow of these days.

"May grace, mercy and peace ever be with you.
"Yours truly, B. M. SMITH."

[*From* REV. DR. R. L. DABNEY.]
"SEMINARY, *December* 13, 1873.

"MY DEAR MRS. WHITE: You need not be assured that we have all watched with the tenderest interest such accounts as the papers brought us of the last sickness of your honored husband. When I learned that he had certainly gone to his rest, I felt that I had lost one of the wisest and truest friends I ever had. I take a pensive pleasure in running over the numerous instances of his hospitality and kindness to me, and the many very happy hours he has given me, since the beginning of our acquaintance, when I came to the University of Virginia, an unfriended and poor young man. Few men have ever held such a place in my estimation, for every quality that ennobles a man and a Christian.

"I do not write, my dear madam, for the purpose of intruding the common-places of consolation. These truths you know; and doubtless the Divine Comforter has already been ministering them to your heart, even from the first day that this bereavement began to cast its shadow upon you. I can only pray that you may experience the fullest supports of a Christian faith and hope; and that your remaining pilgrimage may be made pleasant and comfortable by the tender affection of the children who owe you and their father so much.

"Lavinia asks especially to join me in this prayer and in my hearty acknowledgments of the many kindnesses we have both received from you and your husband. Remember us also affectionately to Harriet and to Professor James White and their families.

"Very faithfully yours, R. L. DABNEY."

[*From* MRS. MARGARET J. PRESTON.]

"MONDAY, *December* 1.

"MY DEAR SORROWING FRIEND: My heart is bowed down with you in your sore grief! I do not know how to take in the thought that dear, dear Dr. White is gone from us for ever. It is better to think that I will never, never see him again. And if *I* feel it so, how does *your* poor, smitten heart bear up under the heavy bereavement! How often he has comforted us in *our* many griefs! how he has sympathized and prayed with us! and now it is only left us to mourn *over* him, not *for* him. Passed, as he has, into the splendor of the ineffable glory, we dare not weep for his going from us, hardly; our sorrow must all be for *you*, dear friend, and his children who will so miss him, and for ourselves, his parishioners, to whom he was always so dear. God comfort you in your loneliness and desolation! The everlasting arms be underneath and around you! If I only had seen him once more! Just after I came home, I was on the street to pay him a visit, and was turned aside; and last week, although twice I went to the house, I felt as if it would be an intrusion to ask to see him. *Now*, I so wish I had. My husband truly mourns for him; he had no deeper affection for any man than for his dear old pastor. But his own heart has been so bowed with grief that he has never paid a visit since Phebe's death.

"Last night as I sat and thought of the dear Doctor, I was so impressed with the idea of his being 'a shock of corn fully ripe,' that I wrote the lines enclosed.[1] I send them, thinking they may have a little comfort in them.

"Dear Mrs. White, I have felt that so many were going to see you, that it would be kinder in us to stay away just now. In a few days, when you feel more like seeing me, I will come. My love to Harriet and true Christian sympathy.

"Ever most affectionately,   MARGARET J. PRESTON."

---

[1] These "lines" were appended to the memorial notice of Dr. White by the session of the church. See p. 239.

CHAPTER XVIII.

ESTIMATES OF HIS CHARACTER BY LIFE-LONG FRIENDS: DR. R. L. DABNEY, DR. T. W. SYDNOR, DR. THEODORICK PRYOR.

THE following estimate of Dr. White was written by Dr. R. L. Dabney to Rev. Dr. J. W. Pratt, successor of Dr. White in the Lexington Church, when the latter had in mind to deliver a "Memorial Discourse" on the former, at the request of the session of the church. It was not written by the author to be printed just as it stands, but for substance and in Dr. Pratt's own language:

"*January* 24, 1874.

"THE REV. JOHN W. PRATT, D. D.

"REV. AND DEAR BROTHER: The first time I ever saw Brother White was, I think, in 1833, when I was a child. I went to the University of Virginia, December, 1839; Dr. White was then pastor of the Presbyterian Church in Charlottesville, a householder and principal of a large and laborious female school. Then commenced a life-long friendship. I went very frequently to Dr. White's church, and have to acknowledge his preaching as one of the chief means for developing whatever Christian character I have. I soon became a welcome visitor at his home, and an occasional witness of that charming domestic life of which it was the scene.

"During the session of 1840–'41 Dr. White was appointed chaplain to the University. He conducted a Bible-class and preached in the forenoon in the University. He preached to his own pastoral charge in the afternoon or night. He gave an evening lecture in the University (in some professor's house) Wednesday night. He taught a seminary of some forty girls through the week, and did his pastoral visiting at night. His preaching was greatly admired by the professors, and he was an excellent chaplain. He had not been long chaplain when the murder of Professor Davis took place. Dr. White appeared to unusual advantage amidst all these agitating scenes: tender, sympathetic, but wise and composed. His funeral sermon, almost an *impromptu*, was an exceedingly happy effort, and the effect could not have been surpassed by any one. It was alluded to in class-room by the professors as a true model of pathetic eloquence.

"Such labors, of course, were too much for any man's health; Dr. White's failed from some disease of the liver, accompanied with great sleeplessness. He lay at death's door; recuperated; got to the Hot baths, and always attributed his bodily salvation to that agency, together with a good *rest* there. I think this was about 1843. About the close of Dr. White's first chaplaincy, the change was made from one to two-year's term of service. As soon as the Presbyterian turn could come around, he was made chaplain again for two years. He did not attempt this time to bear up Atlas, but turned his own congregation over to licentiate (now Dr.) D. B. Ewing. I think it was the year after his second tour of duty (I was a divinity student then), that the great rebellion occurred which, for a time, emptied the University. I was in Albemarle among my relatives just after, and I remember hearing leading gentlemen say, that 'the best thing they could do to reduce the young men to order would be to commit the executive management to Dr. White, for he had more talent of command and sound discretion than the whole faculty.'

"I, having settled at Tinkling Spring just before the beginning of the 'Skinner war,' in 1847, was a member to welcome Dr. White in 1848. We were co-presbyters for five years. He had then become an influential director of this Seminary. No man had a fuller sympathy than he with the convictions of its noble and sagacious founder, Dr. John H. Rice. He saw clearly how vital it was to real progress in the South that we should always rear a *home supply* of ministers. It is to me an interesting circumstance, that Dr. White's zeal for the Seminary was the providential occasion of his settlement in Lexington. He was present at the *very* meeting (at the River Church, near the Rockbridge Baths) at which the 'Skinner war' began, as ambassador from the Seminary Board to Lexington Presbytery, to gain their fuller coöperation. Lexington Presbytery was then very Philadelphianish and Princetonish. My father-in-law, even while a director of Union, sent three Browns to Princeton. Dr. White made a very prudent and attractive speech. This was the means of directing the attention of the Lexington elders to him. The next fall Dr. S. R. Graham died. To his great chagrin Dr. ——— was elected, and coquetted with the Board for a year. I was then—April, 1853—elected by some sort of haphazard or blind groping.

"You ask for my estimate of Dr. White: it is, in every point of view, *very high*. He was an admirable head of a family, firm, wise, generous, and tender. As a business man, he was sagacious and successful. He never *meant to get riches*; had he desired them he would have succeeded, but he was too noble. As a companion, he was unrivalled: a genial humorist, with an exhaustless fund of incident, and a cheerfulness that rarely flagged. His courage was lionlike. He was fond of books and delighted in his study. Those who think otherwise did not know him. But his 'meat was to do the will of his Father and finish his work.' Zeal for souls thrust him out; although it was a true self-denial to him, he always responded. He was right, for who can doubt that the multitudes of spiritual children he thus begot were more to the glory of God than any additional critical accuracy he might have gained by staying in his study? His mind was not formed for critical niceties, and, I presume, was impatient of protracted research. He was a man of action. But I have heard from him many able, well-knit, devotional sermons, especially while chaplain. He wielded a very graceful pen. I rank his *African Preacher* among the English classics: the easy flow, perspicuity and unambitious grace are equal, in my view, to the best popular writings of John Newton or James W. Alexander. His literary taste was very pure.

"As a preacher, Dr. White had nearly every excellency. It was usual to say that he was 'not profound,' 'not scholarly,' etc. He was too wise a 'master of assemblies' to affect the scholastic forms of discussion; his genius taught him better what suited the popular mind. As a preacher he was *eminently gifted* in prayer. His sermons never failed in appropriate unction. His power of appropriate illustration never failed him. He dealt with ideas in the concrete, as do all great, popular leaders. His pathos was great, and he knew where to touch the heart-strings of the people. To my ear his elocution was very fine, flexible, expressive, solemn, manly, noble. The last sermon I ever heard from him was to a part of my charge here, at the last meeting of the trustees he ever attended, to an afternoon congregation in a little 'chapel of ease' we keep down at the village. The morning had been occupied by one of our most admired pulpit orators, in an effort which was generally pronounced 'brilliant.' After dinner, Dr. Smith took Dr. White down in his little carriage, and he preached an unpretending, practical sermon of thirty minutes. To my ear and heart, it carried more true eloquence than the other.

"On the whole, Dr. White was a man of a large and noble build. It has very seldom been my privilege to know such a one, never to have the warm friendship—as I had his—of a nobler. His friendship and counsels I count as one of the great blessings of my life. None of his sons is exactly like him. Hugh was his darling; the least like him in temperament and idiosyncrasy, rare in nobleness, courage and deep piety. Mrs. White was an admirable help-meet for him.

"I find that Dr. White's name stands on our matriculation list in 1825. His family can give you the framework of his history. I have heard him talk much of his early history. He told me once, that his aspirations were due to a word from a kinsman who had emigrated to Florida and there become a distinguished public man. (This was the Hon. Thomas White, who represented Florida in Congress —————.) When Dr. White was a youth at home this kinsman visited his native neighborhood. He said to his young cousin, 'Don't *vegetate* here on the Chick-a-hominy; resolve to *be something*.' These words, he said, enforced by the example of his kinsman's brilliant success, awakened aspirations which were never quenched, and which, chastened by grace, led to his holy and useful career.

"He was in Hampden-Sidney College as a candidate the last terms of Dr. Moses Hoge's presidency, and remembered him well. He also knew and was assisted by Dr. J. H. Rice, then pastor of the First Church, Richmond. Dr. White had to earn his education by teaching. One of his pleasant incidents was this: Being a very young aspirant for a school in Richmond he had ventured to append to his card a reference to Dr. Rice. He took the first opportunity *afterwards* to mention it to the Doctor and ascertain if it was agreeable. He had hitherto known him chiefly in his graver moods (which were *very* grave), and approached him with no little awe. Dr. Rice immediately put him at his ease, thus: 'Well, my young brother, you have taken me at the same disadvantage that old John—(mentioning a familiar old neighbor of Major James Morton at Willington)—used to take of my father-in-law about his turnip-salad. Old John would come by the patch, cut a fine basketful, hide it in the fence corner, and *then* come to the house to ask for salad. You see, if my father-in-law demurred, on the ground that it was getting scarce, he would say: Well, Major, it's cut now; and its too late to jine it to the turnips again.'

"You will see that my statements are not fit in form for citation; the substance is at your service.

"Fraternally yours, R. L. DABNEY.

"POST-SCRIPT.—Perhaps it may be well for me to say more of the religious history of the University, and the change which was taking place in it at the time of Dr. White's chaplaincies.

"Formed by Mr. Jefferson (a low-type, rational Socinian) as a State institution, it was at first of no religion nominally. This turned out, as it generally does, anti-Christian practically. There were no religious observances; many of the professors were skeptical; much Sabbath-breaking, drunkenness and lechery among the students. After a few years they had an epidemic typhoid fever, like that which prevailed in 1855-'56. Many students died. As a sort of 'sop to the Cerberus' of Christian opinion in the State, the Faculty invited Bishop Meade to preach a common funeral sermon in the great rotunda. The Faculty complained that the bishop denounced the pestilence as a visitation of God on them for the godlessness of the institution. The bishop denied using such strong language, and published the text of his sermon in proof. But they said that he had enlarged in the heat of delivery, and the severe things were extempore. These facts I had from Professor Gessner Harrison in person. The bishop's whipping, however, did them good. It was after this, *I think*, that the first movement was made for a chaplaincy, as a tribute to the religious sentiment of the State. If I am rightly informed, the first was ———, a brilliant man, but rather a pulpit charlatan, and a bad man in private character. Dr. Sampson was there then as a student, and by his consistent, modest,

Christian firmness, did more than ———. Dr. Sampson was one of the 'mainspokes' in the first Sunday-school and prayer-meeting. The chaplaincy was, and is, a 'voluntary' movement, on the part of professors and students, who support him by subscription; the Visitors never having given anything but a chapel and a piece of ground for a manse.

"By the time of this movement John A. G. Davis had settled there as law-professor—an evangelical Episcopalian, and a truly holy man. He was of great value to the religious interests until his murder. He recognized the importance of such students as Sampson, and asked Dr. White if Presbyterian families would not send more such, expressing his opinion that the University would do well to *give* them their tuition gratis to get them. From about that time 'candidates' have been free.

"Dr. McGuffey came about 1845, I think. I soon made his acquaintance. He said to me once, remarking on his being an utter stranger in Virginia, that he was very inquisitive and anxious about what manner of man the Presbyterian pastor in Charlottesville should be, because he knew that his comfort and success would depend very much on that. He added that he had found Dr. White just the man after his own heart, who had given him the noblest welcome, and always held up his hands wisely and staunchly.

"Dr. McGuffey began with great discretion. His reputation had been exclusively a Western one. It was, to a good degree, through the representations of Dr. Landon Rives, of Cincinnati, (where Dr. McGuffey had been teacher in Woodward College) to the Hon. William C. Rives, visitor, that Dr. McGuffey got the appointment. It was a surprise to the Virginia people. Dr. James L. Cabell was his chief competitor. Some said, 'Who is this Yankee?' But he came on the scene very quietly and devoted himself the first session *exclusively* to establishing his prestige as an *able teacher*. (He was always devoted to his course of instruction.) This he did triumphantly. He then began to launch out, canvassing for a better class of students, from Christian, and especially from Presbyterian, families. He preached as he had opportunity (being scrupulously punctual at every lecture, and his vacations were devoted, for a year or two, to canvassing tours really; seemingly to public addresses on education and kindred topics. Wherever he was invited, there he would go, speak, form the acquaintance of Christian parents, etc. He also began to exert a Christian influence in the University by Bible-class instruction, etc., *but especially in his lectures on Moral Philosophy.*

"Dr. White used to tell, with his heartiest relish, a story about this 'new departure' of Dr. McGuffey, which bears too hard on Professor ——— to be repeated abroad. This latter, and it seems most of the Faculty, were alarmed at Dr. McGuffey's course. One evening ——— met Dr. White, near the post-office in Charlottesville, and began to complain: 'The University is a *State* institution. It must not be tarnished with sectarianism. Dr. McGuffey is compromising us all by preaching, etc., etc. Dr. White, I wish you would advise your brother preacher to quit preaching altogether. He owes it to his colleagues. Why, sir, he was *elected* here as McGuffey, LL. D. Had we known he was a clergyman, he would never have been elected!' Meantime, Mr Valentine Southall had joined the group. (He was a lawyer, not a church-member, though his wife was; commonwealth's attorney, politician, etc. He was remarkable for a crow-black roach, dark skin, black, heavy eye-brows, gruff voice, and very positive air.) Mr. ———, relying on him as a *secular* man, appealed to him for support. 'Mr. Southall, don't you think Dr. McGuffey ought to demit the pulpit?' Dr. White used to repeat the answer with infinite glee. Knitting his bushy brow and working his raven's roach, as a horse does his mane when a fly bites, he replied, with the most intense dogmatism: 'No, sir; I think no such thing!

I do not profess, like you, to be a Christian, but Virginia is a Christian community. I know the necessity of the influences of this religion; it is for want of them that your University is in danger of going to the devil. Pity but a good many more of you were like Dr. McGuffey—good preachers; then the sensible, prudent parents in Virginia would have more confidence in your institution.' Professor ——— was so utterly taken aback that he turned pale and trembled with excitement, but added nothing.

. . . .

"Now I always regarded Dr. White and Dr. McGuffey colaborers in the work of changing the godless character of the University. Dr. White's two chaplaincies were of great value. His influence with the Faculty was always for good. He gave a new impulse, by his school and pastoral labors, to vital godliness in all that neighborhood and country, and this reacted. He prudently and quietly sought opportunities to bring the students acquainted with leading ministers by getting them to his pulpit and to the University—for instance, Dr. Plumer to deliver a Bible society address at the commencement in 1841 at the anniversary of a Union Bible Society which he had mainly gotten up. Above all, Dr. White exerted a constant and genial influence on the pious students, whether chaplain or not. His study was always open to them.

"I will recall another incident of his earlier ministry which had much to do in shaping his final course. About the time Dr. White was preaching in Scottsville, a discussion was had in the Richmond Presbyterian paper (then Dr. Converse's) known as the 'Aliquis Discussion.' Several ministers wrote under this signature, of whom Dr. White was one. Their object was to argue the detriment to pastoral character and activities of a *secular occupation*. Some went so far as to say that it was a breach of ordination vows, and that no minister ought to accept, and no Presbytery sanction, *any* call which laid the minister liable to such secular labor in any event. They were replied to with a good deal of asperity, as by Dr. Stanton, pastor of the College Church at Hampden-Sidney. Dr. White never went to extremes. Pretty soon his opponents said that he well illustrated the impracticability of the 'Aliquis theory' by immersing himself in a large school. Now, when the Lexington call came in 1848, enabling him to devote himself exclusively to the ministry, he told me that a prominent reason for accepting was his yearning to get rid of secular employment. 'Yes, sir" said he, 'I have verified in my own experience the justice of the more moderate views of us "Aliquis" men. Secular occupation is a bane to a pastor. It disperses his energies, secularizes his heart, and cripples his ministry.'

"I will close with a story on the Cohees. Meeting Dr. White after he had been in Lexington a year, I asked him how he liked them. He remarked upon the habitual caution, often over-caution, of the Scotch-Irish character; he found the Lexington session and people deficient in aggressive boldness for Christ; the community was in name almost all Presbyterian; all nominally on the side of order and righteousness; yet flagrant vice abounded. He said: 'I just lay quiet for a couple of months until I could "take my bearings" well. Then I asked for a full meeting of session to consider the interests of Christ's cause in general. So they all assembled, and wished to know what the business was. I made them a talk, and I began about thus: "Well, brethren, you have a noble church here, etc. But I must say that, with all its excellences, your community is in one respect the queerest I ever lived in. God's people have the reins in their own hands, yet they let the devil do the driving."' Didn't that wake up the elders?   R. L. D."

www.ingramcontent.com/pod-product-compliance
Lightning Source LLC
Chambersburg PA
CBHW032111230426
43672CB00009B/1701